Silbury Hill ½ mile   Falkner's Circle

THE ROUGH GUIDE TO THE
GREAT
WEST WAY®

ROUGH
GUIDES

Contents

INTRODUCTION 4

The route	4	Things not to miss	10
Author picks	5	Itineraries	22
When to go	7		

BASICS 32

Getting around	33	Travel essentials	41
Accommodation	36	Festivals and events calendar	44
Food and drink	37	My Great West Way	47
Sports and outdoor activities	39		

THE GUIDE 50

1 West of London	50	4 The southern and Wiltshire Cotswolds	115
2 West Berkshire	65	5 Bath	125
3 Wiltshire	84	6 Bristol	140

CONTEXTS 158

History	159	Wildlife	179
Film and TV	176	Books	182
Music	178		

DID YOU KNOW...? 185

GREAT WEST WAY AMBASSADOR NETWORK 189

SMALL PRINT & INDEX 194

A ROUGH GUIDE TO ROUGH GUIDES

Published in 1982, the first Rough Guide – to Greece – was a student scheme that became a publishing phenomenon. Mark Ellingham, a recent graduate in English from Bristol University, had been travelling in Greece the previous summer and couldn't find the right guidebook. With a small group of friends he wrote his own guide, combining a contemporary, journalistic style with a thoroughly practical approach to travellers' needs.

The immediate success of the book spawned a series that rapidly covered dozens of destinations. And, in addition to impecunious backpackers, Rough Guides soon acquired a much broader readership that relished the guides' wit and inquisitiveness as much as their enthusiastic, critical approach and value-for-money ethos. These days, Rough Guides include recommendations from budget to luxury and cover more than 120 destinations around the globe, from Amsterdam to Zanzibar, all regularly updated by our team of roaming writers.

Browse all our latest guides, read inspirational features and book your trip at **roughguides.com**.

Introduction to the
Great West Way

The Great West Way reaches west from the UK capital of London to the ex-industrial powerhouse of Bristol, now one of the country's hippest cities, covering a distance of some 125 miles in the process. But this touring route is far from an A to B run between urban centres, it is the world's first multi-modal touring route, a meandering lattice of tracks and trails that include the Kennet & Avon Canal, the Great Western Railway, the River Thames and numerous walking and cycling routes, as well as the main A4 road. However you choose to explore, you'll be travelling through the soul of England, weaving a pathway between ancient market towns with imposing Georgian architecture, quaint villages built in honey-coloured Bath stone and across the patchwork of woodland, downland and farmers' fields that rolls out across this quintessentially English area. There is no mistaking which country you're touring here.

The route

The Great West Way runs between Bristol in the west and western London in the east, passing through the counties of Somerset, Gloucestershire, Wiltshire and Berkshire en route and dipping into the southern parts of Oxfordshire and Buckinghamshire as it approaches the capital.

If you start in **Bristol** and head eastwards along the Great West Way your first major stop is likely to be **Bath**, a city so beautiful – and so historically important – that it has been UNESCO World Heritage-listed as a cultural site. Stretching northeast of Bath and into Wiltshire and Gloucestershire is the **Cotswolds** Area of Outstanding Natural Beauty (AONB), a bucolic paradise of rolling hills and picturesque, somnolent villages that tempts you out onto two feet, or perhaps two wheels.

ABOVE AVEBURY **RIGHT, FROM TOP** THE FAT DUCK; THE BREWHOUSE CLOCK, LACOCK ABBEY; NARROWBOATING, KENNET & AVON C

Author picks

Our author Helen Ochyra grew up on the Great West Way (W GreatWestWay.co.uk). Let her lead you to the very best the route has to offer with her selection of handpicked highlights.

Tasty treats Bristol has recently emerged as a gastronomic hotspot and no visit to the city is complete for me without at least one meal at Cargo, a series of ex-shipping containers turned hip restaurants down by the harbour. One of my favourites is *Woko Ko* (p.155), which does fabulous bao buns. There's now great local dining at pubs along the Great West Way, including *The Three Tuns* in Great Bedwyn (p.92), the *Sign of the Angel* in Lacock (p.107) and *The Snooty Fox* in Tetbury (p.123). Finally, there really is nowhere like Heston Blumenthal's three Michelin-starred *Fat Duck*. My meal here has me raving about it more than a year later and I can't imagine I'll ever enjoy a dinner more (p.71).

Terrific towns Bray in Berkshire is a must-visit for foodies, with not only the *Fat Duck* but also *The Waterside Inn* (p.72) serving up three Michelin-star cuisine and there are lovely walks along the Thames to boot. In the Cotswolds, Lacock is an obligatory stop for *Harry Potter* fans, who might recognise the cloisters at the Abbey, while Tetbury is packed with historic architecture and traditional pubs. Wiltshire is home to several appealing market towns, including Marlborough and Corsham but the top pick has to be my hometown of Devizes (p.98), where you'll find a gorgeous marketplace, a Victorian brewery that still uses Shire horses and the impressive engineering feat of the Caen Hill lock flight.

Brilliant boating There are few better ways to spend a sunny English evening than in a beer garden, glass in hand, with your bed for the night moored just a few metres away. Hire a narrowboat on the Kennet & Avon Canal and every night of your trip can be just like this, with the added joy of pootling along through jade and golden countryside, chatting to locals as you cruise past them at strolling pace. Numerous companies hire out boats and even the most vehicularly challenged will quickly get the hang of driving one (see p.27).

> Our author recommendations don't end here. We've flagged up Helen's favourite places throughout the guide, highlighted with the ★ symbol.

ADVENTURES START HERE

GWR | ENGLAND'S GREAT WEST WAY

East of the Cotswolds is the rest of Wiltshire, a large county that is mostly rural and relatively unknown as a destination in its own right but is nevertheless home to the world-famous prehistoric UNESCO World Heritage site of **Stonehenge** and **Avebury**, the ever-onscreen village of **Lacock** (seen in both *Downton Abbey* and *Harry Potter*) and a large chunk of another Area of Outstanding Natural Beauty, the **North Wessex Downs**. Wiltshire also boasts some of the Great West Way's most appealing towns and villages, including **Marlborough, Corsham, Calne, Devizes, Bradford on Avon, Trowbridge, Chippenham, Malmesbury** and **Castle Combe**, as well as plenty of pubs, tearooms and country walks in the beautiful **Vale of Pewsey**.

Abutting Wiltshire in the heart of the North Wessex Downs is **Berkshire**, an unsung county that runs east into London's environs and hosts big-hitting sites such as **Highclere Castle** (the real "Downton Abbey") and **Windsor Castle** (the world's oldest and largest inhabited castle) as well as the towns of **Hungerford**, **Newbury** and **Reading**. Travel further east along the River Thames to **Henley on Thames** (famous for its annual Royal Regatta), **Marlow** and **Maidenhead**.

The North Wessex Downs give way to the **Chilterns** here, yet another Area of Outstanding Natural Beauty and a wonderful place for a cycle. Finally, the Great West Way comes to its spectacular conclusion in western London where you'll find **Richmond Park**, a royal park home to hundreds of free-roaming deer, and the world renowned **Royal Botanic Gardens, Kew,** a garden that is home to the world's largest and most diverse plant collection.

When to go

England is much-maligned for its changeable weather but the Great West Way traverses the far south and the driest part of the British Isles. Visit in summer and you can expect a reasonable amount of sunshine and warm temperatures that don't require a jacket most of the time. This, though, is peak season and July and August see much of the population taking time off to travel in their own backyard. A better time to visit is the spring (roughly March to June) or the autumn (September and October) when you can still expect plenty of dry weather and the days remain long, with light evenings ideal for sitting in pub gardens. Winter (December to February) is a better time to visit than you might think, with those traditional pubs and tearooms coming into their own. This is a country used to carrying on regardless in chilly, wet weather and you can expect decent heating in your hotel room, roaring fires in the pubs and a "stiff upper lip" attitude that means everyone pretty much shrugs and gets on with it – albeit with more clothing and an umbrella. Christmas is big here too and can be a great time to visit, with tons of events running throughout December. Bear in mind, though, that England largely shuts down between Christmas Eve and New Year's Eve, when many businesses are closed.

Great West Way route map

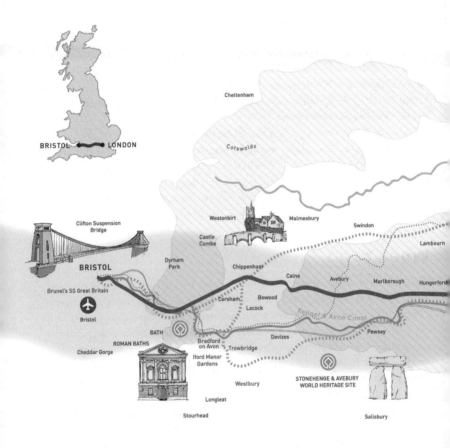

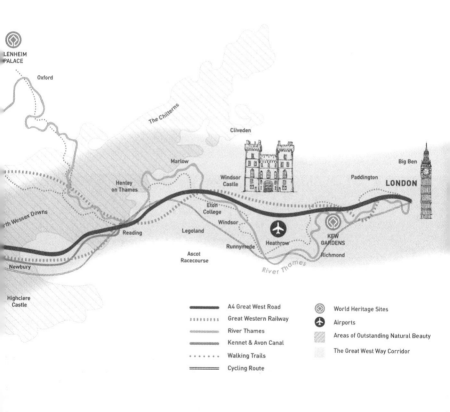

LENHEIM PALACE

Oxford

The Chilterns

Cliveden

Marlow

Windsor Castle

Big Ben

Henley on Thames

Paddington

LONDON

rth Wessex Downs

Eton College

Windsor

Reading

Legoland

Heathrow

KEW GARDENS

Runnymede

Richmond

Ascot Racecourse

Newbury

River Thames

Highclere Castle

▬▬▬ A4 Great West Road	◉ World Heritage Sites
▪▪▪▪▪▪ Great Western Railway	✈ Airports
▬▬▬ River Thames	▨ Areas of Outstanding Natural Beauty
▬▬▬ Kennet & Avon Canal	▨ The Great West Way Corridor
••••• Walking Trails	
═══ Cycling Route	

33

things not to miss

The Great West Way runs through the very soul of England, tempting you to stop regularly and to spend more time exploring and discovering – there is always something new around the next corner. These 33 highlights are some of the best things to see and do along the route.

1

 STONEHENGE
Page 110

This UNESCO World Heritage stone circle is perhaps the world's most famous prehistoric monument. Book well ahead for a Stone Circle Access visit that lets you inside this ring of megaliths – before the site opens to the public for the day.

 ROYAL ASCOT
Page 60

One of England's best horse racing meetings is a four-day extravaganza, starting each day with a royal carriage procession featuring the Queen herself. The perfect an excuse to buy a hat.

 LACOCK ABBEY
Page 103

Harry Potter film fans might recognise some of the rooms off the cloisters in this ancient National Trust country house, which is also where the earliest surviving photographic negative was created.

 WESTONBIRT, THE NATIONAL ARBORETUM
Page 121

Wander through ancient woodland and discover rare, exotic species at Westonbirt, The National Arboretum, home to dozens of so-called "champion trees", the largest or tallest of their kind in Britain.

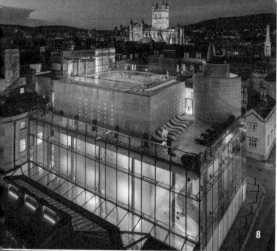

5 THE COTSWOLDS
Page 115 & 123

England's largest designated AONB stretches for miles of rolling hills and quaint villages built in honey-coloured stone. A more perfect landscape is hard to imagine.

6 CLIMBING THE RIGGING AT BRUNEL'S SS *GREAT BRITAIN*
Page 144

Ahoy there, sailor! This is your chance to prove your nautical skills with a clamber up the rigging of this early Victorian ship. You'll reach heights of 82ft above Bristol harbour and the very brave can continue out along the yardarm.

7 NARROWBOATING THE KENNET & AVON CANAL
Page 35

Hire a narrowboat and cruise the Great West Way at walking pace. The 87 miles of canal can be tackled all at once but far better to slow down and just do a section, stopping off at picturesque villages and mooring overnight at canalside pubs.

8 WATSU AT THERMAE BATH SPA
Page 127

Try an in-water massage at Thermae Bath Spa, where the city's natural thermal waters are used in a range of treatments – of which this is the dreamiest. Afterwards soak in the rooftop pool overlooking the city's Georgian heart.

9 MOUNTAIN BIKING IN SWINLEY FOREST
Page 64

Whizz down the mountain biking trails that wind through this ancient woodland, twisting past trees and over jumps as you make your descent. The Red Trail is the most challenging – saddle up if you dare.

10 WINDSOR CASTLE
Page 58

Poke your nose into the castle that is said to be the Queen's favourite residence, checking out the state apartments and gilded reception rooms that have hosted the world's great and good. You'll also see the Gothic St George's Chapel, which hosted Prince Harry's wedding to Meghan Markle.

11 MEETING A RED PANDA AT BRISTOL ZOO GARDENS

Page 148

Have a meet and greet with one of this historic zoo's red pandas. You'll go behind the scenes at their enclosure and come face to face with Lady Hilary or Chota, two red pandas who had their first cub in 2016.

12 AFTERNOON TEA

Page 38

Settle in for a quintessentially English meal, where homemade scones and cakes star and the tea is endless. Most five-star hotels, do them well, notably The Royal Crescent Hotel & Spa (pictured), the only Landmark Building in the world where you can stay and experience as a guest.

13 DEVIZES CARNIVAL CONFETTI BATTLE

Page 98

Nobody knows why this market town started such a weird and wonderful tradition but its annual confetti-throwing event is unique. The riotous "battle" takes place in the town's marketplace and covers everything in flecks of paper before ending with a fireworks display.

14 DEER COUNTING IN RICHMOND PARK

Page 53

Deer have roamed freely in this royal park since the seventeenth century and it's easy to get (fairly) close to the herd here. Autumn is rutting season, when the stags might be seen clashing antlers, while May–July is your best chance of seeing a brand new baby.

15 HAGGLING FOR ANTIQUES IN HUNGERFORD

Page 78

This picturesque Berkshire town is a hotspot for antiques, with numerous shops lining the streets. The best place to head is Hungerford Arcade Antiques, home to more than a hundred dealers in everything from jewellery to pottery.

16 AL FRESCO SWIMMING AT THAMES LIDO

Page 73

England's long-neglected outdoor swimming pools are having a renaissance. This Edwardian lido is leading the charge, reborn as a gorgeous 82ft outdoor pool, complete with adjacent restaurant.

11

12

17 SHOPPING IN BATH
Page 137

Forget the mall, in Bath shopping means strolling Georgian streets in search of the best boutiques and bookshops. We recommend Mr B's Emporium for books and Vintage to Vogue for vintage fashion.

18 RIDING A STEAM TRAIN AT AVON VALLEY RAILWAY
Page 151

Listen out for the whistle of the guard and the whoosh of the steam on a steam train ride through this bucolic valley. Avon Valley Railway volunteers have restored three miles of track and there are 1940s weekends and festive Santa Specials to enjoy.

19 SPOTTING RED KITES IN THE CHILTERNS
Page 181

Red kites were reintroduced to this protected AONB in 1989 and today the population is booming. The southern Chilterns around Henley and Maidenhead is a good spot for sightings, especially from October to April.

20 ROYAL BOTANIC GARDENS, KEW
Page 51

The world's largest collection of plants blooms in the gardens at Kew. It's worth a visit for the two Victorian glasshouses, which house the temperate and tropical collections, but there are numerous other attractions, including the Great Pagoda and Kew Palace. Christmas at Kew is a highlight, when the gardens are lit up with dazzling light installations.

21 HORSE RIDING ON THE MARLBOROUGH DOWNS
Page 35

Gallop across the glorious chalk downland of the Marlborough Downs. Equestrian route PLAP 14 loops out from Hackpen Hill, taking in part of the Ridgeway trail as it passes across the downs, as well as quaint villages and ancient hill forts.

22 STAND UP PADDLE BOARDING THROUGH BATH
Page 138

See Bath's beautiful cityscape from a different angle by taking to the water on a stand up paddle board. Original Wild will teach you how to gain your balance and paddle before leading you on a unique tour of the city.

23 A PROPER ENGLISH PUB
Page 37

There's nothing like a proper English pub. The Great West Way is home to hundreds, where you can savour a pint of local ale, a hearty meal and often a roaring fire or a sun-drenched beer garden. Some of our favourites are The Three Tuns in Great Bedwyn, The Old Bell Hotel in Malmesbury and The Royal Oak in Yattendon.

17

18

19

24

25

24 DELVING INTO PREHISTORY AT WEST KENNET LONG BARROW
Page 88

Duck behind the ancient sarsen stones at the entrance to this Neolithic chambered tomb and walk back into prehistory beneath the rolling English countryside.

25 RIDING THE RAILS OF THE GREAT WESTERN RAILWAY
Page 34

Watch the Great West Way roll past on one of the Great Western Railway's modern trains. Engineered by Brunel, this remains one of England's great railway journeys.

26 BOARDING CONCORDE AT AEROSPACE BRISTOL
Page 151

Follow in the footsteps of the rich and famous at Aerospace Bristol and climb aboard iconic Alpha Foxtrot – the last Concorde aircraft ever built.

27 MEETING THE LIONS AT LONGLEAT
Page 111

Take a safari – in Wiltshire. England's first self-drive safari brings you tantalisingly close to lions, rhinos, giraffes and some very cheeky monkeys.

28 EXPLORING A LOCAL BREWERY
Page 77 & 99

Sup a pint of proper English ale at one of the Great West Way's local breweries. The West Berkshire Brewery in Yattendon has a welcoming tap room, while Devizes' Wadworth Brewery has tours on most days.

30 FEELING LIKE ROYALTY AT HAMPTON COURT PALACE
Page 54
The finest of England's Tudor palaces, this spectacular red-brick royal abode is packed with historic treasures and has glorious gardens designed to rival Versailles.

31 HUNTING FOR BANKSY ON A TOUR OF BRISTOL
Page 154
Check out the work of Banksy and other street artists on an engaging walking tour of Bristol – either in a guided group or by downloading the Banksy Bristol Trail app.

32 DRESSING UP AUSTEN-STYLE IN BATH
Page 136
Don your Regency finest and join the Jane Austen Festival's annual Promenade through the historic streets of Bath.

33 RACING A SPORTS CAR AT CASTLE COMBE CIRCUIT
Page 117
Feel the need for speed? Get behind the wheel of a sports car at Castle Combe Circuit, and put the pedal to the metal.

34 CLIMBING SALISBURY'S SPIRE
Page 113
Salisbury Cathedral towers above the Wiltshire countryside, its spire – at 403ft – the tallest in the country. Take the Tower Tour for a closer look, and one hell of a view.

32

33

Itineraries

The Great West Way isn't just one route – and there isn't just one way to travel it. You could take a tour, go your own way, or perhaps follow one of our itineraries, which link the best sights and attractions for a range of different interests – from Food and Drink, Luxury, and Industrial Heritage to Gardens, the Great Outdoors and places Seen on Screen. Use these as a starting point and build your own adventure.

FOOD AND DRINK

Long gone are the days of joking about England's unimaginative food. Today the country is one of the best places to eat in Europe, where award-winning high-class restaurants rub shoulders with cosy, traditional pubs. The Great West Way is home to some of England's best foodie experiences, with plenty

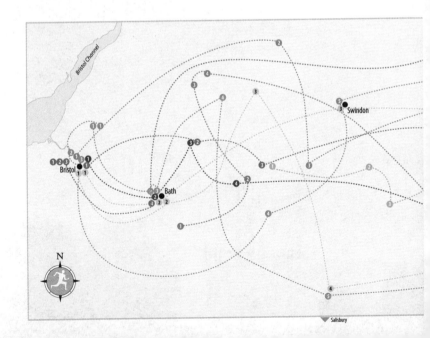

of Michelin stars and a whole galaxy of local food heroes serving up everything from vegetables hand grown in the kitchen garden to just-baked homemade cakes. It's also the home of the famous Wiltshire cure and more than a sprinkling of cosy tearooms and enticing delis.

❶ Paco Tapas Start your Great West Way feast at one of the very best restaurants in Bristol, a city with a vibrant food scene that rivals London's. Leading local chef Peter Sanchez-Iglesias opened this authentic Spanish taperìa in 2016 and it won a Michelin star in its very first year. Order lip-smacking Cinco Jotas jamón, fish fresh from Cornwall and beautifully cooked Galician beef, washed down with a recommendation from the Spanish-focused wine list. **See p.155**

❷ Traditional afternoon tea It doesn't get much more quintessentially English than afternoon tea. There are dozens of places - from luxury hotels to homespun tearooms - to try the traditional scone with cream and jam, but for something really special take a table at *The Tutti Pole* in Hungerford, where the scones are homemade and cakes freshly baked. **See p.81**

❸ Wiltshire ham The Wiltshire cure – where meat is soaked in brine for several days for a succulent, moist texture – was developed in the small town of Calne by the Harris family in the 18th century. Try it in the town of its birth at *Fay's Bistro*, where it's served in a traditional ploughmans, or call in to Buttle Farm to buy it fresh from the farm **See p.104 &107**

❹ A proper English pub The best English villages have a pub at their centre, which serve freshly cooked meals and local ales in front of roaring log fires or in sunny gardens. In Yattendon you'll find a cracker – *The Royal Oak* has oak beams, leather chairs and log fires inside and a beer garden and boules pitch outside. There are bedrooms upstairs too. **See p.81**

❺ West Berkshire Brewery No food and drink tour of the Great West Way would be complete without a visit to a brewery. This microbrewery champions traditional brewing techniques (which you can see on one of their monthly tours) and produces a high-quality range of real ales and craft beers. Sample a pint at the *Taproom*, where wood-fired pizzas are served to soak up those beers. **See p.81**

❻ The Fat Duck Finish your foodie itinerary in Bray, at the restaurant that could claim to be England's best. Chef Heston Blumenthal serves up an unforgettable tasting menu here, with dishes that focus on fun and aim to trigger childhood memories of trips to the seaside. The

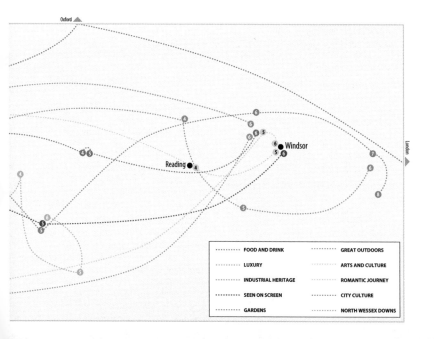

restaurant has been awarded three Michelin stars and everything is exemplary, from the service to the incredible menu. **See p.71**

LUXURY

England knows how to do luxury, from exquisite service and high-class design right down to the little touches that make a journey here so memorable. On the Great West Way you are truly spoiled for choice, where some of the country's leading luxury hotels and most famous fine dining restaurants light the way from one unforgettable sight to the next. Follow this opulent itinerary and you'll get exclusive access to not only one by two UNESCO World Heritage sites, plus plenty of pampering along the way.

❶ Step aboard Concorde Begin your luxury escape by boarding Concorde, the chicest airplane the world has ever seen. The British ones were all assembled in Filton, where the last one to ever fly now stands on ceremony in a vast hangar at the Aerospace Bristol. You may not be allowed to sit in the seats but you can sashay through the aircraft door, poke your nose into the cockpit and let your imagination run riot. **See p.151**

❷ Thermae Bath Spa Few spa treatments are as soothing as a watsu and in Bath this in-water massage is performed in mineral-rich thermal waters direct from the springs beneath the city. After your treatment head up to the roof for a soak in the thermal pool overlooking the rooftops of this gorgeous city cast in honey-coloured stone. **See p.127**

❸ The Gainsborough Bath Spa Stay here for the chance to soak in the city's thermal waters in complete privacy. Some of the opulent rooms at this five-star hotel are plumbed directly into the city's thermal springs, meaning that you can run a bath and soak in them in the comfort of your own room. There's also a lovely pool in the Spa Village downstairs. **See p.134**

❹ Afternoon tea at Whatley Manor Hotel & Spa A luxury manor house, set in 16 acres of gardens near Malmesbury, Afternoon tea is served in either the Garden Roon, Drawing Room, or one of the terraces and includes everything from finger sandwiches to freshly-baked scones with clotted cream. Add a Bellini for a special occasion. **See p.122**

❺ Stone Circle Access visit at Stonehenge Don't let the crowds obscure your view of Stonehenge – book ahead for this exclusive tour and gain access early in the morning before the site is open to the general public. You'll still be in a group but it will be small, with opportunities for you to take pictures of the stones without anyone else in the shot. **See p.111**

❻ The Waterside Inn Finish your trip in style with a stay at one of the Great West Way's very best hotels. Some of the eleven bedrooms here have balconies overlooking the River Thames and dinner is in the Michelin-starred dining room, one of the best in England. The food here is luxuriously French with tasting menus from chef Alain Roux – the Menu Exceptionnel has six courses and is a delight. **See p.72**

❼ Shopping in Bath Bath has unique shopping, with an enticing selection of independent boutiques lining its Georgian streets. Call in to *Vintage to Vogue* for one-off vintage pieces from designer brands, select from fine cheeses at Churchill's favourite, *Paxton & Whitfield*, and pick up antique books at *Bath Old Books*. **See p.137**

INDUSTRIAL HERITAGE

England was the birthplace of the industrial revolution and the Great West Way is the best place to discover the country's industrial heritage. The route is followed by the Great Western Railway, with trains running along the line that Isambard Kingdom Brunel designed in the 1830s and there are many places to stop off and be a part of the story. The Great West Way is also followed by the Kennet & Avon Canal – an engineering feat worthy of exploration by water or land – and is home to two cities that have been at the heart of England's industrial success: Bristol and Swindon.

❶ Aerospace Bristol The city of Bristol has played a leading role in aviation development and was once home to the largest aircraft factory in the world. Visit this fascinating museum and you'll learn the story of how the city became an aviation superstar, including its role in the two World Wars and in building the most famous – and most loved – aeroplane in the world has ever seen: Concorde. **See p.151**

❷ Clifton Suspension Bridge Continue your industrial heritage tour with a spin across Isambard Kingdom Brunel's world-famous bridge. Cars can cross this nineteenth-century suspension bridge for the princely sum of £1, while pedestrians will love peering over the sides to check out the plunging views of the Avon Gorge far below. **See p.147**

❸ **Brunel's SS** *Great Britain* Brunel also designed this passenger steamship hailed as, "the greatest experiment since the creation". The SS *Great Britain* carried emigrants to Australia for many years and was later used for cargo; today she sits in the city where she was built and is open to visitors who can roam her decks and even climb her rigging. **See p.144**

❹ **Caen Hill Lock Flight**, operated by the Canal & River Trust, is the most enticing sight on the Kennet & Avon Canal – a series of 29 locks rising 237ft over 2 miles uphill into the market town of Devizes. Take a stroll up the eponymous hill or hire a narrowboat and travel as so many have done before by pulling open the gates and letting the water carry you up the hill. **See p.99**

❺ **STEAM – Museum of the Great Western Railway** The town of Swindon was once home to the Swindon Works, the main maintenance centre for the railway in the west of England. Today one of the Grade II listed railway buildings has been restored as a museum, where you can have a go in the interactive signal box and drive a steam train simulator. **See p.93**

❻ **Maidenhead Railway Bridge** Another extraordinary design by Brunel, but onlookers were so sceptical that its flat arches would collapse under the weight of the trains crossing it that he had to leave the wooden formwork in place for years after it opened to assuage people's fears. Needless to say, it's survived the test of time and today it still carries the Great Western Railway from London Paddington on its way west towards Bristol. **See p.66**

SEEN ON SCREEN

The Great West Way is quintessentially English, so it's no surprise that many of its cities, villages and castles have appeared on screen. The BBC have made good use of one Wiltshire village in particular, while Bath and Bristol have both starred in global hits and the castles of Highclere and Windsor are familiar to millions. Whether you're a fan of *Harry Potter, Downton Abbey* or the British Royal Family, this itinerary has plenty of places you might just recognise.

❶ **Queen Square, Bristol** Start your on-screen tour in Bristol, where this gorgeous central square was featured in *Sherlock Holmes: The Abominable Bride*, starring Benedict Cumberbatch. A balcony here was used for Emilia Ricoletti's shoot-out before she died; later the square morphed into the exterior of the Diogenese Club. **See p.144**

❷ **Royal Crescent, Bath** Reese Witherspoon spent some time in Bath filming the 2004 movie *Vanity Fair*. The movie was adapted from William Makepeace Thackeray's nineteenth century novel of the same name and used the city's beautiful Georgian architecture to full effect. Scenes were shot in Beauford Square behind the Theatre Royal, in the grand boulevard of Great Pulteney Street and at the sweeping Royal Crescent, a glorious semicircle of thirty golden-hued stone terraced houses. **See p.130**

❸ **Castle Combe** This chocolate box Wiltshire village is most famous on screen for its appearance in Spielberg's *War Horse*, when its main street was transformed into a Devon village whose men were heading off to war. The village's fourteenth-century market cross was bedecked in banners encouraging the village's locals to enlist. **See p.117**

❹ **Lacock** Nowhere on the Great West Way has appeared on screen more times than this National Trust village. There are no phone lines or telegraph poles, making it perfect for historical TV series such as the BBC classics *Cranford* – when it stood in for the Cheshire village of Knutsford – and *Pride and Prejudice*, when it appeared as Meryton. The main street here has also been used in *Downton Abbey* and Lacock Abbey was filmed for several scenes in the *Harry Potter* films, including when Harry sees his parents for the first time, in the *Mirror of Erised*. **See p.103 & 104**

❺ **Highclere Castle** Highclere Castle is "Downton Abbey". This Jacobethan country house is the building Julian Fellowes is said to have had in mind when he wrote the TV drama and although it remains the family home of the Earl and Countess of Carnarvon, visitors can step inside the Great Hall – backdrop to much of Mary and Matthew's romance – and the Dining Room – scene of many a family drama and plenty of acerbic comments from the Dowager Countess. Look out also for the upcoming *Downton Abbey* film, filmed at Highclere as well as at Bowood in Wiltshire. **See p.78**

❻ **Windsor Castle** Not all Great West Way sites to have appeared on screen have done so in fiction. Windsor Castle was seen on millions of TV screens around the world in 2018 when it hosted the wedding of Prince Harry and Meghan Markle, now officially known as the Duke and Duchess of Sussex. **See p.58**

GARDENS

This green-fingered country has long had a nerdy, borderline obsessive fascination with gardening and no visit to England is complete without taking a turn around at least one or two of its fabulous gardens. The Great West Way is home to some of the best, from the world-famous Kew to an organic garden presided over by a Prince. This itinerary hits the highlights.

❶ Iford Manor Gardens Start your Great West Way gardens tour at this romantic Italianate garden designed by Edwardian architect Harold Peto. Tucked into a tranquil valley, the gardens are designed to work with the steep hillside and terracing is an important element of the design. Follow the paths that twist around columns and ancient statues, surrounded by bright and beautiful plants including original wisterias and lilies. **See p.108**

❷ Bowood House and Gardens This dazzling Woodland Garden is open only for flowering season each spring but is worth timing a visit at this time to see its vibrant displays of brightly coloured rhododendrons. More than two miles of paths wend their way through the woodland here and some of the plants date back to when the garden was first planted in 1854 by the 3rd Marquis of Lansdowne. **See p.103**

❸ Westonbirt, The National Arboretum This is the country's National Arboretum and is home to some 15,000 tree specimens from around the world. Walk the STIHL Treetop Walkway to get up into the tree canopy and take a stroll through the Old Arboretum, checking out rare and exotic trees planted in the nineteenth century. Each one is labelled and some are the largest or tallest of their kind in Britain. **See p.121**

❹ Highgrove Royal Gardens Highgrove is the private residence of Prince Charles, who has transformed a mere lawn into a series of glorious organic gardens home to a rich selection of plants and flowers. In the Sundial Garden you'll find elegant delphiniums, while the Cottage Garden features trees, shrubs and herbaceous plants. Four acres of wildflower meadows stretch out in front of the house too. **See p.121**

❺ Highclere Castle After romping across the vast lawn in front of the castle you'll find a series of gardens and woods in the grounds of this

famous mansion, aka "Downton Abbey". In the Secret Garden there are herbaceous borders that come alive with colour in the summer, while the White Border is a picturesque display of climbing white roses and clematis. **See p.78**

❻ Cliveden The gardens at this world-renowned estate are owned by the National Trust and are home to acres of woodland running down to the Thames. The Parterre is the showstopper, with sixteen triangular beds laid out in front of the house are filled with seasonal bedding plants, while the Rose Garden is home to more than nine hundred roses which bloom from mid-June until late September. **See p.68**

❼ Royal Botanic Gardens, Kew No garden lover can resist the pull of Kew, the perfect end point to your trip. This is the largest and most diverse plant collection in the world and there is so much to explore you might want more than one day. Don't miss the Palm House, with its rainforest climate and the Temperate House, home to some of the planet's most threatened plants. **See p.51**

❽ Hampton Court Palace Tucked into a loop of the River Thames, the gardens at this royal palace are exceptional. There are 60 acres of formal gardens, while the 750 acres of parkland are home to the descendants of King Henry VIII's deer herd. The kids will love the maze, the world's oldest. **See p.54**

GREAT OUTDOORS

The Great West Way runs through the heart of England's southern countryside, offering plenty of chances to get outdoors. For those who want to spend just a few hours exploring there are plenty of short walks and bike rides, while those seeking the ultimate Great West Way adventure can tackle long-distance trails, in sections or as a whole. Follow this active itinerary and you'll discover some of the best preserved and most beautiful scenery in the country.

❶ Avon Gorge Start your Great West Way adventure by tackling England's best urban climbing spot. The towering gorge here rises for some 234ft above the River Avon and is home to dozens of routes, some are easy enough for beginners to have a crack at and others are so challenging that they've only been climbed once. **See p.147**

❷ **Cotswold Water Park** There are over 150 lakes puddled across the landscape here and it's easy to escape the crowds and find a spot to call your own. For swimming, the best place is the Cotswold Country Park and Beach which has a sandy beach, plus water sports available across the park, from stand up paddle boarding to water skiing. **See p.41**

❸ **The Ridgeway to Avebury** This long-distance walking route is thought to have been used since prehistoric times, when herdsmen and soldiers used it to pass through the rolling chalk downland that is now protected as the Chilterns AONB and North Wessex Downs AONB. The southern section of the route is part of the Great West Way and you can walk for 87 miles through some of England's most unspoiled countryside and end up at Avebury, home to a stone circle far larger than the more famous one at Stonehenge. **See p.87**

❹ **Chilterns Cycleway** Head out from Henley on Thames on two wheels and explore the southern section of the Chilterns AONB at a leisurely pace. This cycling route is mostly on-road and runs for 170 miles through historic villages and picturesque ancient landscapes. If you'd rather just ride for the day, there's also an 18-mile loop from Henley through the Hambledon Valley. **See p.70**

❺ Swinley Forest This ancient woodland is a great place for a stroll through the trees, but it's better known for its mountain biking. Swinley Bike Hub can hire out bikes and there are three trails that run from here, ranging from the Green, which anyone can take on, to the steep and twisty Red, suitable only for proficient mountain bikers. The Blue is a happy medium, with 6 miles of moderate single track with just a few small obstacles. **See p.59**

❻ Thames Path This long-distance walking route follows the course of the River Thames all the way from its source in the Cotswolds to the Thames Barrier, just a few miles from the sea. Finish your outdoor adventure on the Great West Way by taking on the 11-mile section from Teddington to Putney. Stick to the river's south bank and you'll walk alongside Richmond Park and the Royal Botanic Gardens at Kew as you head into London. **See p.57**

❻ The Kennet & Avon Canal This ex-industrial waterway runs for 87 miles along the Great West Way and is perfect for narrowboating. Pick up your craft in Bradford on Avon and drive it eastwards towards Devizes, where the Caen Hill lock flight is a real challenge – a steep series of 29 locks that must be opened and closed with your own elbow grease. It takes half a day to travel all the way up – or down – the hill. **See p.35**

ARTS AND CULTURE

The Great West Way is home to numerous important art collections, as well as a wide range of significant cultural sites. Follow this arts and culture focused itinerary to get straight to the best of the best.

❶ Bristol Museum and Art Gallery Start your arts and culture tour at Bristol's leading museum, a grand Edwardian Baroque building that houses an eclectic collection. You'll find works by local street artist Banksy here, and the second floor is devoted to art, including one of the best collections of Chinese glass outside Asia and a series of European Old Masters, from Bellini to Bouts. **See p.143**

❷ The Holburne Museum The Holburne Museum was Bath's first public art gallery and remains its finest. The Grade I listed building is home to a hoard of fine artworks built around the original collection by the eponymous Sir William Holburne. Of particular interest are works by Gainsborough, who lived in the city for many years, and the 1750 portrait of local

fashion icon Richard 'Beau' Nash, by Nathaniel Hone. **See p.130**

❸ Swindon Museum and Art Gallery One of the best places on the Great West Way to see twentieth century British art is in Swindon Old Town's beautiful art gallery. The collection was established in the 1940s by a local benefactor and now features some 900 works both two- and three-dimensional, dating from 1880 to 2017. The paintings are arranged by movement, from St Ives to Pop Art and Abstraction, providing a great overview of modern British art. **See p.93**

❹ Reading Museum and Abbey Quarter In Reading's Town Hall, the local museum displays the highlights of the city's 8000-strong art collection. From oil paintings to sculpture, there is plenty to see here, but the highlight is the tin-glazed pottery on display in the Atrium. Outside, the Abbey Quarter is where Henry I established one of Europe's largest royal monasteries in the twelfth century. Although now ruined, a sizeable amount remains standing and it's an atmospheric place for a poke around. Stroll beneath the Abbey Gateway and check out the chapter house and parts of the south transept, which still stand. **See p.72**

❺ Royal Collection, Windsor Castle It will doubtless come as no surprise that the British royal family owns one of the Great West Way's most impressive art collections. Held at Windsor Castle, the Royal Collection has been built up over generations, with monarch's acquiring artwork for centuries. There are paintings by Holbein, Rubens and Van Dyck, as well as an array of artefacts from jewelled snuffboxes to ornate ancient weaponry. **See p.58**

ROMANTIC JOURNEY

Looking for the perfect escape for two? Romance is sure to blossom on this idyllic journey along the Great West Way, taking in beautiful gardens, sweeping views of some of England's most glorious countryside and a sunrise visit to incomparable Stonehenge.

❶ Hot air balloon ride Take off from Ashton Court and soar above the Great West Way countryside on a serene hot air balloon flight with Bailey Balloons. You'll float above the estate's Deer Park and woodland and, depending on the wind direction, could even get a bird's eye view of the world-famous Clifton Suspension Bridge. You'll even get a glass of champagne on landing to toast your romantic flight. **See p.150**

❷ **Thermae Bath Spa** What could be more romantic than a soak "a deux" in Bath's natural thermal waters? At Thermae Bath Spa you can join the throng at the main baths, where you'll get a cracking up-close view of Bath Abbey, or book a couples' massage with soothing aromatherapy in the spa. For something even more romantic why not book the Cross Bath, an intimate open-air thermal bath that can be reserved exclusively. **See p.127**

❸ **The Old Bell Hotel** Cosy up for the night at England's oldest hotel, the Old Bell in Malmesbury. Rooms are romantically decorated (some have four-poster beds) and the Grade I listed building has been thoroughly upgraded to offer elegant afternoon teas and laidback dinners. You're right next to the twelfth-century Abbey too, with all the beauty of this charming market town on your doorstep. **See p.122**

❹ **Sunrise at Stonehenge** One of the most unique ways to see Stonehenge is to visit at sunrise, when the sky is a deep blue above the stones and the site is closed to all but those who have booked tickets for the exclusive Stone Circle Access tour. You can't touch the stones, but you can get them more or less to yourselves. If you're seeking somewhere for a proposal… this might just be the one. **See p.110**

❺ **The Waterside Inn** End your romantic escape in style with a stay at the Waterside Inn in Bray. This is one of only two restaurants in the UK outside of London to hold three Michelin stars and it has an enchanting riverside setting, wonderful French menu and dreamy suites with a shared garden that edges the River Thames and features a "kissing bench". **See p.72**

❻ **Thames river cruise** Book a cream tea hamper and chilled bottle of champagne in advance for your cruise on the River Thames with French Brothers. You'll push off from Windsor Promenade on one of the company's sleek blue and white boats, taking in memorable views of Windsor Castle and Eton before passing Windsor Racecourse and some of Berkshire's prettiest and most bucolic countryside. **See p.64 & 74**

CITY CULTURE

The Great West Way links two of England's most fascinating cities – the peerless capital city of London and the western powerhouse and ex-industrial heavyweight of Bristol. Although most of the GWW is made up of rural land and small towns, there is plenty to see and do by sticking to the cities. Especially when it comes to culture.

❶ **M Shed** Discover the Great West Way's westernmost city of Bristol through the stories of its people. Covering the city's history from the prehistoric era to the present day, this free museum features everything from dinosaurs to antique vehicles. The museum paints an evocative picture, using recreations of homes from the past and first-person tales from local people to bring history to life. **See p.146**

❷ **Banksy street art trail** No cultural visit to Bristol would be complete without checking out at least one of the major works of local street artist Banksy. Born in Bristol in the 1970s, the artist remains anonymous, but their work peppers the city, spicing up walls and alleyways throughout it. Fresh artwork appears on a regular basis so it's best to join a tour, led by a passionate Banksy expert. Alternatively, there is – of course – an app for that. **See p.143**

❸ **CARGO** Bristol's harbourside Wapping Wharf saw a new concept in urban regeneration in 2016: a series of shipping containers stacked on the quay and opened as independent restaurants and retailers. Since its wildly successful opening, CARGO has become the place in Bristol to eat, feasting on fresh fish and chips, ultra-modern British cuisine, Indian street food, tacos and all stops in between with the hip locals of this dynamic city. **See p.155**

❹ **The Roman Baths** Step back in time and into the bathing culture of Roman Bath with a visit to one of England's most important historic cultural sites. These remarkably preserved nearly two thousand-year-old remains are one of the Great West Way's most impressive sights – wander around the still-steaming natural thermal waters, passing behind ancient stone columns as you imagine all that have gone before you. **See p.126**

❺ **Oxford** Veer from the Great West Way for a day trip to Oxford, just a few miles north of the route. This university city is one of England's finest and there are plenty of honey-hued stone buildings and ivy-clad quadrangles to stroll past. Don't miss a visit to the Ashmolean, the city's premier museum and home to a vast collection of cultural artefacts from Egyptian mummies to Hindu bronzes. **See p.82**

❾ Apsley House and Wellington Arch Visit the home of the current Duke of Wellington before celebrating his forefather's victory at the Battle of Waterloo by climbing the towering arch erected just outside, in the middle of Hyde Park Corner. Wellington Arch is one of the finest viewpoints in west London, while Apsley House (aka Number 1 London) is packed with priceless artworks and artefacts including works by Caravaggio and Van Dyck. **See p.54**

NORTH WESSEX DOWNS

❶ Cherhill White Horse The North Wessex Downs are the best place in England to see white horses: equine figures carved into the brilliant white chalk of the hillside. First cut in 1780, the Cherhill White Horse is one of the most appealing: its slender shape seems to gallop across the rolling green hills of the Pewsey Downs. The site is owned by the National Trust and access is free, so take a walk up here and get an up-close look at one of Wiltshire's most famous figures. **See p.88**

❷ Marlborough Few towns in England are as instantly charming as Marlborough, a prosperous market town with the second widest high street in the country. Start your exploration here, popping into boutiques and traditional tearooms, before heading out into ancient Savernake Forest, where many of the large oak trees date back to medieval times. **See p.89**

❸ Crofton Beam Engines When the Kennet & Avon Canal was built around the turn of the nineteenth century, cutting-edge engineering had to be put in place to pump the water needed to the highest point. That engineering remains just south of Great Bedwyn in the shape of the Crofton Beam Engines, the world's oldest working beam engines. Book ahead for a Steam Experience, when you can even have a go at operating them. **See p.90**

❹ Boat trip on the Rose of Hungerford Cruise out from the historic market town of Hungerford aboard the well-maintained 50-seat narrowboat, the Rose of Hungerford. You'll see the beautiful Kennet & Avon Canal as it should be seen – from its waters – and take in the pretty Berkshire countryside between the town and Dunmill Lock at a sedate and peaceful pace. **See p.81**

❺ Bombay Sapphire Distillery Visit the home of one of England's most famous gins, at Laverstoke Mill in the Hampshire Downs. You can check out the 300 year-old paper mill that now houses the distillery on one of the self-guided or guided tours, discover the botanicals that go into the gin in the ultra-modern glasshouse at the building's entrance and, naturally, taste the world-renowned product in the Mill Bar. **See p.80**

❻ Highclere Castle Step inside the real "Downton Abbey" at the palatial home of the Earl of Carnarvon and his family and check out the Dining Room, the Library and even the bedrooms of the Crawley girls. There's also a fascinating Egyptian exhibition, which celebrates the work of the 5th Earl, who was involved in discovering the tomb of Tutankhamun in 1922. **See p.78**

ROWING, HENLEY ON THAMES

Basics

33 Getting around

36 Accommodation

37 Food and drink

39 Sports and outdoor activities

41 Travel essentials

44 Festivals and events calendar

47 My Great West Way

Getting around

Whether you take the wheel and drive, board a train, bus or coach, or brave the English weather by bike or on foot, your mode of transport will define your experience on the Great West Way (Ⓦ GreatWestWay.co.uk). However you choose to travel, remember that the journey is part of the fun and that slow travel always rewards.

By road

Hire – or bring – your own wheels and you can set the pace, following your own itinerary and meandering off track when the mood takes you.

The route of the Great West Way was one of the six Great Roads proposed by King Charles I in the seventeenth century. Today this has become the modern **A4**, running through the towns of Maidenhead, Reading, Newbury, Marlborough and Chippenham before reaching Bath and Bristol. Each of these towns is a useful hub, standing at the meeting point of several major A roads that can get you further off the beaten track.

The Great West Way also follows a similar route to the **M4** motorway, one of England's busiest thoroughfares, crossing the heart of the country's south – from London and Heathrow airport in the east to Bristol in the west. The M4 is used by thousands of commuters and lorries every day and traffic is often heavy, meaning it is best avoided.

Try England's **country roads** instead. These are almost always single carriageway and although they may not cut across the landscape in the most direct way, they tend to yield the greatest rewards.

Renting a car

Renting a car is best done online in advance of your arrival. If you're flying in, Heathrow and Bristol

> ### DRIVING THE GREAT WEST WAY
>
> Driving in England is relatively straightforward, with rules of the road to which – in general – people adhere. Remember to **drive on the left** and travel around roundabouts clockwise, giving way to traffic coming from the right. **Seatbelts** must be worn by everyone in the car (front and back seats) and there are plenty of speed cameras, so stick to the limit. Distances are measured in **miles** not kilometres.

airports are the easiest places to pick up a vehicle and all of the major car rental companies have desks either in the terminal buildings or within walking distance – both airports have Alamo, Avis, Budget, Enterprise, Europcar, Hertz, National and Sixt. The cities of Reading, Swindon and Bath are also good places to pick up a rental car while Practical Car and Van Rental (Ⓦ practical.co.uk) offer pick up and drop off in Chippenham as well as Heathrow. For something a little more special, hire a classic car from Vintage Classics, based in Melksham in Wiltshire (Ⓦ vintage-classics.co.uk).

You'll get the cheapest price by dropping off your vehicle in the same place you picked it up, so planning an itinerary that returns to your starting point can save money. It's possible to pick up and drop off in different places (for example, you could pick up at Heathrow and drop off at Bristol airport) but this often incurs a one-way fee, which can be quite sizeable.

Almost all rental cars in England are **manual**; if you require an automatic you'll need to book further in advance – and be sure to specify that you want an automatic transmission.

To rent a car in England you will need to have

PARKING

Most attractions have designated parking, which is very often free of charge. In towns and cities parking becomes more of a hassle, and **fees** to park can be hefty. A blue sign with a white **P** at its centre denotes a car park and these are usually signposted from the entrance to the town. Look for a **pay and display** ticket machine; most take coins with only a few taking notes and credit cards so try to keep some small change in the car. Increasingly there are options to pay via text or a phone app too.

In Bristol and Bath it is better to leave your car outside the city centre in one of the **park and ride** car parks. These are signposted on the approach to each city and parking is **free**; you simply pay for the bus into the centre. Most larger hotels have parking and others will have an agreement with a particular car park nearby – it's always worth checking when you book what the parking arrangements are and how much you will be charged.

held a full driving licence for at least a year. Some rental companies have a minimum **age limit** (often 21) and drivers under 25 almost always have to pay a surcharge.

Taxis

Taxis are a reliable way to travel short distances, especially in the larger towns and cities where there are often **taxi ranks** outside major transport hubs. London and Bristol have ride-sharing **app** Uber (for now) as well as Gett, which allows users to hail licensed black cabs. Both allow you to input your card details in advance; Gett also allows you to pay in cash.

London's **black cabs** are the best in the world, with drivers having to pass the infamous Knowledge, a test that has been a requirement since 1865 and involves learning every road and landmark within a six-mile radius of Charing Cross. Black cabs can be hailed on the street; those with the yellow light on their roof illuminated are available. Black cabs run on a **meter**, with rates set by Transport for London.

Bear in mind that in rural areas taxis are often limited and need to be booked in advance; even at train stations in quieter areas you won't find cabs idling at a designated taxi rank. If you intend to rely on a taxi for a journey, especially at peak times such as Friday and Saturday nights, it's advisable to book a couple of days in advance.

By rail

One of England's great long-distance railway lines, the Great Western Railway (or GWR), runs along the full length of the Great West Way from London Paddington station to Bristol Temple Meads. Its chief engineer was Isambard Kingdom Brunel and you'll travel the course he plotted back in the 1830s, including his Box Tunnel – famously said to be impossible to build. Before he built it.

In one go the journey is just 1hr 40min, but you'll want to stop en route to explore. There are **major stations** in Reading, Swindon and Bath. The GWR also operates local services, with stops at Windsor & Eton Central and Maidenhead en route from London to Reading. There is also another useful GWR line which diverges at Reading, offering services to Newbury, Hungerford and Bedwyn. A further line runs from Bristol Temple Meads and Bath south through Wiltshire, calling at Bradford on Avon en route to Salisbury. These two lines meet at Westbury in Wiltshire.

ESCORTED TOURS

There are companies offering escorted tours of the Great West Way. Tour & Explore (🔟 tourandexplore.co.uk) has a range of guided itineraries.

Tickets for the Great Western Railway can be bought from ticket offices at stations along the route but can be cheaper when bought in advance. For an easy, hassle-free journey, choose the **Great West Way Discoverer Ticket**. Included in this ticket is unlimited off-peak train travel with Great Western Railway from London Paddington or London Waterloo to Bristol Temple Meads, via the Reading and/or Basingstoke routes, with options to branch off towards Oxford and Kemble in the Cotswolds, as well as to Salisbury on the Wiltshire line through Westbury. Also included is unlimited travel on bus services along the route. One-day, three-day and week-long options are available, with prices from just £24 per person. The best bet is to book **online** at 🔟 gwr.com. The website also has **timetables**. From outside the UK, book online through ACP (🔟 acprail.com) or your travel agent. Collect tickets from the ticket machines at all stations. You just need the credit card you paid with and the confirmation number you will have received by email.

By water

The Great West Way can be travelled entirely by water and incorporates the River Thames, which flows from the Cotswolds in the west to London in the east, the River Kennet (a tributary of the Thames) and the River Avon, which flows from South Gloucestershire to Bristol.

River Thames

There are numerous boat trips available on the Great West Way. One of the best places to get out on the water is Henley, on the River Thames, which hosts the world famous annual regatta and is also a popular jumping off point for cruises along the river with local operator Hobbs of Henley (🔟 hobbsof henley.com). Also on the Thames, French Brothers (🔟 frenchbrothers.co.uk) operate sightseeing cruises to Maidenhead, Runnymede and Hampton Court from Windsor; Salter's Steamers (🔟 salters steamers.co.uk) offers trips between Oxford and Staines and Thames Rivercruise (🔟 thamesriver cruise.co.uk) hosts afternoon tea, jazz and sundowner cruises.

River Avon

On the River Avon, Bristol is a hub for boat trips, with Bristol Packet (⦿bristolpacket.co.uk) and Bristol Community Ferry Boats (⦿bristolferry.com) both operating trips along Avon Gorge and around Bristol harbour.

The Kennet & Avon Canal

The Kennet & Avon Canal runs along the route of the Great West Way for 87 miles and incorporates navigable sections of the River Avon (from Bath to Bristol) and the River Kennet (from Newbury to Reading). There are 105 locks along the way and the waterway can be used to travel from Bristol to London by joining the River Thames at Reading.

Narrowboat rental

There are numerous places along the Kennet & Avon Canal to rent a **narrowboat**. Most places rent boats by the week (seven nights), with some options for shorter rentals, usually either Friday to Monday or Monday to Friday.

Although you don't need a **licence** to drive a narrowboat on the canal, cruising the River Avon or River Kennet requires a licence, as well as experience of narrowboating. For more information and an application form, visit ⦿canalrivertrust.org.uk.

If this is your first time at the tiller you'll need to stick to the canal, which runs for 57 miles between Bath and Newbury. You will probably travel at about two miles per hour and are likely to want to cruise for around four hours a day (including 15 minutes for each lock), so in a week don't plan to cover more than about 50 miles. You will almost certainly have

to return the boat to the original pick-up location.

The following companies, all based on the Kennet & Avon Canal, have narrowboats to **rent**. They get booked up fast so reserve well ahead of your trip: Black Prince (⦿black-prince.com), Canal Holidays (⦿canalholidays.com), Foxhangers (⦿foxhangers. co.uk), Honeystreet Boats (⦿honeystreetboats.co.uk), Moonraker Canalboats (⦿moonboats.co.uk), Sally Narrowboats (⦿sallynarrowboats.co.uk), White Horse Boats (⦿whitehorsenarrowboats.co.uk), Wiltshire Narrowboats (⦿wiltshire-narrowboats.co.uk).

The Kennet & Avon Canal is looked after by the Canal & River Trust, who are responsible for some 2000 miles of waterways across England and Wales. The Trust maintains the waterway and locks, issues licences and maintains an informative website, which has more information about the canal (⦿canalrivertrust.org.uk).

Driving a narrowboat

You don't need a licence to drive a narrowboat on the canal and for the most part, manoeuvring one is easy. The driver stands at the back end of the boat at the tiller, a type of long lever that is pushed left to steer to the right and vice versa. Unlike in a car, movement takes a few seconds to happen so planning ahead is key, though the **speed limit** on all canals is only 4 miles per hour – nothing happens too quickly. You'll also find that steering from the back means you can see the whole boat ahead of you, as well as where you are going.

The Kennet & Avon Canal has a large number of **locks**, used to change the water level so that your boat can travel either up or downhill. Two boats can fit in most locks at once and it is good **canal practice** to ensure you are travelling with another boat where possible. This saves water and means there are two crews to operate the locks. Since they are opened and closed using very heavy wooden gates this can really speed things up. You might find an audience gathers at some locks too, keen to

---

---

get involved.

The longest section of locks is the Caen Hill flight outside the town of Devizes. This incorporates 29 locks in total, with 16 of them marching in a straight line up the hillside and takes at least half a day to travel up (or down). This is best for longer itineraries.

If you'd rather avoid locks altogether there are some stretches of the canal that are entirely **lock-free**. East of Devizes there are several miles up to Pewsey Bridge without locks and you can rent a narrowboat from Honey Street, in the centre of this section. Rent in Bradford on Avon and there is just one lock, then none until Bath.

Life on a narrowboat

Mooring is allowed more or less anywhere along the canal, as long as you tie up on the towpath side and do not block a lock, bridge or water point. There are often metal rings to tie onto and narrowboats all come with mooring pins and a gangplank.

Most narrowboats are small, with limited amounts of storage. On most boats the dining table converts into a bed, so if you are told it sleeps four this almost certainly means two in one separate bedroom and two in the living space. If you want to avoid the nightly reconfiguration of your dining space it can be worth booking a boat that can take a larger number of people than you need it to – and always check the number of actual **bedrooms** you'll get.

You can expect a reasonably well-equipped **kitchen** (called the galley) complete with a cooker and a fridge, as well as a bathroom with shower and toilet. Bikes are almost always welcome onboard and can be stored on the roof of the boat.

By bike

Cycling the Great West Way can be extremely rewarding and there are numerous bike-friendly routes you can

---

BATH SELF CATERING

Bath can be a particularly tricky place to find well-priced accommodation. This is where the Bath Area Self-catering Association comes in, bringing together the cream of independently owned self-catering properties in and around the city. Properties range from small one-bedroom cottages right up to chic Georgian townhouses that can sleep twelve or more. Check out what's on offer at Ⓦ bathselfcatering.com.

---

take. These are highlighted throughout the guide.

Bike rental is easily organised in most places and Bristol and Bath both have bike sharing schemes. A good resource for cycling on the western end of the Great West Way, around Bristol and Bath, is Ⓦ betterbybike.info, which has information on routes and bike rental. In Wiltshire, Ⓦ connecting-wiltshire.co.uk has bike rental listings.

On foot

Much of the Great West Way is best explored on foot and there are hundreds of short walks and trails through its parks, around its castles and country houses and along its canal and rivers.

The best **trails** have been highlighted throughout the guide but walking is the freest way to travel and the best **walks** on the Great West Way often start with the words "Let's just see what's around that corner". If you'd rather join an organized waling group tour, check out Alison Howell's Footrails (Ⓦ foottrails.co.uk) for itineraries.

Accommodation

Accommodation on the Great West Way ranges from large five-star hotels to quaint B&Bs with a handful of rooms. Hotels here are often in interesting old buildings – former coaching inns, converted mansions and manor houses – which offer heaps of historic atmosphere. Accommodation does tend towards the expensive, but there are bargains to be had.

A nationwide **grading system**, annually updated, awards **stars** to hotels, guesthouses and B&Bs. The system does lay down minimum levels of standards and service. However, not every establishment participates and you shouldn't assume that a particular place is no good simply because it doesn't. In rural areas some of the best accommodation is to be found in **farmhouses** and other properties whose facilities may technically fall short of official standards. There are hotel recommendations throughout this guide, as well as on the official website (Ⓦ Great-WestWay.co.uk).

Hotels

English hotels vary wildly in size, style, comfort and

price. The starting price for a **basic** hotel is around £80 per night for a double or twin room, breakfast usually included; anything more **upmarket**, or with a bit of boutique styling, will be around £100 a night, while at the **top-end** properties the sky's the limit, especially in London or in resort or country-house hotels. Many city hotels in particular charge a room-only rate.

B&Bs, guesthouses and pubs

At its most basic, the typical English **bed and breakfast** (**B&B**) is an ordinary private house with a couple of bedrooms for paying guests. Larger establishments with more rooms, style themselves as **guesthouses**, but are much the same thing.

At the extreme budget end of the scale – basic B&Bs under £70 a night – you'll normally experience small rooms, fairly spartan facilities and shared bathrooms (though there are some fantastic exceptions). You'll pay a few pounds more for en-suite shower and toilet, while at the top end of the range you can expect real style, fresh flowers, gourmet breakfasts, king-sized beds and luxurious bathrooms. Many top-notch B&Bs – say around £100–120 or more per night – offer more luxury and far better value pound for pound than more impersonal hotels. In this category you can also count **pubs** (or inns), and the increasingly popular "**restaurants with rooms**". Both will often have only a handful of rooms, but their atmosphere – and the lazy option of laying your head in the same place that you eat and drink – may make them a good choice.

Self-catering

Holiday self-catering properties range from city penthouses to secluded cottages. **Studios and apartments**, available by the night in many cities, offer an attractive alternative to hotels, with prices from around £90 a night (more in London). Rural **cottages and houses** work out cheaper, though the minimum rental period may be a week. Depending on the season and location, expect to pay from £350 for a week in a small cottage, considerably more for a larger property in a popular tourist spot.

Food and Drink

England no longer has to feel ashamed of its culinary offerings. Over the last couple of decades changing tastes have transformed supermarket shelves, restaurant menus and pub blackboards, with an increasing importance placed on good-quality and sustainable eating – not only sourcing products locally, but also using free-range, organic, humanely produced ingredients. London continues to be the main centre for all things foodie and fashionable, though great restaurants, gastropubs, farmers' markets and interesting local food suppliers can be found across England, often in surprisingly out-of-the-way places. Bristol is certainly hot on London's heels and the Great West Way is home to some of the country's leading restaurants, including two which at the time of writing held three Michelin stars, the highest award possible.

English cuisine

For some visitors the quintessential English meal is **fish and chips**, a dish that can vary from the succulently fresh to the indigestibly greasy. Local knowledge is the key, as most towns, cities and resorts have at least one first-rate fish and chip shop ("chippie") or restaurant. Other **traditional English dishes** (steak and kidney pie, bacon sandwiches, roast beef, sausage and mash, pork pies) have largely discarded their stodgy image and been poshed-up to become restaurant, particularly gastropub, staples. Many hitherto neglected or previously unfashionable English foods – from brawn to brains – are finding their way into top-end restaurants, too, as inventive restaurateurs, keen on using seasonal produce to reinvent the classics. The principles of this "nose to tail" eating cross over with the increasingly modish **Modern British cuisine**, which marries local produce with ingredients and techniques from around the world.

Vegetarians need not worry, veggie restaurants are fairly easy to find in towns and cities and practically every restaurant and pub will have at least one vegetarian option. You'll find that Italian, Indian and Chinese restaurants usually provide a decent range of meat-free dishes, too. Veganism is a growing movement in English cuisine as well – many restaurants now have **vegan** options on their menus and plenty of top fine-dining places have developed vegan tasting menus. Thanks to England's multi-ethnic population you also shouldn't have any trouble finding places that adhere to religious requirements such as halal and kosher, especially in the main towns and cities.

The wealth of **fresh produce** varies regionally, from hedgerow herbs to fish landed from local boats and, of course, seasonally. Restaurants are increasingly making use of **seasonal** ingredients and in rural areas many farms offer "Pick Your Own" sessions, when you can come away with armfuls of delicious berries, orchard fruits and root vegetables. Year-round you'll find superlative **seafood** – from crabs to cockles, oysters to lobster – fine cheeses and delicious free-range meat. Check out the growing profusion of **farmers' markets** and farm shops, usually signposted by the side of the road in rural areas, to enjoy the best local goodies and artisan products.

Cafés, tearooms and coffee shops

Though still a nation of tea-drinkers, Brits have become bona fide **coffee** addicts, and international chain outlets dot every high street. However, there will usually be at least one independent coffee shop, even in the smallest places, and **artisan** coffee, brewed with obsessive care by super-cool baristas, can be found in London, Bristol and other major centres. Despite the encroaching grip of the coffee chains, every town, city and resort in England should also have a few cheap **cafés** offering non-alcoholic drinks, all-day breakfasts, snacks and meals. Most are only open during the daytime and have few airs and graces; the quality is not guaranteed.

A few more genteel **teashops** or **tearooms** serve sandwiches, cakes and light meals throughout the day, as well, of course, as tea – the best of them will offer a full afternoon tea, including sandwiches, cakes and scones with cream and jam.

Pubs and gastropubs

The old-fashioned English **pub** remains an enduring social institution and is often the best introduction to town or village life. In some places it might be your only choice for food. England's foodie renaissance, and a commercial need to diversify, means that many have had to up their game and quality is increasingly dependable.

The umbrella term **gastropub** can refer to anything from a traditional country inn with rooms and a restaurant to a slick city-centre pub with stylish dining room, but generally indicates a pub that puts as much emphasis on the food as the drink. Some are really excellent – and just as expensive as a regular restaurant, though usually with a more informal feel – while others simply provide a relaxed place in which to enjoy a gourmet pork pie or cheese platter with your pint.

Restaurants

Partly by dint of their size, London and Bristol have the broadest selection of **high-end restaurants**, and the widest choice of cuisines on the Great West Way, but there are some seriously fine dining options in some much more out of the way locations. Indeed, wherever you are in England you're rarely more than half an hour's drive from a really good meal.

The going rate for a meal with drinks in most modest restaurants is more like £30–40 per person. If a restaurant has any sort of reputation, you can expect to be spending £40–60 each, and much, much more for the services of a top chef – tasting menus (excluding drinks) at the best-known Michelin-starred restaurants cost upwards of £80 per person. However, **set meals** can be a steal, even at the poshest of restaurants, where a limited-choice two- or three-course lunch or "pre-theatre" menu might cost less than half the usual price. There are restaurant recommendations throughout this guide, as well as on the official website (W GreatWestWay. co.uk).

Drinking

Originating as wayfarers' hostelries and coaching inns, **pubs** – "public houses" – have outlived the church and marketplace as the focal points of many a British town and village. They are as varied as the townscapes: in larger market towns you'll find huge oak-beamed inns with open fires and polished brass fittings; in more remote villages there are stone-built pubs no larger than a two-bedroomed cottage. In towns and cities corner pubs still cater to local neighbourhoods, the best of them stocking an increasingly varied list of local beers and craft brews, while chain pubs, cocktail bars, independent music venues and wine bars all add to the mix. Most pubs and bars serve food in some shape or form.

Most pubs are officially open from 11am to 11pm, though cities and resorts have a growing number of places with extended licences, especially at weekends. The legal **drinking age** is 18 and many places will have a special family room (particularly outside cities) or a beer garden, often with playground, where young children are welcome, even into the evenings.

Beer and cider

Beer, sold by the pint (generally around £3.50–5) and half pint (often just a touch over half the price), is England's staple drink and has been a mainstay of the local diet for centuries, dating back to times when water was too dangerous to drink.

Ask simply for a "beer", though, and you'll cause no end of confusion. While lager is sold everywhere, in recent years there's been a huge resurgence in regional beer-brewing, and England's unique glory is its **real ale** or **cask ale**, a refreshing beer brewed with traditional ingredients, without additional carbonation, pumped by hand from a cask and served at cellar temperature (not "warm", as some jibes imply). If it comes out of an electric pump it isn't the real thing (though it might be a craft beer).

The most common ale is known as **bitter**, with a colour ranging from straw-yellow to dark brown, depending on the brew. Other real ales include golden or **pale ales**, plus darker and maltier **milds**, **stouts** and **porters**. For more on cask ales, check the website of the influential **Campaign for Real Ale** (Ⓦ camra.org.uk), who remain the bastions of this traditional brewing scene.

Complementary to real ale are the **craft beers** produced by hundreds of small, independent breweries that have flourished in recent years, influenced at least in part by the American craft-brewing scene. Though hoppy pale ales predominate, the range of English craft beers is overwhelming. They cover everything from German-style lagers to IPAs (Indian Pale Ales) and Belgian-influenced *sour saisons*; name a beer style and an independent English brewer will have tried making it – in small batches, probably in a shed in the suburbs or under the railway arches in a former industrial zone. Along the Great West Way names to look out for include the Bristol-based Wiper and True, West Berkshire Brewery and Richmond Brewery Company.

The resurgence of independent breweries means that, unlike a decade ago, in many pubs across the country you'll see a row of quirky hand pumps and keg clips lined up along the bar, boasting local provenance and unusual names. It's worth asking if there's a good local brewery whose beers you should try (and a good pub will let you taste first).

Though many pubs are owned by large breweries who favour their own beers, this beer revolution has increased the choice in most places. Still best, however, is a **free house** – an independently run pub that can sell whichever beer it pleases.

The Great West Way's other traditional pint is **cider**, made from fermented apple juice and usually sparkling, with most brewers based in the west. There's also a variant made from pears, called **perry** and **scrumpy**, a potent and cloudy beverage, usually flat, dry and very apple-y. In most pubs you'll only find a few of the big-name brands, though you will find more ciders the further west you travel. In recent years "real" cider – which the Campaign for Real Ale defines as containing a minimum of ninety percent fresh apple juice, along with a few other requirements – has been gaining popularity, ranging from sweet, sparkling golden ciders to cloudy, unfiltered ones from small local producers.

Wine

Now is the time for English **wine**. It has firmly shucked off its image as inferior to its more established European counterparts, with nearly five hundred small-scale vineyards producing delicious tipples, mainly in southeastern England, where the conditions – and rising temperatures – are favourable. The speciality is sparkling wine, and the best of these have beaten French champagnes in international blind-tasting competitions. There are a couple of high-quality small producers on the Great West Way, including a'Beckett's just outside Devizes, Quoins Organic Vineyard near Bradford on Avon and Alder Ridge near Hungerford. For more, see Ⓦ englishwineproducers.co.uk.

Sports and Outdoor Activities

As the birthplace of football, cricket, rugby and tennis, England boasts a series of sporting events that attract a world audience. For those who wish to participate, the UK caters for just about every outdoor activity, in particular walking, cycling and water sports, but there are also opportunities for anything from rock climbing to pony trekking.

Spectator sports

Football (soccer) is the national game in England, with a wide programme of professional league matches taking place every Saturday afternoon from early August to mid-May, with plenty of Sunday and midweek fixtures too. It's very difficult to get tickets to **Premier League** matches involving the most famous teams (Chelsea, Arsenal, Manchester United, Manchester City, Liverpool), but it is often possible to get tickets to the lower-league games.

Bristol is home to two football teams: Bristol City and Bristol Rovers. There is a fierce rivalry between the two teams but at the time of writing they were in different leagues, with Bristol City in the Championship (the league below the Premier League) and

Bristol Rovers one league below them, in Football League One. There are also decent teams in Reading and Swindon; at the time of writing Reading FC were in the Championship and Swindon Town in Football League Two.

Rugby comes in two codes – 15-a-side **Rugby Union** and 13-a-side **Rugby League**, both fearsomely brutal contact sports that can make entertaining viewing even if you don't understand the rules. In England, rugby is much less popular than football, but Rugby League has a loyal and dedicated fan base in the north, while Rugby Union has traditionally been popular with the English middle class. Key Rugby Union and League games are sold out months in advance, but ordinary fixtures present few ticketing problems. The Rugby Union season runs from September to just after Easter, Rugby League February to September.

Cricket is English idiosyncrasy at its finest. People from non-cricketing nations – and most Brits for that matter – marvel at a game that can last several days and still end in a draw, while many people are unfamiliar with its rules. International, five-day "Test" matches, pitting the English national side against visiting countries, are played most summers at grounds around the country, and tickets are usually fairly easy to come by. The domestic game traditionally centres on four-day County Championship matches between English county teams, though there's far bigger interest – certainly for casual watchers – in the "Twenty20" (T20) format, designed to encourage flamboyant, decisive play in three-hour matches.

Horse racing is a national obsession, with a history dating back centuries. Along the Great West Way are some of the country's leading racecourses and there are race meetings throughout the year. The highest profile event is Royal Ascot, a five-day meeting at Ascot Racecourse attended by the Queen, while Newbury Racecourse hosts high profile races including the Lockinge Stakes in May.

The Great West Way is also home to the Kennet & Avon Canal, which hosts the annual Devizes to

---

THE NATIONAL CYCLE NETWORK

The National Cycle Network (🖥 sustrans. org.uk) is a network of traffic-free on-road cycling routes. **Route 4** follows the Great West Way, running from London westwards towards Wales over a total distance of 423 miles.

CYCLING TOURS

There are companies offering cycling tours of the Great West Way. Active England (🖥 activeenglandtours.com) has four- and six-day guided itineraries.

Westminster Canoe Race.

Finally, if you're in England at the end of June and early July, don't miss the country's annual fixation with **tennis** in the shape of the **Wimbledon Championships**. It's often said that no one gives a hoot about the sport for the other fifty weeks of the year, though the success of Scottish champion Andy Murray, changed that somewhat, and has meant the crowds at Wimbledon and watching on screens across the country were for years no longer rooting for an underdog. Advance tickets for main courts are hard to come by, but you can join the queue for ground passes (🖥 wimbledon.com).

Walking

There are numerous **walking routes** along the Great West Way, including three National Trails. For shorter walks, you could check out the **National Trust** website (🖥 nationaltrust.org.uk), which details picturesque routes of varying lengths that weave through or near their properties. If you're travelling on public transport, consult the user-generated site **Car Free Walks** (🖥 carfreewalks.org), which details hundreds of routes that set off and finish at train stations and bus stops, providing OS map links and elevation profiles for each. Various **membership associations**, including the Ramblers Association (🖥 ramblers.org.uk) and Walkers are Welcome (🖥 walkersarewelcome.org.uk), also provide information and route ideas online. There is also lots of information on walking the Great West Way on the official website (🖥 GreatWestWay.co.uk).

Even for short hikes you need to be **properly equipped**, follow local advice and listen out for local **weather** reports – British weather is notoriously changeable and increasingly extreme. You will also need a good **map** – in most cases one of the excellent and reliable Ordnance Survey (OS) series, usually available from local tourist offices or outdoor shops.

Cycling

The **National Cycle Network** is made up of 14,500 miles of signed cycle route and the Great West Way is home to several hundred miles of trails.

Sustrans (W sustrans.org.uk), a charitable trust devoted to the development of environmentally sustainable transport, publishes an excellent series of waterproof cycle maps (1:100,000) and regional guides and has a useful website. England's biggest cycling organization, **Cycling UK** (W cyclinguk.org), provides lists of tour operators and rental outlets, and supplies members with touring and technical advice, as well as insurance.

Water Sports

The Great West Way may not include any coastline but that doesn't mean there are no **water sports** along the route. The **Cotswold Water Park**, an area of more than 150 lakes stretching across some 40 square miles has a beach for **swimming** plus operators offering everything from **sailing** to **water skiing**. It is also possible to do stand up paddle boarding, kayaking and canoeing along the Kennet & Avon Canal, River Thames in Bristol and Bath. SUP Bristol (W supbristol.com) operate paddle boarding adventures around Bristol Harbour.

Travel essentials

Costs

Faced with another £5 pint, a £25 main course and a £20 taxi ride back to your £100-a-night hotel, England can seem expensive – at least in the tourist hotspots. Couples staying in B&Bs, eating at local pubs and restaurants and sightseeing should expect to splash out around £70 per person each day, while if you're renting a car, staying in hotels and eating at fancier places, budget for at least £120 per person. Double this last figure if you choose to stay in a stylish city or grand country house hotel, while with any visit to London work on the basis that you'll need an extra £30–50 per day.

Crime and personal safety

Terrorist attacks in Europe may have changed the general perception of how safe England feels, but it's still extremely unlikely that you'll be at any risk as you travel around, though you will be aware of heightened **security** in places such as airports, major train stations and high-profile sights.

You can walk more or less anywhere on the Great West Way without fear of harassment, though the big cities such as London and Bristol can have their edgy districts and it's always better to err on the side of caution, especially late at night. Leave your passport and valuables in a hotel safe (carrying **ID** is not compulsory, though if you look particularly youthful and intend to drink in a pub or buy alcohol in a shop it can be a good idea to carry it) and exercise the usual caution on public transport. If you're taking a **taxi**, always make sure that it's officially licensed and never pick one up in the street, unless it's an official black cab in London.

Other than asking for directions, most visitors rarely come into contact with the **police**, who as a rule are approachable and helpful. Most wear chest guards and carry batons, though regular street officers do not carry guns. If you are robbed, report it straight away to the police; your insurance company will require a **crime report number**. For **police, fire** and **ambulance** services phone ☏ 999.

Electricity

The **current** is 240V AC. North American appliances will need a transformer and adaptor; those from Europe, South Africa, Australia and New Zealand only need an adaptor. The UK uses plug type G, which has three pins; adaptors can be purchased at the airport and in high street electrical shops.

Emergencies

For **police, fire** and **ambulance** services phone ☏ 999. If you require urgent medical assistance but it is not an emergency you can call the free 24hr NHS helpline on ☏ 111.

Entry requirements

At the time of writing citizens of all European countries – except Albania, Bosnia and Herzegovina, Macedonia, Montenegro, Serbia and all the former Soviet republics (other than the Baltic states) – can enter England with just a **passport**, for up to three months (and indefinitely if you're from the EU, European Economic Area or Switzerland). Americans, Canadians, Australians and New Zealanders can stay for up to six months, providing they have a return ticket and funds to cover their stay. Citizens of most other countries require a **visa**, obtainable from their British consulate or mission office. Check with the **UK Border Agency** (W ukvisas.gov.uk) for up-to-date information about visa applications, extensions and all aspects of residency.

The 2016 referendum, when the UK voted **to leave the European Union**, has, in theory, put many visa and entry requirements to the UK in flux, particularly for work or longer stays for citizens of the EU, EEA and Switzerland. In reality, the status quo will most likely continue for short-term visits, when visas are unlikely to be required, but check in advance as work, study and longer-term visa requirements may be subject to change.

Health

No vaccinations are required for entry into England. Citizens of all EU and EEA countries and Switzerland are entitled to free medical treatment within the National Health Service (**NHS**) on production of their **European Health Insurance Card** (EHIC) or, in extremis, their passport or national identity card. However, this could change when the UK leaves the EU, so check in advance.

Some Commonwealth countries also have reciprocal healthcare arrangements with the UK. If you don't fall into either of these categories, you will be charged for all medical services – except those administered by accident and emergency units at NHS hospitals – so health insurance is strongly advised.

Pharmacists (**chemists**) can advise you on minor conditions but can dispense only a limited range of drugs without a doctor's prescription. Most are open standard shop hours; there are also late-night branches in large cities and at 24-hour supermarkets. Minor complaints and injuries can be dealt with at a **doctor's (GP's) surgery**. For serious injuries, go to the 24-hour **Accident and Emergency (A&E)** department of the nearest **hospital**, and in an **emergency**, call an ambulance on ☏999. For non-emergencies call the NHS's 24-hour **helpline** on ☏111.

LGBTQ travellers

England offers one of the most diverse and accessible **LGBTQ** scenes anywhere in Europe. Nearly every sizeable town has some kind of organized LGBTQ life – from bars and clubs to community groups. Listings, news and reviews can be found at *Gay Times* (Ⓦgaytimes.co.uk) and *Pink News* (Ⓦpinknews.co.uk). The website of the campaigning organization Stonewall (Ⓦstonewall.org.uk) is also useful, with directories of local groups and advice on reporting hate crimes, which. The age of consent is 16.

Maps

Petrol stations in England stock large-format **road** atlases produced by the AA, RAC, Collins, Ordnance Survey and others, which cover all of Britain, at a scale of around 1:250,000, and include larger-scale plans of major towns. The best of these is the Ordnance Survey road atlas, which handily uses the same grid reference system as their folding maps. Overall, the **Ordnance Survey** (OS; Ⓦordnance survey.co.uk) produces the most comprehensive maps, renowned for their accuracy and clarity. Their 1:50,000 (pink) *Landranger* series shows enough detail to be useful for most walkers and cyclists, and there's more detail still in the full-colour 1:25,000 (orange) *Explorer* series – both cover the whole of Britain. The full OS range is only available at a few big-city stores or online, but you can get the OS app, which also converts any paper OS map you buy into a digital version.

Money

England's currency is the **pound sterling** (£), divided into 100 pence (p). Coins come in denominations of 1p, 2p, 5p, 10p, 20p, 50p, £1 and £2. Bank of England notes are in denominations of £5, £10, £20 and £50. At the time of writing, £1 was worth US$1.29, €1.11, Can$1.68, Aus$1.75 and NZ$1.93. For current **exchange rates**, visit Ⓦxe.com.

The easiest way to get hold of cash is to use your **debit card** at an **ATM**; there's usually a daily withdrawal limit, which varies depending on the money issuer, but starts at around £250. You'll find outside banks, at all major points of arrival and motorway service areas, at large supermarkets, petrol stations and even inside some pubs, rural post offices and village shops (though a charge of a few pounds may be levied on cash withdrawals at small, standalone ATMs – the screen will tell you).

Credit cards are widely accepted in hotels, shops and restaurants – MasterCard and Visa are almost universal, American Express less so.

Paying by plastic involves inserting your credit or debit card into a "chip-and-pin" terminal, beside the till in shops, or brought to your table in restaurants, and then keying in your PIN to authorize the transaction. **Contactless payments**, where you simply hold your credit or debit card on or near a card reader without having to key in a PIN, are prevalent for transactions up to £30, including on many bus services (including all services in London). Note that the same overseas transaction fees will apply to contactless payments as to those made with a PIN. Contactless has increased the number of establishments that take cards – even

---

THE NATIONAL TRUST

The National Trust was founded in 1895 and works "to preserve and protect historic places and spaces". In practice this means looking after a staggeringly vast line-up of historic houses, landscapes and nature reserves across the country (as well as in Wales and Northern Ireland).

The Great West Way is home to dozens of National Trust properties, listed throughout this guide. There are also numerous properties just off the route. Some worth making a detour for include Montacute House, Barrington Court, Lytes Cary Manor and Tintinhull Garden, all in Somerset. Membership of the Trust costs £69 for a year so if you plan to visit a lot of their properties it can be cheaper to sign up, especially when you consider that membership also includes free parking. Find out more about the Trust and its work at ⓦ nationaltrust.org.uk.

---

market stalls may – though some smaller places, such as B&Bs and shops, may accept cash only, and occasionally there's a minimum amount for card payments (usually £5 or £10). Apple Pay is increasingly widely accepted too, though it shouldn't be relied upon.

You can change currency or cheques at **post offices** and **bureaux de change** – the former charge no commission, while the latter tend to be open longer hours and are found in most city centres and at major airports and train stations.

Smoking

Smoking is banned in all public buildings and offices, restaurants and pubs, and on all public transport. In addition, the vast majority of hotels and B&Bs no longer allow it. E-cigarettes are not allowed on public transport and are generally prohibited in museums and other public buildings; for restaurants and bars it depends on the individual proprietor.

Time

Greenwich Mean Time (GMT) – equivalent to Coordinated Universal Time (UTC) – is used from the end of October to the end of March; for the rest of the year Britain switches to **British Summer Time** (BST), one hour ahead of GMT.

Tipping

All tipping in the UK is optional, despite what some restaurants might have you believe. It is typical to add 10 percent in restaurants, cafés and pubs where table service has been provided and this can be left in cash, though there is often an option to add a tip when paying by card. It is becoming more common to find a 12.5 percent service charge added on to your bill. Note that this is not obligatory.

In taxis it is customary to round up the fare to the nearest reasonable whole number (ie from £9.10 to £10 or £47 to £50), though again this is optional. It is also typical to tip hairdressers and beauticians if using their services.

At the more luxury hotels tipping is somewhat more American-style, with a small cash tip customarily given to the concierge for their advice, to porters for carrying luggage or to valet parking staff when returning your vehicle, especially at the end of your stay. You do not need to tip housekeeping staff but it is not inappropriate to do so.

Tourist information

The Great West Way **website** (ⓦ GreatWestWay .co.uk/plan-your-way) is the best source of information for planning your trip, with an interactive map, listings of accommodation providers, attractions and places to eat, as well as plenty of **practical travel information**.

Tourist offices (also called Tourist Information Centres, or "TICs") exist in major tourist destinations, though local cuts have led to closures over recent years, and services can depend on volunteers. They tend to follow standard shop hours (roughly Mon–Sat 9am–5.30pm), though are sometimes also open on Sundays, with hours curtailed during the winter season (Nov–Easter). We've listed opening hours in the Guide.

Travellers with disabilities

On the whole, England has good facilities for travellers with disabilities. All new public buildings – including museums, galleries and cinemas – are obliged to provide **wheelchair access**; airports and (generally) train stations are accessible; many buses have easy-access boarding ramps; and dropped kerbs and signalled crossings are the rule in every city and town.

However, old buildings and Victorian infrastructure still create problems for accessibility in some places (not all of London's tube system is wheelchair accessible, for example). The number of accessible hotels and restaurants is growing, and reserved parking bays are available almost everywhere, from shopping centres to museums. If you have specific requirements, it's best to talk first to your travel agent, chosen hotel or tour operator.

People with disabilities including visual and hearing impairments or epilepsy are eligible for the **Disabled Persons Railcard** (£20/year; ⓦ disabled persons-railcard.co.uk), which gives a third off the price of most tickets for you and someone accompanying you. There are no bus discounts for disabled tourists in most areas though wheelchair and mobility-scooter users travel for free on London buses and trams at all times and do not need a travelcard or pass.

In addition to the resources listed below, for detailed reviews of some of England's leading attractions – museums, markets, theatres – written by and for disabled people, download the free **Rough Guide to Accessible Britain** (ⓦ accessibleguide.co.uk).

USEFUL CONTACTS

Open Britain ⓦ openbritain.net. Accessible travel-related information, from accommodation to attractions.
Tourism For All ⓦ tourismforall.org.uk. Listings, guides and advice for access throughout England.
VisitWiltshire ⓦ visitwiltshire.co.uk. Listings, information and inspiration covering the whole of Wiltshire.

Travelling with children

Facilities in England for travellers with children are similar to those in the rest of Europe. Breast-feeding is permitted in all public places, including restaurants and cafés, and **baby-changing** rooms are widely available, including in shopping centres and train stations. Children aren't allowed in certain licensed (alcohol-serving) premises, though this doesn't apply to restaurants, and many pubs have family rooms or beer gardens where children are welcome. Some

---

PUBLIC HOLIDAYS

Jan 1 (New Year's Day)
Good Friday
Easter Monday
First Monday in May (May Day)
Last Monday in May
Last Monday in August
Dec 25 (Christmas Day)
Dec 26 (Boxing Day)

B&Bs and hotels won't accept children under a certain age (usually 12) and there are some adults-only hotels that are restricted to over 18s only.

Under-5s generally **travel free** on public transport and get in free to attractions; 5-16-year-olds are usually entitled to concessionary rates. Many public museums and attractions have kids' activity packs, **family events**, play areas, and playgrounds.

Festivals and events calendar

JANUARY

Clarence House Chase ⓦ ascot.co.uk The horse-racing year kicks off at Ascot in mid-January with this Grade 1 National Hunt steeplechase.

FEBRUARY

Slapstick Festival ⓦ slapstick.org.uk Silent films are screened to live music at Bristol's annual silent comedy festival, which also includes magicians and circus acts.

EASTER

Devizes to Westminster Canoe Race ⓦ dw.marsport.co.uk Annual canoe marathon that sees competitors paddle from Devizes in Wiltshire to Westminster in London, a distance of some 125 miles. See them off at Devizes Wharf.
Howard's Day at Castle Combe ⓦ castlecombecircuit.co.uk Easter Monday is the traditional start to the motor racing season at Castle Combe circuit and is marked by this popular race day.

MAY

The Bath Festival ⓦ bathfestivals.org.uk Having celebrated its 70th birthday in 2018, this 17-day festival celebrates music and literature, bringing prominent writers, musicians and cultural figures to the city.
Highclere Country Show ⓦ highclerecountryshow.co.uk The estate better known as "Downton Abbey", Highclere hosts one of England's best country shows, with falconry, gundog displays and the chance to have a go at clay shooting.
Swindon Festival of Literature ⓦ swindonfestivalofliterature .co.uk This fortnight-long literary festival has been running since the 1990s. Expect readings and talks from celebrated writers, poets and storytellers.

JUNE

Royal Ascot ⓦ ascot.co.uk Arguably England's most famous – and grandest – horse racing event, with four days of races each kicked off by a royal carriage parade – your chance to wave at the Queen.
Reading Waterfest ⓦ reading.gov.uk/waterfest A boat parade along

the Kennet & Avon Canal and events among the Abbey ruins including Civil War and archery demonstrations, plus music and dance.

JULY

Bath Carnival ⓦ bathcarnival.co.uk Bath's biggest party features a procession of more than a thousand dancers and musicians through the city plus plenty of world music on the sound systems and at Party in the Park in Sydney Gardens.

Bristol Harbour Festival ⓦ bristolharbourfestival.co.uk Bristol's largest annual event fills the harbour from SS *Great Britain* to the city centre with tall ships, music stages, dance areas and food markets. Expect water displays and circus acts too.

Bristol Shakespeare Festival ⓦ bristolshakespeare festival.org.uk Throughout July each year Bristol celebrates the national Bard with a fresh line-up of contemporary performances of Shakespeare's work, often in unusual spaces.

Devizes Beer Festival ⓦ devizescamra.org.uk Long-running beer festival at Devizes Wharf with a hundred-odd beers to try, some from the Wadworth Brewery just along the canal. Local music too.

Henley Royal Regatta ⓦ hrr.co.uk Established in 1839, this annual regatta attracts rowing crews from around the world to its five days of head to head knockout competitions and is regarded as an integral part of the English social season.

South Cotswold Beer and Music Festival Chipping Sodbury hosts this annual beer-based shindig, where more than eighty real ales and craft beers can be sampled. Running over two days, it also features a line-up of live music.

Kew the Music ⓦ kew.org Kew Gardens hosts six nights of laidback picnic concerts, from big names in every genre of music from pop and rock to classical and jazz.

Upfest ⓦ upfest.co.uk Europe's largest street art and graffiti festival brings together talented artists both local and international to paint live in locations around Bedminster and Southville in Bristol. There's affordable art for sale too.

WOMAD ⓦ womad.co.uk Global fiesta of music, dance, art and food that started in Charlton Park, Wiltshire and has since taken the party to more than 27 countries worldwide.

AUGUST

Bristol International Balloon Fiesta ⓦ bristolballoon fiesta.co.uk Europe's largest annual meeting of hot air balloons brings colour to the sky above Bristol with twice-daily mass balloon launches and the chance to take a ride yourself.

Devizes Carnival Confetti Battle ⓦ devizes.org.uk Nobody knows why it started, but Devizes Carnival's Confetti Battle is surely the most fun you can have with torn up bits of coloured paper. Get stuck in to the battle in the marketplace and stay for the fireworks.

Highclere Castle Battle Proms Concert ⓦ highclerecastle.co.uk This open-air picnic concert features air displays by World War II Spitfire planes and the Red Devils parachute team, live cannon fire and a lot of flag waving to rousing British classical anthems such as *Land of Hope and Glory*.

Reading Festival ⓦ readingfestival.com One of England's biggest and best-loved music festivals, featuring big-name acts from around the world – think of popular bands such as Kings of Leon.

SEPTEMBER

Jane Austen Festival ⓦ janeaustenfestivalbath.co.uk Get your top hats, bonnets and lace out for this 10-day celebration of all things Austen. Highlights include a costumed Promenade through the city, and the Regency Costumed Masked Ball, with dancing in the Pump Room of the Roman Baths.

Heritage Open Days ⓦ heritageopendays.org.uk This national event sees normally closed places throw their doors open to the public over two weekends. Highlights along the Great West Way include Reading Synagogue, Sevington Victorian School in Wiltshire and the Rolls-Royce Heritage Trust in Bristol.

Marlborough Literature Festival ⓦ marlboroughlitfest.org A vibrant literary festival that celebrates the best writing and includes author talks, workshops and performances. Past speakers have included Louis de Bernières, Fay Weldon and Will Self.

OCTOBER

Henley Literary Festival and Children's Literary Festival ⓦ henleyliteraryfestival.co.uk This highly-regarded literary festival (and accompanying children's literary festival) attracts some of the biggest and brightest names in books, such as Sir Michael Morpurgo and Jodi Picoult.

Legoland Fireworks Spectacular ⓦ legoland.co.uk Make your visit to Legoland even more spectacular by timing it to coincide with the annual fireworks spectacular, part of the theme park's spooky Halloween season.

NOVEMBER

Bonfire Night The Saturday closest to November 5th sees towns along the Great West Way celebrating the failure by Guy Fawkes to blow up the Houses of Parliament in London in 1605. This uniquely British event usually involves a huge bonfire, where effigies of Guy Fawkes are burned, as well as large fireworks displays.

Newbury Christmas Country Show Dog shows, a circus, celebrity chefs and the chance to meet Father Christmas, this festive-themed country show at Newbury Showground has something for everyone.

DECEMBER AND CHRISTMAS

Bath Christmas Market ⓦ bathchristmasmarket.co.uk More than two hundred chalets set up in Bath's Georgian streets around the Abbey as part of this German-style Christmas market. Buy local crafts, sip mulled wine and listen to live music.

Christmas at Kew ⓦ kew.org A trail of festive light installations runs through Kew Gardens from late November until early January. More than a million lights are installed along the route.

Windsor On Ice ⓦ windsoronice.com From mid-November until early January Alexandra Gardens in Windsor plays host to two ice rinks – one indoor and one outdoor – and plenty of other fairground rides, plus the chance to visit Father Christmas.

National Trust

Find famous places and hidden gems with the National Trust

There are spaces to relax, gardens to explore, countryside to tramp through and stories to discover at 15 National Trust places along the Great West Way.

nationaltrust.org.uk/south-west

#nationaltrust

When you visit, donate, volunteer or join the National Trust, your support helps us to look after special places in the South West such as Tyntesfield, Avebury, and Prior Park, for ever, for everyone.

My Great West Way

Rob Dean, Chairman, Kennet & Avon Canal Trust
Devizes, Wiltshire, ⓦ katrust.org.uk

How long have you lived on the Great West Way?

I've been on the Kennet & Avon Canal which runs through the heart of the Great West Way for nearly 15 years.

What does the Great West Way mean to you?

The Kennet & Avon Canal sums up everything that's so great about the Great West Way: beauty, variety, heritage and tranquillity. From bustling towns like Reading and Newbury, to the placid beauty of the Vale of Pewsey, a journey along the Great West Way provides so much to experience and enjoy. All you have to do is slow down.

What inspires you most about your area?

The mix of natural beauty and industrial heritage can be best appreciated by a visit to the Georgian steam-driven pumping station at Crofton, or the amazing flight of 29 locks at Caen Hill near Devizes. I feel honoured to play a part in looking after these special places and presenting them to visitors.

What is your favourite thing to do along the Great West Way?

I most like to be on a boat, which is how I spend much of my time. Ideally early morning gliding through the early mist looking out for kingfishers, herons and water voles. I never tire of it!

David Glass, Head Gardener, Bowood
Wiltshire, ⓦ bowood.org

How long have you lived on the Great West Way?

I have lived in the area for over forty years and have never felt I needed to move anywhere else!

What does the Great West Way mean to you?

The Great West Way is a fantastic opportunity to promote a wonderful part of the country that has so much to offer.

What inspires you most about your area?

It's such a diverse place. Just a few miles southeast are rolling chalk downs and a few miles west are the beautiful Cotswolds. In between we have restored canals, stately homes and many ancient historic sites.

What is your favourite thing to do along the Great West Way?

We as a family are very keen walkers and there are many fantastic walks in the area including around Castle Combe. The towpath of the Kennet & Avon Canal can take you all the way into Bath with plenty of opportunities to stop for tea and cake. And there are some amazing views to take in along the Ridgeway.

Tom McEwen, Customer Service Delivery Manager, Bristol Airport
Bristol, ⓦ bristolairport.co.uk

How long have you lived on the Great West Way?

Eighteen years, having moved to Bristol for work.

What does the Great West Way mean to you?

Sheer variety, from the Georgian elegance of Bath to the proudly independent places to eat and drink in Bristol, typified by the shipping containers lining Wapping Wharf, with easy access to beautiful countryside when you want a break from city life.

What inspires you most about your area?

The vibrancy of Bristol, known around the world for the creations of Isambard Kingdom Brunel and now proud of its culture and diversity.

What is your favourite thing to do along the Great West Way?

Rowing the River Avon from Bath to a pub at Bathampton Mill for Sunday lunch is certainly recommended – and makes having dessert guilt-free!

Mark Hanks, Head Concierge, Royal Crescent Hotel

Bath, ⓦ royalcrescent.co.uk

How long have you lived on the Great West Way?

I have lived my entire life on the Great West Way. I was born near Marlow, have progressed westward, and am now living in Bath.

What does the Great West Way mean to you?

The Great West Way has long been travelled commercially between London and Bristol – by stagecoach, canal, rail or nowadays by road. Sadly most of us charge along the M4 with no awareness of the history and natural beauty that we are passing through. The Great West Way seeks to change that.

What inspires you most about your area?

I don't believe that anyone can tire of Bath's architecture. The local limestone from which the majority of the city is built truly enhances the elegant proportions of its buildings.

What is your favourite thing to do along the Great West Way?

With many picturesque villages and historic sites to visit it is hard to identify a favourite along the route, though I am biased by all that Bath has to offer.

Andrew Smith, Director, Westonbirt, The National Arboretum

Westonbirt, Gloucestershire, ⓦ forestryengland.uk/westonbirt-the-national-arboretum

How long have you lived on the Great West Way?

Nine years.

What does the Great West Way mean to you?

It's a lifestyle thing – the opportunity to live in a city like Bristol that is both cultural and environmentally aware, but also to work in the Cotswolds among verdant scenery. I pass a lot of people going in the other direction on my daily commute! Then on days off we get to enjoy all the things tourists come here for – whether that's cycling, walking or messing about on the river.

What inspires you most about your area?

The fact we're following in the footsteps of visionaries like Brunel, who built our transport links, or Robert Holford, who created the National Arboretum at Westonbirt. It's a real privilege to benefit from their legacy and to be responsible for its ongoing care.

What is your favourite thing to do along the Great West Way?

To experience the awakening of spring at Westonbirt, The National Arboretum, starting with the flowering of magnolias in February through to the riot of colour from the rhododendrons culminating in May.

Cpt. Les Brodie, former Concorde pilot and Aerospace Bristol

'Flight Ambassador'

Bristol, ⓦ aerospacebristol.org

How long have you lived on the Great West Way?

Since 1974, so almost 45 years!

What does the Great West Way mean to you?

It's a marvellous place to live. It's particularly wonderful to be so close to beautiful countryside along the banks of the River Thames and the Kennet & Avon Canal. I'm fascinated by Crofton Beam Engines, which still operate on the canal, more than 200 years after they were built.

What inspires you most about your area?

I'm most inspired by the history of the area and our engineering achievements. The Clifton Suspension Bridge is a masterpiece of engineering and I flew Concorde over the bridge on her last ever flight. It was a very special moment to pilot one masterpiece of engineering over another! I'd encourage anyone to visit both the bridge and Concorde at Aerospace Bristol.

What is your favourite thing to do along the Great West Way?

My favourite pastime is to take my boat out on the river. It's a fantastic way to relax and take in the stunning countryside along the Great West Way.

Kate Davies, Stonehenge Director

Wiltshire, ⓦ english-heritage.org.uk

How long have you lived on the Great West Way?

I've lived on the Great West Way for 15 years and I love it!

What does the Great West Way mean to you?

Coming from South Wales, the places along the Great West Way have been a large part of my life. Heading east means setting out on new adventures and heading west is home to family and childhood memories. It will always be a special place to me whichever direction I'm travelling.

What inspires you most about your area?

This part of the world is packed with history. Just casting your eye around the landscape surrounding Stonehenge, you can see Bronze Age barrows and Neolithic earthworks. It's incredible that these monuments have survived more than 5000 years and yet we still know relatively little about what they were for and how they were built. The potential to unlock the secrets of our ancestors is inspiring.

What is your favourite thing to do along the Great West Way?

Wiltshire is a treasure trove of pretty villages, beautiful countryside and vibrant towns and cities. I love the Wiltshire Museum in Devizes which houses a nationally important Bronze Age collection and the Salisbury Museum in the Cathedral Close, which tells the story of the city and surrounding landscape. Of course, it's not all about history: the shopping and food are pretty good too!

Will Twomey, Head Brewer, West Berkshire Brewery

Berkshire, ⓦ wbbrew.com

How long have you lived on the Great West Way?

I have lived on The Great West Way my entire life (35 years).

What does the Great West Way mean to you?

I grew up in Bucklebury and have spent the last 13 years working at West Berkshire Brewery in the idyllic countryside surrounding Yattendon. I have poured my life and soul into the brewery and so it has a very special place in my heart.

What inspires you most about your area?

What inspires me the most on The Great West Way is the brewery, but more specifically my colleagues inspire me with their enthusiasm and passion for their work.

What is your favourite thing to do along the Great West Way?

My favourite thing to do along The Great West Way is probably a good pub walk, there's a walk on the Ridgeway that leads to a pub supplied with West Berkshire Brewery called The Bell, in Aldworth, it's one of my favourites.

Alana Wright, National Trust

Lacock, Wiltshire ⓦ nationaltrust.org.uk/lists/national-trust-on-the-great-west-way

How long have you lived on the Great West Way?

Nearly nine years. I've worked in and around Bath, Bristol and Wiltshire.

What does the Great West Way mean to you?

The Great West Way feels like a recognition of just how great this area is and an invitation to visitors to discover it for themselves. I've also found it a nudge to me, as someone who's lived here for so long, to get out and explore further.

What inspires you most about your area?

The history. It's amazing to be able to see hundreds of years of history in one place. It's humbling to stand by the stones at Avebury or in the cloisters at Lacock and think about the people who've stood there before; how different their lives were, and what they'd think if they could see us now.

What is your favourite thing to do along the Great West Way?

I love exploring new places. We're lucky to have such incredible variety – from bustling cities like Bristol to historic houses like Tyntesfield, peaceful gardens like Dyrham Park's and amazing museums like those in Bath as well as traditional villages and beautiful countryside – there's always somewhere new to visit and something new to see.

West of London

The fabulous freneticism of the English capital is shaken off as you travel westwards along the River Thames and embark upon the Great West Way. The River Thames was once the "Great Highway of London" and boats still plough their way up the Thames from central London to the Royal Botanic Gardens at Kew and the picturesque riverside at Richmond.

HIGHLIGHTS

❶ **The Royal Botanic Gardens, Kew** Check out the world's largest living plant collection and marvel at the Victorian glasshouses that display many of them at this UNESCO World Heritage-listed garden. Bring a picnic – this one takes all day. **See below**

❷ **Hampton Court Palace** Henry VIII once lived at this royal palace and William and Mary had Christopher Wren spruce it up in the seventeenth century – which gives an idea of just how magnificent it is. Plus, there's the world-famous maze. Challenge accepted? **See p.54**

❸ **Windsor Castle** If you visit just one castle in England make it this one. The Royal Collection of paintings would be impressive in a plain museum but here, on the ancient walls of the gilded State Rooms, they are gawp-worthy. The Changing of the Guard adds pomp and ceremony to the occasion of your visit. **See p.58**

❹ **Royal Ascot** Place your bets and cheer on the horses in the most exclusive horse racing event Britain has to offer. The Queen leads a Royal procession daily at 2pm – start practising your bow/curtsey. **See p.60**

❺ **Swinley Forest Bike Hub** Test your mettle on the three mountain bike tracks through undulating Swinley Forest. No points for the easy Green, but you'll get full marks (hopefully not literally) for racing down the gnarly Red Trail. **See p.59**

This quintessentially English area – all rowing boats and royal castles – is the eastern extremity of the Great West Way. Heathrow Airport lies between the London suburbs of Kew and Richmond to the east and the Berkshire town of Windsor to the west, making this an easy region to visit just before or after an international flight.

Kew and Richmond are well-to-do enclaves, home to some of West London's wealthiest residents, and are a popular excursion out of the city for their world-class attractions: the UNESCO World Heritage-listed Royal Botanic Gardens at Kew and Hampton Court Palace, with its famous maze. Add in parks such as Richmond Park, with its free-roaming deer and easy walks, Windsor Great Park with its gorgeous gardens, and Swinley Forest with its mountain biking trails and there's plenty to keep you occupied – and active – on a visit here.

Kew and around

The name **KEW** is synonymous with horticulture and most visitors to this leafy suburban idyll on the River Thames in the west of London are here for the **Royal Botanic Gardens**. Kew is also home to the **National Archives** – and many a wealthy west Londoner. The local church, St Anne's on Kew Green, is the burial place of English artist Thomas Gainsborough.

Just to the south – and upriver – is the desirable suburb of Richmond, a lively riverside town that is best known for the vast **Richmond Park,** home to several hundred freely-roaming deer. Further along, around one more bend in the Thames is **Hampton Court**, famous for its fiendish maze as well as for its royal history – it is one of only two of Henry VIII's palaces to survive into the 21st century.

Royal Botanic Gardens, Kew

Kew Green or Kew Road, TW9 3AE • Feb daily 10am–5pm, March daily 10am–6pm, April–Aug Mon–Thurs 10am–7pm, Fri–Sun 10am–8pm; Sep daily 10am–7pm, Oct daily 10am–6pm; Nov & Jan daily 10am–4pm; Dec daily 10am–3.30pm, last entry one hour before closing • £17.75 • ☎ 020 8332 5655, ⓦ kew.org • ⊖ Kew Gardens, then a 500 yard walk down Lichfield Rd to Victoria Gate

Established in 1759, the **Royal Botanic Gardens at Kew** manage the extremely difficult task of being both a world leader in botanic research and an extraordinarily beautiful and popular public park. There's always something to see, whatever the season, but to get the most out of the place – and the world's largest living plant collection – come between spring and autumn, bring a picnic and stay for the day.

Of all the glasshouses, the most celebrated is the **Palm House**, a curvaceous mound of glass and wrought iron, designed by Decimus Burton in the 1840s to house the plants being brought back to Britain by the explorers of the day. Its drippingly humid atmosphere nurtures most of the world's known palm species in a recreated rainforest climate. The **Temperate House** is the largest Victorian glasshouse in the world and reopened in 2018 after extensive restoration. Here you can see 1500 species of plants, some of which are extinct in the wild.

Elsewhere in the gardens, you'll find the **Treetop Walkway**, which lifts you 60ft off the ground and gives you a novel view of the tree canopy, a 163ft-high Pagoda, an art gallery, and various follies and semi-wild areas, including an extensive **arboretum** of some 14,000 trees, many of which cannot be found anywhere else in Britain. The newest addition is **The Hive**, a 57ft-high honeycomb structure that takes you inside the world of honeybees using 900 LED lights and the sound of forty thousand bees. At the time of writing, work was also underway on a new **Children's Garden**, an educational play area for 2–12 year olds, which will open in May 2019.

The three-storey red-brick mansion of **Kew Palace** (April–Oct only), to the northwest of the Palm House, was bought by George II as a nursery and schoolhouse for his umpteen children. Later, George III was confined to the palace and subjected to the dubious attentions of doctors who attempted to find a cure for his "madness".

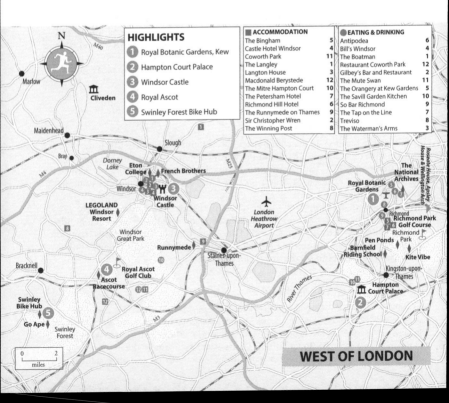

HIGHLIGHTS

1. Royal Botanic Gardens, Kew
2. Hampton Court Palace
3. Windsor Castle
4. Royal Ascot
5. Swinley Forest Bike Hub

■ ACCOMMODATION	
The Bingham	5
Castle Hotel Windsor	4
Coworth Park	11
The Langley	1
Langton House	3
Macdonald Berystede	12
The Mitre Hampton Court	10
The Petersham Hotel	7
Richmond Hill Hotel	6
The Runnymede on Thames	9
Sir Christopher Wren	2
The Winning Post	8

● EATING & DRINKING	
Antipodea	6
Bill's Windsor	4
The Boatman	1
Restaurant Coworth Park	12
Gilbey's Bar and Restaurant	2
The Mute Swan	11
The Orangery at Kew Gardens	5
The Savill Garden Kitchen	10
So Bar Richmond	9
The Tap on the Line	7
Treviso	8
The Waterman's Arms	3

WEST OF LONDON

HEATHROW AIRPORT

Located around 15 miles west of central London, Heathrow (𝕨 heathrowairport.com) has five terminals (though Terminal 1 was officially closed in 2015) and three train/tube stations: one for Terminals 2 and 3 and separate ones for each of Terminals 4 and 5. This is London's (and by most measures, Europe's) busiest airport and it is generally well set up for the number of passengers it handles – 80 million in 2018. For departing passengers there are numerous shops and restaurants once you're through security in every terminal.

For arriving passengers Heathrow is an excellent **gateway** for the Great West Way. All the major car rental companies have large fleets here and you'll find their desks in all four terminals. The airport is just off the M4 motorway, which speeds westwards towards Reading, Swindon and Bristol.

There are also **direct rail** services to Hayes and Harlington, where you can pick up the Great Western Railway (daily 5.30am–midnight; every 30min; journey 5–10min; £6.20 one-way, 𝕨 tfl. gov.uk). National Express **coaches** run to most major UK cities from Heathrow Airport, including Reading (35min), Bath (2hr) and Bristol (2hr). Fares start from £10.50 one-way, 𝕨 nationalexpress.com.

If you're heading into London the **Heathrow Express** trains are your fastest option. They travel nonstop into Paddington station (daily 5.15am–11.45pm; every 15min; journey 15min; from £12.10 one-way off-peak when booked in advance, 𝕨 heathrowexpress.com).

The **Underground** is far cheaper, though a lot slower. The Piccadilly tube line runs directly into central London (daily 5am–11.30pm; Fri & Sat 24hr from terminals 2, 3, 4 & 5 only; every 5min; journey 50min–1hr); £3.10 off-peak, £5.10 peak (Mon–Fri 6.30–9.30am) with Oyster or contactless card. Cash fares are higher (£6). There are also National Express bus services direct to Victoria Coach Station (daily 4.20am–10.10pm; every 20min–1hr; journey 40min–1hr; £6–£13.50 one-way).

The National Archives

Bessant Dr, TW9 4DU • Tue & Thurs 9am–7pm, Wed & Fri–Sat 9am–5pm • free • ☎ 020 8332 5655, 𝕨 nationalarchives.gov.uk

The National Archives is the official archive of the UK government, recording and storing everything from Shakespeare's will to the Foreign Office's latest tweets. A treasure trove of information is available in the reading rooms here, while the Keeper's Gallery displays temporary exhibitions to tie in with current events – in 2018 this focused on the Suffragette movement to celebrate a hundred years of UK women having the vote. If you have family history in the UK this is the place to research it.

Richmond Park

Daily: March–Sept 7am–dusk; Oct–Feb 7.30am–dusk • Free • ☎ 0300 061 2200, 𝕨 royalparks.org.uk • #371 bus from Richmond to Richmond Gate or #65 from Richmond to Petersham Gate

Richmond's greatest attraction is the enormous **Richmond Park**, at the top of Richmond Hill – 2500 acres of undulating grass and woodland, as wild as anything in London. It was created by Charles I in the seventeenth century as a deer park and at eight miles across at its widest point, this is Europe's largest city park, famed for its 650-odd red and fallow deer and for its ancient oaks.

At the Roehampton Gate car park you can hire a trail or road bike by the hour from Parkcycle (from £8/1hr, 𝕨 parkcycle.co.uk). A pleasant route to cycle is the circular **Tamsin Trail**, which loops around the outside of the park on 7.5 miles of gravel and tarmac track. The route is shared with walkers, who can also strike off through the park at will – and who shouldn't miss **King Henry's Mound**, for its unobstructed view all the way to St Paul's Cathedral in central London. This view is protected by law; nothing can be built to obscure it and the trees must be kept trimmed.

Richmond Park Golf Course has two 18-hole courses and several local horse riding stables can organise rides through the park.

1

APSLEY HOUSE AND WELLINGTON ARCH

It's an easy journey into central London from this area, and well worth undertaking for the chance to visit two of the city's most interesting historic sites.

Apsley House (Hyde Park Corner, Wed–Sun 11am–5pm, £10 or £12.70 combined with Wellington Arch, Ⓦ english-heritage.org.uk) was the home of the first Duke of Wellington and is little changed since his historic victory at the Battle of Waterloo in 1815 – it is even still occupied by the current Duke of Wellington. Once known as Number 1 London, the Georgian house is sumptuous, with glittering chandeliers and priceless artworks adorning every room, including works by Caravaggio and Van Dyck. The Duke was showered with gifts from around Europe to thank him for his successes in various battles – look out for the neo-classical silverware from Portugal in the dining room and the colossal statue of Napoleon at the bottom of the grand staircase.

Just outside, Wellington Arch (Hyde Park Corner, winter daily 10am–4pm, summer daily 10am–5pm, £5.40 or £12.70 combined with Apsley House, Ⓦ english-heritage.org.uk) was built as an original entrance to Buckingham Palace but later became a victory arch celebrating the outcome of the Battle of Waterloo. A new exhibition was installed on the third and fourth floors to mark the 200th anniversary, while the balconies at the top of the arch are an unbeatable viewpoint over the Royal Parks to the Houses of Parliament – this is a great place to watch the Changing of the Guard. It is also topped with Europe's largest bronze sculpture, depicting the Angel of Peace riding the Quadriga chariot of war.

Hampton Court Palace

Hampton Court Rd, KT8 9AU • **Palace** Daily: April–Oct 10am–6pm; Nov–March closes 4.30pm; last entry 1hr before closing • £21.20 (includes Magic Garden and maze) • **Magic Garden** April–Oct daily 10am–6pm, last admission 5.15pm • £7.70, kids aged 3–15 £5.80 (includes Maze) • ☏ 020 3166 6000, Ⓦ hrp.org.uk

Hampton Court Palace, a sprawling red-brick ensemble on the banks of the River Thames, is the finest of England's royal abodes. Built in 1516 by the upwardly mobile Cardinal Wolsey, Henry VIII's Lord Chancellor, it was purloined by Henry himself after Wolsey fell from favour. In the second half of the seventeenth century, Charles II laid out the gardens, inspired by what he had seen at Versailles, while William and Mary had large sections of the palace remodelled by Wren a few years later.

Audio guides are available and free guided tours are led by period-costumed historians who bring the place to life. It's a good idea to take a day to explore fully as Hampton Court is huge – but the most rewarding sections are: **Henry VIII's Apartments**, which feature the glorious double-hammer-beamed Great Hall and Chapel Royal, with vaulted ceiling adorned with gilded cherubs; **William III's Apartments**, covered in militaristic *trompe-l'oeil* paintings; **Henry VIII's Kitchens**; and the **Cumberland Art Gallery**, which display a superb selection of works from the Royal Collection.

Overlooked by Wren's magnificent South Front is the formal **Privy Garden**, laid out as it would have been under William III. Here is the palace's celebrated Great Vine, whose grapes are sold at the palace each year in September. Close by is the gallery housing The Triumphs of Caesar, a series of heroic canvases by Andrea Mantegna from around 1486. To the west, the magnificent **Broad Walk** runs north for half a mile from the Thames. Halfway along lies the indoor Royal Tennis Court, used for real tennis, an arcane precursor of the modern game.

To the north of the palace the informal Wilderness area contains the famous trapezoidal **Maze**, commissioned by William III and laid out in 1714. This fiendish puzzle covers a third of an acre (about 7 tennis courts) and is the UK's oldest surviving hedge maze. The average time to complete it is about twenty minutes. Also on this side of the palace grounds is the gorgeous **Rose Garden** and an elaborate adventure playground for kids called the **Magic Garden**.

RIGHT, FROM TOP APSLEY HOUSE; HAMPTON COURT PALACE

1

ARRIVAL AND INFORMATION

BY TRAIN
Kew Gardens and Richmond are one stop apart on the District tube line and London Overground line. Journey times from central London are around 30min (one way fares from £2.80 off peak with an Oyster or contactless card, ⓦ tfl.gov.uk).Hampton Court and Kew Bridge stations can both be reached on direct trains from London Waterloo in about 30min (one way fares from £4.20 with an Oyster or contactless card, ⓦ southwesternrailway.com).

BY BUS
The 65 bus stops at Kew Bridge, Kew Gardens and Richmond station on its journey from Ealing Broadway to Chessington. There is no direct bus from central London. The R68 bus travels to Hampton Court from Richmond (single fare £1.50, ⓦ tfl.gov.uk). There is a coach service linking Windsor Castle with Hampton Court, enabling you to visit both in one day (ⓦ surbitoncoaches.com, daily 12.15pm–2.30pm, every 45min, £10 one way, must be booked in advance).

BY CAR
Kew and Richmond are best reached on public transport as

KEW AND AROUND

west London's streets are extremely busy. If you do drive, Kew Gardens' car park is located close to the Brentford Gate on Ferry Lane (TW9 3AF, £7/day). There is some free parking on Kew Road after 10am. At Richmond Park, parking is free.

Hampton Court is easy to reach by car, signposted off junctions 10 and 12 of the M25. There is parking on-site (£1.60/hr, cash or card).

BY BIKE
Bikes are not allowed in Kew Gardens but there are bike racks at all four entrance gates. At Brentford Gate they are in the car park, under a covered shelter.

The long-distance National Cycle Network route 4 runs through Richmond Park and past Hampton Court palace. At the palace there are bike racks in the car park and next to the main entrance.

BY BOAT
Thames River Boats (☎ 020 7930 2062, ⓦ wpsa.co.uk) operate a daily river boat service from Westminster Pier to Kew (£22 return), Richmond (£25 return) and Hampton Court (£27 return).

ACCOMMODATION

The Bingham 61–63 Petersham Road, Richmond ☎ 020 8940 0902, ⓦ thebingham.co.uk; ⊖ Richmond; map p.44. This classy riverside retreat has stylish contemporary rooms, some with freestanding copper baths and views of the Thames. The restaurant serves upmarket British cuisine. £129.

The Mitre Hampton Court Hampton Court Road ☎ 020 8979 9988, ⓦ mitrehamptoncourt.com; ⌦ Hampton Court; map p.44. A fine hotel right outside Hampton Court Palace and right on the river. Rooms have a historical flavour, with wooden four-poster beds and fireplaces in some. The riverside terrace has lovely views and a straightforward menu including fish and chips (£14) and burgers (£14). £94.

★**The Petersham Hotel** Nightingale Lane, Richmond ☎ 020 8940 7471, ⓦ petershamhotel.co.uk; ⊖ Richmond; map p.44. Family-owned hotel that oozes luxury from every understated room. The bedrooms are classic – think plush carpets and tartan cushions – and there's a restaurant serving fresh, modern dishes. The

hotel's location on the side of Richmond Hill yields cracking Thames views. £80

Richmond Hill Hotel 144–150 Richmond Hill, Richmond ☎ 020 8940 2247, ⓦ richmondhill-hotel .co.uk; ⊖ Richmond; map p.44. Choose between Georgian rooms in the old house and the more contemporary Hill Collection rooms – all decorated in bright colours and with luxury linens. Cedars Health and Leisure Club is in the grounds and has a sauna, steam room and gym plus fitness classes; access is complimentary for hotel guests. The hotel can recommend local walking and cycling routes and if you book direct you'll get free parking. £140

Roseate House 3 Westbourne Terrace, W2 3UL, ☎ 020 7479 6600, ⓦ roseatehotels.com; ⊖ Paddington; map p.44. Luxury hotel near Paddington Station, the eastern-most terminus of the GWW. You're also a short walk from Hyde Park here and rooms are classically beautiful with antique furniture and period features. £144

EATING AND DRINKING

★**Antipodea** 9 Station Approach, Kew ☎ 020 8940 6532, ⓦ antipodea.co.uk; ⊖ Kew Gardens; map p.44. Come for breakfast, of eggs benedict (£11.50), or sweetcorn fritters (£11.90), pop in for lunch (burgers and pides start at £10.50) or relax over a long dinner Aussie-style in this

laidback café restaurant. At dinner the wood-fired pizzas are a hit (from £7) and there's whole grilled lobster for just £33. There's another branch in Richmond too, at 30 Hill St. Sun–Wed 7am–10pm, Thur–Sat 7am–11pm.

The Mute Swan 3 Palace Gate, Hampton Court

1

WALK: THAMES PATH

The Thames Path (🖥 nationaltrail.co.uk/thames-path) follows the eponymous river for 184 miles – all the way from its source in the Cotswolds to the sea just east of London, hugging the Great West Way and linking many of its best attractions. One of the most rewarding sections is the short (roughly 6 miles) segment from Kew to Teddington Lock, which runs from Kew Bridge on an easy path along the side of the Royal Botanic Gardens and southwards past the sixteenth-century pile of Syon House to Richmond. Further along the river are Petersham Meadows – a bucolic haven dotted with munching cattle – and Ham House, a seventeenth-century Stuart house now managed by the National Trust.

☎020 8941 5959, 🖥 brunningandprice.co.uk; 🚆 Hampton Court; map p.44. Opposite the gates of the palace is this welcoming pub serving an extensive range of British ales, gins and whiskies. Downstairs you'll find a pubby vibe, while upstairs is a more refined restaurant. The same menu is served on both floors – lamb shoulder is £17.95, rump steak £19.95. Mon–Thurs 11am–11pm, Fri & Sat 11am–midnight, Sun 11am–10.30pm.

The Orangery at Kew Gardens Near Elizabeth Gate 020 8332 5655, 🖥 kew.org; 🚇 Kew Gardens; map p.44. If you're spending a full day at Kew you'll need lunch, and the Orangery is top pick. There's a serve-yourself salad counter (£6.95) and hot food is served from noon–3.30pm. Expect the likes of roast chicken (£8.95) and fish and chips (£12.50). Mon–Thurs 10am–6pm, Fri–Sun 10am–7pm.

So Bar Richmond 10 Brewers Lane, Richmond ☎020 8940 0427, 🖥 sobar-richmond.co.uk; 🚇 Richmond; map p.44. Classic cocktails and long drinks are served at this stylish bar, where exposed brick walls and warm, moody lighting make for a relaxed, cosy atmosphere. The

old fashioned (£9.50) is especially good and there are bar snacks (chicken skewers, nachos) to keep you going until the small hours. Mon–Wed 5pm–midnight, Thurs 5pm–1am, Fri 4pm–1am, Sat noon–1am, Sun 3pm–1am.

The Tap on the Line Station Approach, Kew ☎020 8332 1162, 🖥 tapontheline.co.uk; 🚇 Kew Gardens; map p.44. On the platform at Kew train station is this lively pub – the perfect place to wait for your train. Ales on tap include London Pride and the food menu features lemon sole (£19.50), bacon chop (£14.50) and ribeye (£25). Mon–Thurs 8.30am–11pm, Fri 8am–11pm, Sat 9am–11pm, Sun 10am–10.30pm.

Treviso 94 Kew Road, Richmond ☎020 8940 0033, 🖥 treviso-restaurant.co.uk; 🚇 Richmond; map p.44. Proper Italian food is served at this neighbourhood restaurant. The pasta dishes include a melt in the mouth tagliatelle carbonara (£10.95) and rich penne al ragu (£11.95) while the secondi include sea bass (£16.75) and salmon (£16.75). Mon–Fri noon–3pm & 6pm–11pm, Sat & Sun 11am–midnight.

ACTIVITIES

Fishing In Richmond Park fishing is available at Pen Ponds. ☎0300 061 2200, 🖥 royalparks.org.uk; 🚇 Richmond, then bus 371 or 65 to Petersham Gate; map p.44. Permits can be purchased at Holly Lodge and the season runs from June 16 to March 14.

Golf Richmond Park Golf Course, Norstead Place SW15 3SA ☎020 8876 3205, 🖥 glendalegolf.co.uk; 🚇 Putney then bus 85 to Ringwood Gardens; map p.44. There are two 18-hole courses at this low-key pay and play club in Richmond Park. The Prince's Course is shorter (5487yd), with lovely views across the park, while the Duke's Course (6359yd) is more challenging, with plenty of water hazards. Green fees from £14.40; no dress code. There is also a 15-bay covered driving range.

Horse riding Barnfield Riding School offer hacks in Richmond Park (1hr; £45) ☎020 8546 3616, 🖥 barnfieldridingschool.org; 🚇 Richmond then bus 371 to Wingfield Road; map p.44.

Power Kiting At Robin Hood Gate in Richmond Park, Kite Vibe offer beginners lessons and courses in power kiting – being pulled along by a kite a whole lot more powerful than the one you had as a kid. Taster sessions with a two-line kite last an hour and cost £30 (minimum age ten). ☎07866 430979, 🖥 kitevibe.com; 🚇 Putney then bus 85 to Robin Hood Lane; map p.44

1

Windsor and around

Just west of Heathrow airport and cut off from London by the M25 motorway, the area around **WINDSOR** has a more pastoral feel than the London suburbs of Richmond and Kew. The River Thames loops through here, dividing Windsor and the iconic **Windsor Castle** from **Eton** and its world-famous school and there are parks aplenty – **Windsor Great Park** chief among them.

This area is a popular escape from the capital and there's plenty of fun to be had. **Legoland Windsor Resort**, a theme park ever popular with children, sits to Windsor's south, as does **Ascot Racecourse**, home to the most famous racing event in England, Royal Ascot. There's also rowing at the purpose-built **Dorney Lake** and the site of the signing of the Magna Carta at **Runnymede.**

Windsor Castle

Windsor, SL4 1NJ • Daily: March–Oct 9.30am–5.15pm; Nov–Feb 9.45am–4.15pm; last entry 1hr 15min before closing • £21.20 • ☎ 0303 123 7304, ⓦ royalcollection.org.uk/visit/windsorcastle

Towering above the town on a steep chalk bluff, **Windsor Castle** is an undeniably imposing sight, its grey walls, punctuated by mighty medieval bastions, continuing as far as the eye can see. This is the oldest and the largest occupied castle in the world and the Queen spends most of her private weekends here – this is truly her home.

The castle was founded by William the Conqueror in the eleventh century and 39 monarchs have made their home here since. The **State Apartments** are the centrepiece of it all, a gilded line-up of grand rooms with painted ceilings, and you're sure to spend plenty of time gawping at the grandeur of it all. The real highlight though is perhaps the **Royal Collection** of paintings which line the walls. There are works by Holbein, Van Dyck and Rubens and many of the paintings remain hanging in the same place they were collected or commissioned to fill by previous monarchs.

The impressive **St George's Chapel** out in the grounds is one of the finest examples of Gothic architecture in England. This is the resting place of many monarchs, including Henry VIII and Charles I and has also hosted numerous royal weddings, most recently the 2018 nuptials of Prince Harry and Meghan Markle.

On Tuesdays, Thursdays and Saturdays at 11am (though subject to change) you can watch the **Changing of the Guard** ceremony at the castle. This is the handover from one group of Household Troops – in their characteristic scarlet jackets and black bearskin hats – to the next and has all the pomp and ceremony you would expect from a British tradition.

THE GREAT WEST WAY'S ROYAL CONNECTIONS

Windsor is the epicenter of all things royal and the sort of place to have Union Jack bunting fluttering in the streets all year round. Windsor Castle is where the current Queen, Elizabeth II, spends much of her time and the town that surrounds it has long been the haunt of monarchs.

Windsor Great Park started life as a hunting ground for William the Conqueror and Virginia Water was used by Queen Victoria as a place to entertain guests. Today, the Duke of Edinburgh is the Ranger of Windsor Great Park. It isn't just here though that the Great West Way (ⓦ GreatWestWay.co.uk) has royal connections. The Duchess of Cambridge, was a pupil at Marlborough College in the eponymous Wiltshire town and Prince Charles and Camilla, the Duchess of Cornwall, live at Highgrove House near Tetbury in the Cotswolds. It is here that Prince Charles has cultivated an organic garden and daily tours are offered – though you won't get a peek at the royals themselves.

Windsor Great Park

The Great Park, Windsor, SL4 2HT · Daily dawn/7.45am–dusk/7pm · Free · ☎ 01753 860222, ⓦ windsorgreatpark.co.uk

Stretching south from Windsor, this 5000-acre **Royal Park** is a welcome respite from the crowds at the castle. The **Long Walk** is the highlight, running for three miles from the castle along a tree-lined avenue to the towering Copper Horse statue (which depicts George III). You're sure to see deer grazing wherever you wander here – there are around five hundred red deer roaming freely and there are some lovely woodland trails through the Valley Gardens. The gardens run down to Virginia Water, a man-made lake with an ornamental waterfall. A pleasant 4.5mile path – partly paved and partly natural – leads around the lake and is suitable for pushchairs.

The Savill Garden

The Great Park, Windsor, SL4 2HT · Summer 10am–6pm, winter 10am–4.30pm, last admission 1hr before closing · £10.50 · ☎ 01753 860222, ⓦ windsorgreatpark.co.uk

Tucked away within **Windsor Great Park** is this woodland garden designed by Sir Eric Savill in the 1930s. Thanks to the collection of international plants there is something to see here at all times of the year, but the highlight is the **Rose Garden**, where the Queen Elizabeth rose was recently planted to mark the Queen's entrance into the history books as the world's longest serving monarch.

Swinley Forest

The Great Park, Windsor, SL4 2HT · Daily year-round; car park Apr–Sep 7am–8.30pm, Oct–Mar 7am–6pm · Free; parking £2/4hr, £4 all day · ☎ 01753 860222, ⓦ windsorgreatpark.co.uk

Linked to Windsor Great Park, this 3000-acre undulating woodland is more for adventure seekers than strollers. There are three purpose-built **mountain biking** trails here, totalling more than 15 miles – the Green Trail is suitable for children and bike trailers, while the Red cuts in and out of the pine forest on a thrilling adventure for experienced riders.

There's also a **Go Ape** high ropes course through the trees.

Eton College

Windsor, SL4 6DW · Tours May–Sept Fri 2pm & 4pm; Museum of Eton Life Sun 2.30–5pm · £10 · ☎ 01753 370600, ⓦ etoncollege.com

Eton College boarding school for boys dates back to 1440, when it was founded by Henry VI and has been educating England's aristocracy ever since. Each year some 1300 students pass through its hallowed halls and although the fees are steep (around £13,000 a term, with three terms each academic year) the school today admits a sizeable number of boys free of charge. Former pupils of the school are known as Old Etonians and include Princes William and Harry, the current Archbishop of Canterbury Justin Welby and nineteen former British Prime Ministers including David Cameron.

As a school for young boys, Eton College is rightly highly restrictive of entry to the public. Your only chance to have a proper peek inside is on Friday afternoons, when

---

THE MAGNA CARTA

The **Magna Carta**, or "Great Charter", was issued in 1215 by King John of England. For the first time in history it enshrined into law the principle that everyone, including the king, was subject to the law. The most famous clause is the 39th which gives all "free men" the right to justice and a fair trial.

The core principles of the Magna Carta are said to have influenced the **United States Bill of Rights**, the **Universal Declaration of Human Rights** and the **European Convention on Human Rights**.

1

two tours take in the School Yard, the splendid **Gothic College Chapel** and the **Museum of Eton Life**. This uncovers the school's traditions and explains how pupils learn, eat and live at the school today.

Dorney Lake

Off Court Lane, Windsor SL4 6QP • Open daily; access restricted during events • Free; parking £2.50 • ☎ 01753 832756, ⓦ etoncollege.com

Owned by Eton College, **Dorney Lake** is a beautifully manicured area of parkland surrounding a 2200-metre eight-lane rowing course – used in the London 2012 Olympics and Paralympics. The arboretum is a pleasant place for a stroll on quiet days but the real attraction here is the lake, which hosts three large annual regattas – the **Wallingford Regatta** in May and the **Metropolitan** and **Marlow Regattas** in June.

Legoland Windsor Resort

Winkfield Rd, SL4 4AY • March–May, Sept, Oct & Dec weekends and selected weekdays 9.30am–5/6pm (until 7pm selected days for Halloween), June & July daily 9.30am–5/6pm, Aug daily 9.30am–6pm, Dec most weekends & week before Christmas 10am–7pm • £32–60 • ☎ 0871 222 2001 ⓦ legoland.co.uk

Legoland theme park opened in 1996 and is aimed squarely at young children. Although there are more than fifty rides, shows and attractions, this isn't a place for teenagers – the rides are nowhere near daring enough. There's plenty to entice younger children though, with kid-friendly boats, cars and even hot air balloons to drive, a submarine "voyage" complete with real fish and a raft ride with a Viking theme. Adults will probably be more impressed with Miniland, where 42 million Lego bricks have been employed to create iconic buildings from Europe and the US.

At **Halloween** the park is lit to look spooky, with rides operating in the dark and a fireworks display, while Legoland at **Christmas** sees Father Christmas (not just a Lego version) visit the park.

ASCOT, HENLEY ON THAMES AND WIMBLEDON

The English "season" of social events evolved in the seventeenth and eighteenth centuries but reached its fashionable height in the nineteenth, when anyone who was anyone would be in London throughout the summer in order to attend events from debutante balls to sports fixtures. Today, many of the events persist and the three most famous are still going strong: **Royal Ascot**, the **Henley Royal Regatta** and **Wimbledon** tennis championships.

Royal Ascot features five days of horse racing at **Ascot Racecourse** and is attended by the Queen, who leads a **Royal Procession** each day at 2pm before racing begins. A strict dress code is enforced in the more exclusive Queen Anne Enclosure and the Royal Enclosure – where men must wear top hats. In the Windsor Enclosure more or less anything goes, and the atmosphere is more nightclub than society event. Tickets from £37 for the Windsor Enclosure, £75 for the Queen Anne Enclosure.

The Henley Royal Regatta was first held in 1839 and today sees five days of competitive rowing take place on the Thames in early July. The course is about 1.3 miles in length and outside of the official enclosures anyone can take to the river. The Steward's Enclosure is the most exclusive here, open only to members and their guests – mobile phones are banned and ladies are not allowed to wear trousers. The Regatta Enclosure is open to all, including children. Tickets from £25. ⓦ hrr.co.uk.

Wimbledon is the most relaxed of the three events (it has no dress code for spectators) and runs for two weeks in late June and/or early July. Although tickets are mostly sold in advance through a ballot it is possible to buy tickets (even for **Centre Court**, where the top matches are played) on the day – news broadcasts feature plucky would-be spectators being interviewed in their tents having camped out all night without fail around this time. Tickets from £8 for grounds admission, £60 for Centre Court. ⓦ wimbledon.com.

1

Runnymede

Windsor Road, TW20 0AE · Daily dawn to dusk · Car park £1.50/hr, £7/day; free to National Trust members · ☎ 01784 432891, ⓦ nationaltrust.org.uk

The site of the sealing of the **Magna Carta** stands in unremarkable meadows running down to the River Thames. It's a peaceful spot for a walk and is marked by the official **Magna Carta Memorial**, a circular stone dome supported by slender columns that was erected here in 1957 by the American Bar Association.

An area of land nearby was donated by the Queen to the USA in 1965 and holds a memorial in Portland stone to President John F Kennedy. It's also worth taking the walk up Coopers Hill to the **Commonwealth Air Forces Memorial**, inscribed with the names of more than 20,000 men and women who lost their lives in World War II and have no known grave. There are beautiful views from this high point across the Berkshire countryside and along the River Thames.

Ascot Racecourse

Ascot SL5 7JX · ☎ 0344 346 3000, ⓦ ascot.co.uk

With a race calendar of only a dozen or so days a year there'll be nothing to see at **Ascot Racecourse** for months at a time and then suddenly it's literally stopping traffic. The biggest event here is **Royal Ascot** in June, when local traffic has to be rerouted because of the crowds, but there is racing throughout the summer and on selected autumn dates too.

Horse racing at Ascot dates back to 1711 when Queen Anne rode out here from Windsor and saw the potential for "horses to gallop at full stretch". The course is 1 mile and 6 furlongs long and famed for being tough, rising 73ft from its lowest point at Swinley Bottom to the highest at The Winning Post.

ARRIVAL AND INFORMATION

BY TRAIN

The train is the best way to visit Windsor, Eton and their attractions. Windsor and Eton are served by two centrally located train stations, a seven-minute walk apart. Windsor & Eton Central train station has trains from London Paddington via Slough (every 30min; 25min; from £10.50 single; ⓦ gwr.com), while Windsor & Eton Riverside railway station has direct trains from London Waterloo (every 30min; 1hr; from £10.50 single; ⓦ southwesternrailway.com). If you're coming from Oxford or Reading, you'll need to change at Slough. Ascot is served by trains from London Waterloo (every 15min; 50min; from £12.60 single).

BY BUS

The Greenline 702 bus links London Victoria to Reading via Windsor and Legoland (every 60min; 1hr 15min to Windsor, 1hr 30min to Legoland, from £7 single. The Greenline 703 starts from Heathrow airport instead of Victoria (every 60min; 40min to Windsor; 55min to Legoland; from £4 single; ⓦ greenline702.co.uk). Both also call at Slough.

BY CAR

A car is the best way to get to Windsor Great Park, Swinley

WINDSOR AND AROUND

Forest and Runnymede. Windsor Great Park is easily reached from the M25 London orbital motorway and there are several car parks: at the Savill Garden (TW20 0UJ), Virginia Water (GU25 4QF) and Virginia Water South (SL5 7SB). All cost £2.50/hr or £10 for 3hr+ on weekdays; £3/hr or £12 for 3hr+ on weekends.

Swinley Forest is close to the M3 and M4 motorways. Parking here is at the Look Out Discovery Centre (RG12 7QW, £2/4hr, £4/day).

Runnymede is less than 10min from the M25 and parking is free for National Trust members (otherwise £1.50/hr or £7/day).

At Legoland parking costs £6. The park is within easy reach of the M3, M4 and M25 and is signposted with easy-to-follow brown signs.

BY BOAT

French Brothers (ⓦ frenchbrothers.co.uk) have return boat services to Windsor from Maidenhead (May–Sept, Tues–Sat, departs 11am, arrives 12.30pm, returns 3.45pm, £21.50 return). and Runnymede (March–Sept, Wed, Fri, Sat & Sun, departs 11am, arrives 12.30pm, returns 4pm, £21.50 return).

ACCOMMODATION

Castle Hotel Windsor 18 High St SL4 1LJ ☎01753 252800, ⓦcastlehotelwindsor.com; map p.44. An enviable location on Windsor's High Street makes this historic hotel (it's in one of the town's oldest buildings) a convenient place to stay. Its most recent incarnation is as an MGallery hotel, the boutique brand from the Accor group, and the feel is elegant and intimate. Rooms are understated, with bathrobes, Nespresso machines and Lanvin toiletries. The restaurant serves a traditional English menu with a focus on steaks. £109.

★**Coworth Park** Blacknest Rd, Ascot SL5 7SE ☎01344 876600, ⓦcoworthpark.com; map p.44. The most luxurious option in the area, Coworth Park is five-star from its crystal-lit swimming pool right down to its impeccable service. This is a proper 21st-century country house hotel and you'll find everything from afternoon tea served in the drawing room to a Polo Academy and Equestrian Centre. The grounds are extensive – and lovely for a stroll – and the spa is one of England's best. £321.

The Langley, a Luxury Collection Hotel Uxbridge Rd, Iver, SL3 6DW, ☎020 7236 3636, ⓦmarriott.com; map p.44. Brand new hotel in a former royal hunting lodge, with landscaped gardens originally designed by Lancelot "Capability" Brown. The 41 rooms are divided between the main house and the Brew House and the spa has indoor and outdoor pools and a thermal area. Free parking on site too. £375

Langton House 46 Alma Rd, Windsor SL4 3HA, ☎01753 858299, ⓦlangtonhouse.co.uk; map p.44. This friendly bed and breakfast is superb value for money, set in a Victorian town house on a leafy street a five-minute walk from Windsor town centre. Rooms are classic and comfortable;

one family room can sleep up to four, one of the doubles has a four-poster and all bathroom are en suite. £65.

Macdonald Berystede Hotel & Spa Bagshot Road, Sunninghill, Ascot SL5 9JH ☎0344 879 9104, ⓦmacdonaldhotels.co.uk; map p.44. This is the closest four-star hotel to Ascot Racecourse and is ideal for drivers – it has secure gated parking and is close to the main road. You wouldn't know you were surrounded by so many tourist attractions here though – with gated entry leading through secluded gardens to the hotel itself you'll feel like you're staying somewhere far more rural. The 120 rooms are traditionally styled (some have four-poster beds) and many have garden or countryside views. The spa and leisure club has both indoor and outdoor pools. £112.

The Runnymede on Thames Hotel & Spa Windsor Rd, Egham TW20 0AG ☎01784 220600, ⓦrunnymede hotel.com; map p.44. Two miles along the Thames from the Magna Carta Memorial and just off the M25 motorway, this chic but simple hotel has cosy doubles with river views, Hypnos beds and ESPA toiletries. Guests have use of the pools (indoor and outdoor), spa and gym, where there are numerous fitness classes. Three of the rooms are dog-friendly, with direct access to the riverside. £175

Sir Christopher Wren Thames St, Windsor SL4 1PX ☎01753 442400, ⓦsirchristopherwren.co.uk; map p.44. On the riverfront by Eton Bridge, this modern four-star is ideally located for exploring both Windsor and Eton on foot. The 133 rooms are arranged across three historic buildings and there are also seven serviced apartments with kitchenettes. All guests get complimentary access to the Wren's Club with its spa and three-storey gym. Book direct for a free drink in the bar. £155.

EATING AND DRINKING

The Boatman 10 Thames Side, Windsor SL4 1QN ☎01753 620010, ⓦboatmanwindsor.com; map p.44. This is Windsor's only pub to actually be on the River Thames and it has a lovely terrace overlooking the water. Classic British food is served, from smoked haddock fishcakes (£12.95) to lamb shoulder (£17.95). There are also steaks, pastas and lighter salads. The bar has local ales (from the Windsor & Eton Brewery) and gin cocktails. Dog-friendly. Daily 10am–11.30pm.

Restaurant Coworth Park Blacknest Rd, Ascot SL5 7SE ☎01344 876600, ⓦcoworthpark.com; map p.44. A vast copper chandelier hangs over this Michelin-starred dining room, where chef Adam Smith cooks up a showcase of a tasting menu, which features dishes such as Cornish turbot with salted grapes and Highland wagyu short rib (£110 for 7 courses). There's also wine pairing from the extensive list (£75) and a three-course a la carte option for £80. Wed & Thurs 6.30–9.30pm, Fri & Sat 12.30–2pm &

6.30–9.30pm, Sun 12.30–2.30pm.

Gilbey's Bar & Restaurant Eton 82-83 High St, Eton SL4 6AF ☎01753 854921, ⓦgilbeygroup.com; map p.44. A garden tucked away out the back makes this brasserie-style restaurant a real find. Food is traditional, with plenty of seafood on the menu (a starter of Loch Duart salmon is £11.95, a main course of pave of North Atlantic cod £22.95) and there's a cracking selection of British cheeses (£10 for three). A set menu is served at lunchtimes only – two courses will cost you just £15. Tues–Sun lunch from noon; daily dinner from 6pm.

The Savill Garden Kitchen The Savill Garden, Windsor Great Park; map p.44. A pleasant spot for lunch in the park, this airy café serves a range of pizzas, burgers and salads daily from noon. Pizzas start at £9.25; mains include sausage and mash for £10.50. Breakfast is also served daily until 11.30am (Full English £11). Mon–Fri 9.30am–4pm, Sat & Sun 9.30am–5pm.

1

ACTIVITIES

Boat trips French Brothers ☎01753 851900, ⊛french brothers.co.uk; map p.44. Year-round sightseeing boat trips of 40min and 2hr for views of Windsor Castle and Eton College from the water. The longer trips (March–Oct only) cruise further upstream. From £9.

Golf Royal Ascot Golf Club Winkfield Rd, Ascot SL5 7LJ ☎01344 624656, ⊛royalascotgolfclub.co.uk; map p.44. Royal Ascot is a parkland course in the southwest corner of Windsor Great Park with a history that dates back to 1887, when it was established and named by Queen Victoria. Any golfer with a handicap certificate is welcome to play up to six times in any year. Book in advance with the Pro Shop. Green fees start from £40 for a weekday, £50 at weekends. No visitors can play before noon on weekdays and under 18s can only play accompanied by an adult.

Go Ape Swinley Forest ⊛goape.co.uk; map p.44. Go Ape Tree Top Adventure runs for 770yd through Swinley Forest, across challenging rope crossings and down zip wires up to 175yd long. The experience lasts for 2–3hrs and children must be at least ten years old and 4ft 6in tall. For littler ones there's Tree Top Junior (£14.40). £26.40.

Mountain biking Swinley Bike Hub, The Look Out Discovery Centre, RG12 7QW ☎01344 360229, ⊛swinleybikehub.com; map p.44. Swinley Bike Hub hires out bikes for tackling Swinley Forest's mountain biking trails. The one-mile Green Trail is suitable for novices and children, the 6.25-mile Blue Trail can be tackled by anyone with intermediate bike skills and the gnarly 8-mile Red Trail is for those with good off-roading skills only. Coaching sessions also available. Bike hire from £20. April–Oct 9am–6pm (5pm Sun), Nov–Mar 9am–4pm.

Segway Swinley Forest ⊛goape.co.uk; map p.44. One-hour Segway adventures through the forest. 10+ years only. £28.

NORTH WESSEX DOWNS

West Berkshire

Berkshire covers a diverse swathe of terrain immediately west of the capital, starting with Maidenhead in the east and continuing along the Great West Way to the town of Reading and the rolling chalk hills of the North Wessex Downs which rise above Newbury and Hungerford.

2

HIGHLIGHTS

❶ **The Fat Duck** Simply the best restaurant the Great West Way has to offer, with three Michelin stars and an inventive menu that will have you buzzing for weeks. **See p.71**

❷ **Cliveden Estate** Romp through the grounds of this classic country estate, once embroiled in a scandal that nearly brought down the government and today reborn as a super-luxury hotel. **See p.68**

❸ **Thames Lido** England is gradually rediscovering its traditional al fresco swimming baths and Reading's Thames Lido is one of the best. **See p.73**

❹ **Highclere Castle** Wander the halls of the real "Downton Abbey", which is the family home of the Earl and Countess of Carnarvon. Visitors can see the Great Hall, backdrop to much of Mary and Matthew's romance and the Dining Room, scene of many a family drama and plenty of acerbic comments from the Dowager Countess. **See p.78**

❺ **Maidenhead Heritage Centre** Have a go at flying a Spitfire and find out how the female pilots of the Air Transport Auxiliary helped the war effort. **See below**

The River Thames flows through the heart of West Berkshire, linking the pleasant town of Maidenhead with the villages of Cookham and Marlow upstream. In Cookham a gallery displaying works by the local twentieth-century artist Stanley Spencer gives a bucolic insight into a now-lost rural idyll, while Marlow is a wealthy town with a Michelin-starred restaurant. Immediately to the north, the beautifully unspoiled Chiltern Hills stretch into Buckinghamshire and Oxfordshire, while just to the west and just into Oxfordshire, Henley on Thames is a superb place for messing about in boats.

Maidenhead and around

The sizeable market town of **MAIDENHEAD** stands in lovely countryside on the banks of the River Thames just a few miles upriver from Windsor. It is an attractive if unexciting place, useful as a hub for visiting the sights that surround it, which include the gorgeous (and famously gastronomic) village of Bray and, a little further upriver, the villages of **Marlow** (over the border in Buckinghamshire) and **Cookham**. Just across the border in Oxfordshire is the rowing centre of **Henley on Thames**, known for its annual regatta. This is a region of quiet beauty, more about wandering at will through a sublime English landscape than visiting formal attractions – getting lost here is often well rewarded.

Maidenhead is an important calling point on the Great Western Railway and in the town itself you'll find Brunel's **Maidenhead Railway Bridge**. Its wide twin arches were built in 1838 and were so flat that people did not believe they would hold the trains that steamed across it. Brunel, of course, knew better and the bridge still stands, as sturdy as ever, today, carrying trains along the Great West Way.

Maidenhead Heritage Centre

18 Park St, SL6 1SL • Tues–Sat 10am–4pm • Free • ☎ 01628 780555, ⓦ maidenheadheritage.org.uk

Maidenhead has a fascinating history, notably during World War II when the Air Transport Auxiliary (ATA) was headquartered at White Waltham Airfield just outside the town. This civilian-run air service ferried planes between factories, maintenance units and airfields and was the first British government organisation to pay its women and men equally The **Maidenhead Heritage Centre** hosts the permanent Grandma Flew Spitfires exhibition which tells the story of the ATA and features a Spitfire simulator. The Story of Maidenhead gallery tells the history of the town, from Roman times to its role as a key point on the Great Western Railway.

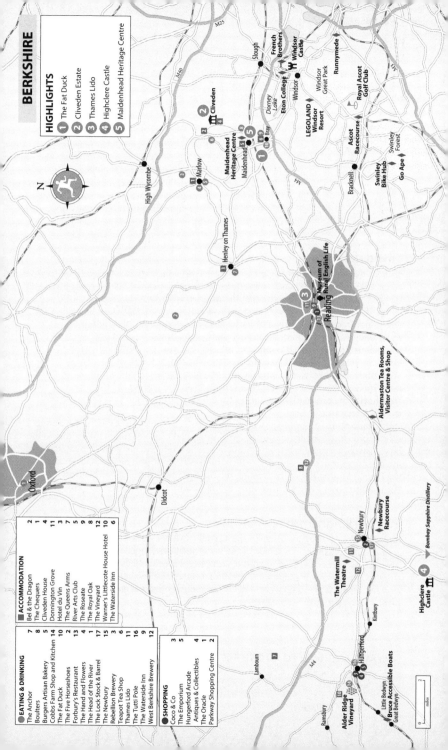

BERKSHIRE

HIGHLIGHTS

1. The Fat Duck
2. Cliveden Estate
3. Thames Lido
4. Highclere Castle
5. Maidenhead Heritage Centre

● EATING & DRINKING

The Anchor	7
Boulters	8
Burgers Artisan Bakery	5
Cobbs Farm Shop and Kitchen	14
The Fat Duck	10
The Five Horseshoes	2
Forbury's Restaurant	13
The Hand and Flowers	4
The Head of the River	1
The Lock Stock & Barrel	17
The Newbury	15
Rebellion Brewery	6
Teapot Tea Shop	11
Thames Lido	16
The Waterside Inn	9
West Berkshire Brewery	12

■ ACCOMMODATION

Bel & the Dragon	2
The Chequers	1
Cliveden House	4
Donnington Grove	11
Hotel du Vin	3
The Queens Arms	7
River Arts Club	5
The Roseate	9
The Royal Oak	8
The Vineyard	12
Warner's Littlecote House Hotel	10
The Waterside Inn	6

● SHOPPING

Coco & Co	3
The Emporium	5
Hungerford Arcade	4
Antiques & Collectibles	1
The Oracle	2

Parkway Shopping Centre

Bray

With a population of under five thousand and, as of 2018, a whopping seven Michelin stars, **BRAY** could surely claim to have the most stars per capita of any village or town in the world – a good feed is the main reason to come here. There is also three miles of River Thames frontage and a very pretty High Street.

Cookham

The attractive village of **Cookham** and the quintessentially English countryside that surrounds it are said to have inspired Kenneth Grahame's *Wind in the Willows*. The author grew up near here and the village itself is certainly pretty enough for the suggestion to be believable. Today Cookham is chiefly of interest for its **Stanley Spencer Gallery**, home to a collection of works by the eponymous local painter and located in the old **Wesleyan Chapel** where the family used to attend church (High St; daily 10.30am–5.30pm; £6; ⓦstanleyspencer.org.uk).

Cliveden Estate

Taplow, SL1 8NS, 1 mile east of Cookham • Grounds Daily: mid-Feb to Oct 10am–5.30pm; Nov & Dec 10am–4pm • £16; National Trust members free • House tours April–Oct Mon, Tues & Thurs 11am–1pm; 30min • £2; NT • ☎ 01628 605069, ⓦ nationaltrust.org.uk/cliveden

Perched on a ridge overlooking the Thames, **Cliveden** (pronounced cliv-dun) is a grand Victorian mansion, designed with sweeping neoclassical lines by Sir Charles Barry, architect of the Houses of Parliament in London. Its most famous occupant was Nancy Astor, the first female MP, though the house remains best known for the scandalous **Profumo Affair**. Conservative cabinet minister John Profumo met nineteen-year-old model Christine Keeler at a party at Cliveden in 1961 and had a brief affair with her. Keeler, meanwhile, was also involved with a number of other men, including a Soviet intelligence officer. Profumo was forced to resign in 1963 after having lied to parliament, and Prime Minister Harold Macmillan resigned shortly afterwards.

The **National Trust** now owns Cliveden. Visits focus on the grounds, where a large slice of broadleaf woodland is intercepted by several themed gardens and a maze. The house is now a luxury hotel, with non-guests admitted only on guided tours. Its lavish interiors feature acres of wood panelling and portraits of past owners, culminating in the French Dining Room, containing the fittings and furnishings of Madame de Pompadour's own eighteenth-century dining room.

Into Buckinghamshire: Marlow

MARLOW sits on the River Thames, its attractive white-painted suspension bridge connecting Berkshire on one side of the water with Buckinghamshire on the other. This is a wealthy riverside playground, complete with chic high street **shopping**, one of Britain's premier rowing clubs and a pub that holds two Michelin stars (*The Hand and Flowers*). There is also a brewery – Rebellion, which has tours and a good shop – and plenty of opportunity for boat trips.

WALK: MARLOW TO COOKHAM

Marlow and **Cookham** are best explored on foot and there is an attractive riverside walk between the two, making use of a 5-mile stretch of the waymarked, long-distance Thames Path. Midway you can stop off at Bourne End, once home to author **Enid Blyton** and crime writer **Edgar Wallace**.

THE CHILTERNS AONB

The **Chilterns** were designated an Area of Outstanding Natural Beauty in 1965, joining the roster of landscapes across England (and Wales) that are recognised as some of the finest, and most unspoilt, areas of the country.

The AONB covers 324 square miles and runs from the Thames through Buckinghamshire and Bedfordshire to Hitchin, north of London in Hertfordshire, putting much of its southern reaches on the Great West Way.

The bedrock here is chalk, giving rise to gently undulating hillsides of chalk downland criss-crossed by chalk streams, a **rare habitat** that is found almost entirely in England and is home to some of the country's most threatened plants and animals, such as the brown trout and the water vole. The countryside here may be protected but this is no museum piece, this is a working area where some two thirds of the land are given over to farming and pretty villages go about their business in quiet valleys. This is quintessential **English countryside** at its very best.

2

Into Oxfordshire: Henley on Thames

On the very edge of the **Chilterns Area of Outstanding Natural Beauty**, sandwiched between this region of wooded hills and rambling fields and the river Thames, **HENLEY** is a supremely attractive town just 7 miles west of Maidenhead.

Here the Thames flows beneath an eighteenth-century stone bridge, while historic pubs, traditional tearooms and boutique shops jostle for prime position along the ancient streets. The best time to visit is during the annual **Henley Royal Regatta**, when the river is packed with boats of all shapes and sizes and plays host to some of the world's leading rowers in a series of races.

The River & Rowing Museum

Mill Meadows, RG9 1BF · Daily 10am–5pm · £12.50 · ☎ 01491 415600, ⓦ rrm.co.uk

Everything you ever wanted to know about **rowing** and plenty more besides is on display in the galleries of this family-friendly museum. There is also a gallery devoted to discussing rivers more generally, as well as one on local history and another focused on the works of English artist John Piper. A multimedia *Wind in the Willows* **exhibition** brings Kenneth Grahame's beloved story to life.

Stonor Park

Henley-on-Thames, RG9 6HF · **House and chapel**: April–June Sun & hols 1.30–5pm, July & Aug Thurs–Sun & hols 1.30–5pm, Sept Sun 1.30–5pm; **Gardens and Wonder Woods**: late March–Oct Wed–Sun 10am–5pm (daily during local school hols) · £10; **Garden and Wonder Woods** £6.50 · ☎ 01491 638587, ⓦ stonor.com

The Stonor family have lived at **Stonor Park** for some 850 years – making this one of the oldest family homes in England to still be lived in. The simple red brick frontage belies the extravagant sights within, which include a very grand Gothic revival hall and a seventeenth-century library. The highlight though is the **Chapel**, built atop a prehistoric stone circle (one of the stones can still be seen in the southeast corner). Mass has been celebrated here for over eight centuries (every Sun, 10.30am).

Stonor is set in a valley and there is plenty of lush **parkland** to explore here. A herd of fallow deer roams the green slopes beneath centuries-old beech and ash trees and there are three more **formal gardens** – an arboretum, a kitchen garden and a seventeenth-century Italianate pleasure garden. Spring is an ideal time to visit, with daffodils in bloom in the pleasure garden and apple and plum trees blossoming in the kitchen garden.

For children there is also the Wonder Woods adventure playground, complete with towers, slides, a giant swing and 164-ft zip wire.

Greys Court

Rotherfield Grays, Henley on Thames, RG9 4PG · **Grounds** Daily: summer 10am–5pm; winter 10am–4pm; **House** summer Daily 1–5pm, winter Sat & Sun 1–4pm · £13; National Trust members free · ☎ 01491 628529, ⓦ nationaltrust.org.uk/greys-court

Nestled in the Chiltern hills, this sixteenth-century Tudor mansion and its peaceful gardens were home to the Brunner family until the early twenty-first century. It still has the feel of a family home, albeit a very grand one, with comfortable living rooms and a country-style kitchen, and the gardens are a delight, with a wisteria walk, rose garden and kitchen garden where produce is grown for the tearoom. There are rambling **walks** through the estate too and a den-building area for the kids.

ARRIVAL AND INFORMATION

BY TRAIN

Maidenhead has a sizeable train station, from which Great Western Railway (ⓦgwr.com) operate services to London Paddington via Slough (up to four an hr, 45min, £12.70 single). There are also services to Reading (every 15min, 15min, £6.50 single) and a branch line from Maidenhead out to Marlow (20min, £4.50 single) via Cookham (10min, £3 single) which runs hourly.

To reach Henley on Thames you'll need to take the branch line from Twyford, a stop on the Maidenhead-Reading line (every 30min, 10min, £3.80 single).

BY BUS

National Express (ⓦnationalexpress.com) run non-stop buses from London Victoria to Slough (hourly, 1hr 15min, £10), where you can change onto First bus (ⓦfirstgroup.com) route 4 (every 30min, 30min, £3). It is easier and often cheaper to take the train.

Cookham is served by Arriva (ⓦarrivabus.co.uk) route 37 from Maidenhead (hourly, 15min, £4.60/day). Arriva also have services from Reading to Marlow (1hr) and Henley (40min, every 20min, £4.60/day). Red Eagle (ⓦredeagle.org.uk) also operate a weekly service from Maidenhead to Marlow (Wed 10.20am, 20min, £4 single).

BY CAR

Maidenhead is just off the M4 motorway at junction 8/9 and on the A4. The council operate several car parks in the town centre. West Street (SL6 1RL, £3.50/3hr, 3hr max stay, free Sun) and The Broadway (SL6 1NT, £3.10/3hr, £8/5hr, no max stay, free Sun) are good bets.

In Cookham there is free parking at Cookham Moor, a 5min walk west of the town centre. In Marlow most car parks are free overnight (7pm–7am); during the day try

MAIDENHEAD AND AROUND

West Street (SL7 2LS, £2/4hr, £3/6hr). Bray has a small free car park off the High Street (SL6 2AR, 2hr max stay). The best place to park in Henley is at the station (RG9 1AY, £1.20/3hr, £5/day).

BY BOAT

This is a good area for travelling the Great West Way by water. Salter's Steamers (ⓦsalterssteamers.co.uk) have boat services along the Thames from Marlow to Cookham (45min, £9.10 single), Maidenhead (1hr 45min, £12.60 single) and Windsor (3hr 45min, £18.50 single) every Monday in summer (departs 9.30am, returns 2.30pm). There are also services to Henley from Marlow (Tues–Fri, departs 1pm, returns 4.15pm, 2hr 15min, £12.50 single) and from Reading (Tues–Sun, departs 10.30am, returns 4.15pm, 2hr 15min, £13 single).

BY BIKE

The Chilterns Cycleway runs through Henley. The route is mostly on minor roads and links up with National Cycle Network (ⓦsustrans.org.uk) route 5 for its final few miles south to Reading. National Cycle Network route 4 links Maidenhead with Slough and London to the east and Reading to the west.

ON FOOT

The Thames Path (ⓦnationaltrail.co.uk/thames-path) runs along the River Thames, passing through Maidenhead, Cookham, Marlow and Henley, making this a great section of the Great West Way to tackle on foot. It is approximately 6 miles from Maidenhead to Cookham, 3 between Cookham and Marlow and 8 miles from Marlow to Henley. Upriver from Henley it's a further 9 miles to Reading.

TOURS

★**Hobbs of Henley** ☎01491 572035, ⓦhobbsofhenley.com. Cruises on the Thames including sightseeing trips, vintage afternoon teas, gin tasting and, at Christmas, Santa cruises. Two-hour sightseeing cruise £16.50.

Salters Steamers ☎01865 243421, ⓦsalterssteamers.co.uk. Summer Thames river cruises from Henley and Marlow, lasting around 40–45min. £7.

ACCOMMODATION

The Chequers 53 High St, Marlow, SL7 1BA, ☎01628 482053, ⓦthechequersmarlow.co.uk; map p.58. Pub on the High Street with nine contemporary bedrooms. The best is the signature room, which is split level with a rolltop bath. __£90__

Hotel du Vin New St, Henley, RG9 2BP, ☎01491 877579, ⓦhotelduvin.com; map p.58. A cluster of Georgian buildings that was once a brewery has been reimagined as Henley's leading hotel, part of the upmarket

Hotel du Vin chain. The 43 rooms come with plush beds decked out in fine linens and deep bathtubs as standard, lending a romantic feel that is best suited to couples. £105.

★**Cliveden House**, Taplow, SL6 0JF, ☎01628 607107, ⓦclivedenhouse.co.uk; map p.58. Few hotels are as famous as Cliveden – setting of the Profumo affair – or as romantic. Take a room in the Garden Wing and you'll get views over the spa garden and – in some – a hot tub tucked privately into your terrace. There's also a wonderful restaurant from chef André Garrett, where English ingredients star on the eight-course tasting menu. The trump card here though is the 376-acre National Trust estate that surrounds the hotel, its formal gardens the sort of place you could happily lose yourself in for days. There's direct access to the River Thames for a jaunt and a spot of lunch on a vintage boat, and plenty of pleasant walks to work off the essential afternoon tea, served in the imposing Great Hall. £445

River Arts Club Guards Club Rd, Maidenhead, SL6 8DN, ☎01628 631888, ⓦriverartsclub.com; map p.58. A Victorian riverside mansion is reborn as a stylish hotel with funky, bright rooms. There's a gorgeous riverside garden, an honesty bar and *Ophelia*, a traditional river launch which can be chartered for trips on the river or as a taxi to nearby restaurants. £150.

The Waterside Inn Ferry Rd, Bray, SL6 2AT, ☎01628 620691, ⓦwaterside-inn.co.uk; map p.58. The Waterside is a restaurant with rooms, so only those dining can book a stay. The eleven rooms are located in cottages dotted around the restaurant and are classic in style. A continental breakfast is served in your room in the morning. £260.

Bel & the Dragon, High St, Cookham, SL6 9SQ, ☎01628 521263, ⓦbelandthedragon-cookham.co.uk; map p.58. Country inn with 10 fresh, simple rooms including one for families. Breakfast is £12.50pp extra. £95

EATING AND DRINKING

The Anchor 58 Friday St, Henley, RG9 1AH, ☎01491 574753, ⓦtheanchorhenley.co.uk; map p.58. Close to the Thames just south of Henley Bridge this traditional pub has a south-facing walled garden for summer and wood-burning stove for winter. Dishes are a cut above standard pub fare, including three fish bouillabaisse (£14.95) and wild mushroom ravioli (£12.95). Daily noon–midnight.

Boulters Boulters Lock Island, Maidenhead, SL6 8PE, ☎01628 621291, ⓦboultersrestaurant.co.uk; map p.58. Located on its own island in the Thames this riverfront restaurant has matchless views and a contemporary English menu. At lunch there's a fixed price menu (two courses £15.95) while dinner is a la carte and features dishes such as smoked salmon fishcake and pan-fried seabream (£16.50). Mon–Sat 9.30am–11pm, Sun noon–8pm.

Burgers Artisan Bakery The Causeway, Marlow, SL7 1NF, ☎01628 483389, ⓦburgersartisanbakery.com; map p.58. Family owned bakery which bakes artisan bread fresh every day. The tea room has bay windows overlooking Marlow High Street and a full range of breakfasts (muesli, porridge, the full English) plus main meals at lunchtime, from a ploughman's lunch (£5.85) to ham, egg and chips (£5.95). There's a wonderful range of cakes too, including fresh cream cakes, Danish pastries and jam doughnuts (from £1.80). Mon–Fri 8am–5pm, Sat 8.30am–5pm.

★**The Fat Duck** High St, Bray, SL6 2AQ, ☎01628 580333, ⓦthefatduck.co.uk; map p.58. Simply superlative restaurant from highly regarded English chef Heston Blumenthal. Awarded three Michelin stars for its creative menu, which takes guests on a sensory journey to the seaside and begins before you even arrive, with a phone consultation. Expect to be dazzled – and to be talking about it for years. Bookings essential, and well in advance. Tues–Sat from noon for lunch and 7pm for dinner; allow four hours.

The Five Horseshoes Maidensgrove, RG9 6EX, ☎01491 641282, ⓦthefivehorseshoes.co.uk; map p.58. Gorgeous sixteenth-century pub with a garden and a conservatory with glorious views. The menu is upmarket pub classics and includes lobster (£25 for half) and roast haunch of local venison (£18.50). Wed–Fri noon–2.30pm & 6.30–9pm, Sat noon–11pm (food served noon–3pm & 6.30-9pm), Sun noon–4pm.

The Hand and Flowers 126 West St, Marlow, SL7 2BP, ☎01628 482277, ⓦthehandandflowers.co.uk; map p.58. This was the first pub to achieve two Michelin stars but it remains a relaxed place to settle in for some proper English dishes, including a fabulous Sunday roast. Chef Tom Kerridge serves up sophisticated yet familiar dishes – think half roast chicken with oak gravy and pork belly with roasted pineapple and chorizo mayonnaise. Mon–Sat noon–2.45pm & 6.30–9.45pm, Sun noon–3.15pm.

★**Rebellion Brewery** Bencombe Farm, Marlow, SL7 3LT, ☎01628 476594, ⓦrebellionbeer.co.uk; map p.58. This local brewery has a monthly public night on the first Tuesday of the month, when visitors can sample their beers and order from the barbecue. £13.50 inc five drinks.

Teapot Tea Shop 1-2 Clieve Cottages, Cookham, SL6 9SJ, ☎01628 529514, ⓦteapot-teashop.co.uk; map p.58. Diane and Madga's shabby chic tearoom is a welcoming spot for a cup of tea and a simple lunch. The menu includes welsh rarebit made with homemade cheese sauce (£5.50) and a ploughman's (£7.05). You can also create your own sandwiches and there are homemade cakes and cream teas to boot. Daily 10am–5pm.

The Waterside Inn Ferry Rd, Bray, SL6 2AT, ☎ 01628 620691, ⓦ waterside-inn.co.uk; map p.58. Unashamedly French and truly exquisite restaurant serving three-Michelin-star cuisine from the kitchen of Alain Roux.

The best tables are in the picture window, with views of the river, and the menu changes four times a year. Le Menu Exceptionnel is the premier choice, a six-course tasting menu, costing £167.50pp. Feb–Dec Wed–Sun noon–2pm and 7–10pm.

2

Reading and around

READING, 35 miles west of London, is the first major town on the Great West Way when travelling westwards and is a lively, modern place with historic connections to Oscar Wilde and Jane Austen.

There are some lovely parks within easy striking distance of the town and every August Little John's Farm hosts the world's longest running rock festival, the Reading Festival. Oscar Wilde fans may also be interested in the prison (no public access), a severe-looking structure on Forbury Road, where the writer was incarcerated in the 1890s and wrote his poignant *Ballad of Reading Gaol*. There is a short Oscar Wilde Memorial Walk along the River Kennet in the shadow of the prison.

Reading is prominent today as a transport hub: the huge train station is one of the busiest in the country, standing at the junction of lines from London, Cornwall, South Wales, the West Midlands and the south coast, and with a direct train to Gatwick Airport and express coach to Heathrow.

Reading Museum

Blagrave St RG1 1QH • Tues–Sat 10am–4pm • Suggested donation £3 • ☎ 0118 937 3400, ⓦ readingmuseum.org.uk

Reading's **museum** is in the Town Hall. Its permanent galleries hold displays on local history, including the Huntley and Palmers biscuit factory that once dominated the town, and finds from nearby **Roman Silchester**. The Bayeux Gallery houses a Victorian replica of the **Bayeux Tapestry** recording William the Conqueror's invasion of England in 1066. It was made by 35 female embroiderers in 1885 and is 230ft long. There are weekly tours of the tapestry (Sat, 2.15pm, £5).

Abbey Quarter

Via Forbury Gardens or from Chestnut Walk • Daily dawn–dusk • Free • T 0118 937 3400, ⓦ readingabbeyquarter.org.uk

After discovering Reading's history at the museum, the nearby **Abbey Quarter** is a worthy detour. This is the site of the former Reading Abbey, founded by Henry I in the twelfth century. A sizeable amount remains, including the chapter house and parts of the south transept, the refectory, dormitory and treasury. The Abbey Gateway also still stands. This once divided the public part of the Abbey grounds (now Forbury Gardens) from the private areas and later was part of the Reading Ladies Boarding School, attended by **Jane Austen**. After its collapse in a storm in 1861 the arch was rebuilt by Sir George Gilbert Scott, who also designed Reading Gaol.

Riverside Museum

Blake's Lock, Kenavon Dr, RG1 3DH • April–Sep daily 10am–6pm • Free • ☎ 01491 628529, ⓦ readingmuseum.org.uk

A branch of Reading Museum, located in two former waterworks buildings, tells the story of the town's two rivers: the Kennet and the Thames. The **Screen House** holds the museum's permanent collection, including a gypsy caravan built by Reading firm Dunton and Sons and a medieval wooden water wheel that was uncovered during the building of the Oracle shopping centre. The Victorian **Turbine House** spans the River Kennet and houses turbine machinery as well as regular local exhibitions.

The Museum of English Rural Life

6 Redlands Rd, Reading RG1 5EX3DH • Tues–Fri 9am-5pm, Sat–Sun 10am–5pm, last Thurs of month 9am-9pm • Free • ☎ 0118 378 8660, ⓦ merl.reading.ac.uk

Part of Reading University, the Museum of English Rural Life is home to the country's most extensive collection of artefacts focused on the history of food, farming and the countryside. Find out about the farming year, both past and present, and discover rural English life in all its grime and glory.

2

Thames Lido

Napier Rd, RG1 8FR • Public swim sessions Mon–Fri 1–4pm • £20 • ☎ 0118 207 0640, ⓦ thameslido.com

The Edwardian **Kings Meadow** swimming pool, next to the River Thames was recently restored and is now the area's most enticing place for a swim. Non-members can swim and use the saunas and hot tub during the public swim sessions, when the 25-metre **pool** tends to be at its busiest. During other hours there are pricier packages, which can include breakfast, lunch or dinner in the waterside **bar and restaurant** (from £35). There is also a **spa** offering massages.

Basildon Park

Lower Basildon, RG8 9NR • **House** Daily noon–5pm, **grounds** Daily 10am–5pm; tours daily at 11am & noon, 45min • £14, National Trust members free • ☎ 01491 672382, ⓦ nationaltrust.org.uk/basildon-park

The Georgian manor house at **Basildon Park** stands in 400 acres of historic **parkland** and **gardens**. The house was built in Bath stone by architect John Carr for the wealthy East India Company magnate Francis Sykes and later saw service as a wartime convalescent home, D-Day training camp and prisoner of war camp. It was bought and restored in the 1950s by Lord and Lady Iliffe, who returned it to its former glory but also added central heating and a modern kitchen. The result is a fascinating mix of eighteenth- and twentieth-century styles.

In the surrounding parkland there are four clearly signposted **walks** but the real joy is in exploring off the beaten track, taking in the spring bluebells or summer orchids in the hidden valley and looking out for the belted Galloway cattle who roam freely here. The parkland was used for tank training during the World War II and Nissen huts were built to house prisoners of war, the foundations of which can still be seen in some places.

Beale Park

Lower Basildon, RG8 9NW • Feb, March, Oct & early Nov Daily 10am–5pm, April–Sep daily 10am–6pm, last admission 1hr before closing • Feb, March, Oct & early Nov £8, Apr–Sept £11, £1 discount when booked online 48hrs in advance • ☎ 01189 767 480, ⓦ bealepark.org.uk

Beale Park is home to numerous attractions, including plenty of **wildlife** and lots of **family-friendly** things to do. There's an adventure playground, paddling pool and sandpit as well as a miniature railway and model boat collection. Adult visitors might enjoy the **Treasured Toys** museum, where toys from the 1950s, 60s and 70s, both British and international, are displayed in a row of contemporary shop windows – look out for Action Man, Sindy and the Thunderbirds. Animals you can see in the wildlife park include ring-tailed lemurs, squirrel monkeys and red-necked wallabies.

ARRIVAL AND INFORMATION
READING

BY TRAIN
Reading is a major stop on the Great Western Railway (ⓦ gwr.com) mainline from London to Bristol. There are regular services from London Paddington (every 15min; 30min; £20 single), Bristol Temple Meads (every 30min; 1hr 15min; £11.50 single) and all points in between including Swindon and Bath. There is also a direct service from Gatwick airport (hourly; 1hr 20min; £19 single).

The nearest station to both Basildon Park and Beale Park is Pangbourne, which has services from Reading (every 30min; 10min; £3.70 single). It's a 2.5 mile, 40min walk to Basildon Park and a 1.4-mile, 25min walk to Beale Park. Alternatively,

2

taxis can be prebooked with Atlantic Cars (☏ 01189 101 010, ⓦ atlanticcars.co.uk). On Saturdays, the Going Forward bus (ⓦ goingforwardbuses.com) route 142 runs from Pangbourne to both parks (4 daily; 3min; £2 single).

BY BUS

National Express (ⓦ nationalexpress.com) have regular coach services from London Victoria coach station to Reading (roughly 10 daily; 1hr 45min; £5 single). National Express also have non-stop services from Bristol (roughly 10 daily; 1hr 30min; £14) and Bath (roughly 6 daily; 1hr 40min; £5 single). The X25 Railair coach (ⓦ firstgroup.com) shuttles between Reading and Heathrow Airport (daily every 20min–1hr; 1hr; from £15 return).

BY CAR

Reading is one of the key towns on the M4 motorway, with three junctions (J10 for Reading East, J11 for Central & South and J12 for Reading West) plus a substantial service station. The A4 runs through the town centre. There are plenty of car parks around the town centre, though prices are extortionate – you can expect to pay around £4/hr. The Oracle car parks, Holy Brook (RG1 2LR) and The Riverside (RG1 2AG), are slightly cheaper – £4 will get you 2hr here. Both car parks also have electric car charging points. Reading also has three park and ride car parks, at the Madejski Stadium (RG2 0FL, near J11 of M4), Winnersh

Triangle (RG41 5RD, near J10 of M4) and Mereoak (RG7 1PB, near J11 of M4). Bus services into town are provided by Reading buses (ⓦ reading-buses.co.uk, every 10–20min, £4 return after 9.30am).

BY BIKE

Sustrans (ⓦ sustrans.org.uk) National Cycle Routes 4 and 5 meet at Reading. Route 4 continues east to London and west through Newbury, Wiltshire and Bath to Bristol; Route 5 runs north to Oxford.

BY BOAT

The River Kennet runs through Reading, linking the town to the Kennet & Avon Canal further west along the Great West Way. Eight miles west of Reading at Aldermaston you'll find the Aldermaston tea rooms, visitor centre and shop, run by the Kennet & Avon Canal Trust (☏ 01189 712868, ⓦ katrust.org.uk).

Thames River Cruise (ⓦ thamesrivercruise.co.uk) run services from Caversham pier in Reading to Beale Park on selected summer dates (departs 10.30am, returns 3.45pm, 2hr, £18 return).

ON FOOT

The Thames Path (ⓦ nationaltrail.co.uk/thames-path) runs along the eponymous river through Reading. It's 9 miles downriver to Henley.

TOURS AND ACTIVITIES

Bozedown Alpacas Bozedown Farm, RG8 7QY, ☏ 0118 9843827, ⓦ bozedown-alpacas.co.uk. Fancy owning an alpaca? Join one of Bozedown Farm's beginners day to learn the basics of husbandry, shearing and nutrition. £45 including lunch.

Thames Canoe Hire Scours Lane, Tilehurst, RG30 6AY, ☏ 01189 412777, ⓦ thamescanoehire.com. Canoe and kayak hire from Tilehurst on the Thames, which is about two miles upriver from Reading. All boats are full equipped with licences, paddles and buoyancy aids. Single kayak from £25/4hr, two-man canoe £45/day.

Thames River Cruise ☏ 01189 481088, ⓦ thames

rivercruise.co.uk. Range of sightseeing cruises on the Thames departing from Caversham Pier in Reading. The 30min trip (£6.50) gives a brief intro to the river, longer 45min (£7.50) and 80min (£9.50) cruises take in more local scenery, while Sundowner (£12.50) and afternoon tea (£25 inc tea) cruises allow for two hours cruising. The bar is open on all cruises.

★ **Tours 2 Order** ☏ 07827 715353, ⓦ tours2order.com. Graham Horn is a Blue Badge Tourist Guide with a wealth of knowledge on the south of England including Berkshire and Wiltshire. Graham offers bespoke tours for individuals and small groups, both by coach and on foot, including an enlightening and entertaining 2hr town tour of Reading.

ACCOMMODATION AND EATING

Forbury's Restaurant 1 Forbury Sq, RG1 3BB, ☏ 01189 574 044, ⓦ forburys.co.uk; map p.58. Upmarket French restaurant on modern Forbury Sq. The menu includes classic dishes such as steak tartare (£18.50) and guinea fowl with wild mushrooms (£21) and there is some outside seating. Tues–Sat noon–2.15pm & 6–9.30pm.

The Roseate 26 The Forbury, RG1 3EJ, ☏ 01189 527 770, ⓦ roseatehotels.com; map p.58. Luxury hotel right next to Forbury Gardens in Reading town centre. The 55 bedrooms are warmly decorated and very comfortable, all with

king-size beds. Suites have a sofa and the Forbury Suite has a four-poster bed, steam room and dining area. The Cerise restaurant (mains from £20) and Secret Garden outdoor bar are found downstairs and there's 24hr room service. **£125**

★ **Thames Lido** Napier Rd, RG1 8FR, ☏ 0118 2070640, ⓦ thameslido.com; map p.58. Unpretentious restaurant at Reading's outdoor swimming baths with a charcoal grill and wood-fired oven. The menu has a Spanish/Mediterranean feel and changes daily. Packages are available, including a swim. Mon–Fri 1–4pm for non-members.

RIGHT, FROM TOP READING ABBEY QUARTER; THE MUSEUM OF ENGLISH RURAL LIFE

SHOPPING

The Oracle RG1 2AG, ☎0118 965 9000, ⓦtheoracle .com, map p.58. Large shopping mall on the banks of the River Kennet with more than 80 shops, including brands

such as Jones the Bootmaker, Fat Face and Reiss. There's a large cinema and plenty of chain restaurants here too.

West Berkshire

Away from the major sprawl of Reading **West Berkshire** has a more rural feel, with small **market towns** acting as hubs for an area that remains largely unspoiled by modern development. **Newbury** is the largest town hereabouts and has long been a vibrant centre of local industry, while **Hungerford** sits on the border with **Wiltshire**, tempting passing visitors with its excellent independent shops. The most famous attraction in this area by far is **Highclere Castle**, aka the real "Downton Abbey", but it is the lesser-known attractions such as **Donnington Castle** and **Thatcham's Nature Discovery Centre** that show off bucolic Berkshire at its most serene.

Newbury

NEWBURY might be small, but it certainly punches above its weight when it comes to both historic attractions and modern vibrancy. The town centres around the **market square** with its medieval Cloth Hall and fifteenth century St Nicholas Church, while further away from its ancient core it is home to Vodafone UK's headquarters and a growing number of tech companies.

The town was founded in the eleventh century and was a centre of the booming **cloth trade** in the sixteenth, before seeing further success in the eighteenth century as a staging post on the Great West Road between London and Bath – the town stands almost exactly halfway between the two cities on what is today the A4, making it an important part of the history of the Great West Way. It is also on the edge of the **Berkshire Downs**, part of the **North Wessex Downs AONB**, making it an ideal base for country pursuits.

Newbury Racecourse

RG14 7NZ · ☎01635 40015, ⓦnewburyracecourse.co.uk

Founded in 1905, Newbury Racecourse is one of England's most famous racecourses and is currently undergoing an extensive redevelopment to add top of the range facilities for racegoers. The calendar of events runs year-round, with the course hosting a full line-up of flat and jumps races. The course has its own train station.

West Berkshire Museum

The Wharf, RG14 5AS · Wed–Sun & hols 10am–4pm · Free · ☎01635 519562, ⓦwestberkshireheritage.org

The small **West Berkshire Museum** tells the story of West Berkshire's history, including displays on the **Greenham Common** protests and English Civil War **Battles of Newbury**, which all occurred nearby. There is also information about the landscape and geology of the area as well as details about the town's successful sixteenth-century cloth-making industry and local leading clothier Jack of Newbury.

Shaw House

Church Rd, RG14 2DR · Feb–Sep Sat & Sun 11am–4pm, school hols also Mon–Fri 10am–4pm · Free · ☎01635 279279, ⓦwestberkshireheritage.org

Shaw House was built by wealthy cloth merchant Thomas Dolman in the sixteenth century and survives as a great example of an Elizabethan H-plan **mansion**. The local council now hire out the house for events and it is open to visitors most weekends. The

NORTH WESSEX DOWNS AONB

The **North Wessex Downs** was designated an Area of Outstanding Natural Beauty in 1972 and is one of the country's largest continuous areas of **chalk downland**. It runs from West Berkshire into Wiltshire, Oxfordshire and Hampshire and appears on a map as a C-shaped area of land with its northeastern-most extremity abutting the Chilterns AONB at the River Thames. The Berkshire Downs, the Vale of Pewsey and Savernake Forest are all part of the North Wessex Downs.

2

extensive grounds are a great place for a picnic and there are giant **garden games** in the summer months.

Donnington Castle

Donnington, RG14 2LE; 5 miles north of Newbury • Daylight hours • Free • Ⓦ english-heritage.org.uk

Although only the twin-towered gatehouse of fourteenth-century **Donnington Castle** remains, it is an imposing sight and well worth a short visit. During the **English Civil War** in the 1640s Charles I sent Sir John Boys to capture the castle from Parliamentarian John Packer and defences were built around the castle in a star shape, the remains of which can still be seen. The building was attacked many times and did not survive the onslaught, being mostly demolished in 1646, but the gatehouse that still stands retains its finely vaulted ceiling and elegant stone string courses.

The Nature Discovery Centre, Thatcham

Muddy Lane, Lower Way, Thatcham, RG19 3FU • April–Oct Daily 10.30am–5pm, Nov–March Tues–Sun 10.30am–4pm • Free • ☎ 01635 874381, Ⓦ bbowt.org.uk/nature-discovery-centre

The Berkshire, Buckinghamshire and Oxfordshire Wildlife Trust own this unspoilt area of lakes and reedbeds, which provides a **habitat** for numerous **birds**, including large groups of wintering wildfowl, and dozens of butterflies, dragonflies and beetles. It's a lovely place for a **walk**, along designated paths that run around the main lake, out to Thatcham Reedbeds, and along the Kennet & Avon Canal.

The Living Rainforest

Hampstead Norreys, Thatcham, RG18 0TN • Daily 10am–5pm, last admission 30min before • £11.50 • ☎ 01635 202444, Ⓦ livingrainforest.org

The Living Rainforest's three glasshouses host a lush tropical rainforest complete with all the sounds and smells you might expect. More than 650 different rainforest plants and animals have been gathered together here, many of them rare and endangered species, and there are 1hr and 2hr **Keeper Experiences** where visitors can meet and even feed their favourite animals (from £45).

West Berkshire Brewery

The Old Dairy, Yattendon, RG18 0XT • **Tours** 1 day/month, Taproom Sun–Tues 11am–6pm, Wed–Sat 11am–11pm, **Shop** Daily 10am–6pm • Tours £15 • ☎ 01635 767090, Ⓦ wbbrew.com

The independent **West Berkshire Brewery** has been using traditional brewing techniques to make **real ales** and **craft beers** for more than 20 years. The brewery itself is cutting-edge and can be seen on one of the monthly tours. During the rest of the month it's still worth popping in to the taproom to try the full range of beers, with views of the brewhouse through large glass windows on one side and of the Berkshire countryside on the other.

Bucklebury Farm Park

Bucklebury, RG7 6RR • Early spring–late autumn Daily 9.30am–6pm (last admission 5pm), Oct–Jan 9.30am–5pm • £9.95–£11.45 depending on season • ☎ 01189 714 002, ⓦ bucklebburyfarmpark.co.uk

Spread over 77 acres in the Pang Valley, **Bucklebury Farm Park** is home to a small herd of rare breed Berkshire pigs, pygmy and Anglo-Nubian goats, Dexter cattle, ponies, donkeys, poultry, guinea fowl and reindeer. Admission includes a free **tractor ride** through the deer park (15min) and there is plenty to keep the **kids** active, including a nature trail, zip wire and bounce mat. There's also an indoor play area for rainy days.

2

Highclere Castle

Highclere Park, RG20 9RN • July–early Sep 9.30am–5pm, last admission 1hr before • £23 including Egyptian exhibition, £16 castle and gardens, £7 gardens only • ☎ 01635 253204, ⓦ highclerecastle.co.uk

Highclere Castle will be very familiar to fans of ITV's hit period drama, *Downton Abbey*, which was filmed here. Home to the Earl of Carnarvon and his family, the house is approached via a long drive that winds through a stunning 5000-acre estate and is surrounded by beautiful **gardens** designed by **Capability Brown**. Inside the house, Downton Abbey aficionados will enjoy loitering in the Drawing Room and the Library, scene of many a drama and quivering stiff-upper-lip of Lord Grantham and his family, while upstairs you can peer into the bedrooms of the Crawley girls. In the castle cellars, an **Egyptian Exhibition** celebrates the real-life 5th Earl of Carnarvon, who, in 1922, discovered the tomb of **Tutankhamun** with Howard Carter, and who funded many of Carter's expeditions. Since the house is still a family home and is also sometimes closed for filming, its opening hours vary from month to month and year to year; call or check the website for details.

Hungerford

HUNGERFORD is a handsome town in a bucolic setting – the River Kennet and River Dun meet here and are joined by the Kennet & Avon Canal, while the North Wessex Downs AONB encircles the town. The High Street is a good example of a traditional English shopping street, with several good **antiques** stores, while Hungerford Wharf is a lovely place to stroll along the canal. There is a weekly **market** (Wednesday) and on the last Saturday of the month, a large antiques fair in the town hall. Hungerford is a useful hub, with a mainline railway station and easy access to both the A4 and M4.

Alder Ridge Vineyard

Cobbs Farm, Bath Road, Hungerford, RG17 0SP • Tours May–Sep, 45 mins • ☎ 01488 686770, ⓦ alderridge.co.uk

Alder Ridge started life as a vineyard back in 2009 and its land in the North Wessex Downs AONB is south-facing, with some similarities to the terroir of Champagne. The wines produced here are excellent and can be sampled after one of their tours. Group bookings can also be catered for.

ARRIVAL AND INFORMATION

WEST BERKSHIRE

BY TRAIN

Newbury is served by Great Western Railway (ⓦ gwr .com) trains from London Paddington (2-3/hr; 1hr; £6 single) which run via Reading (30min; £6.50 single). Hungerford is on the same line from London though fewer services stop here (1-2/hr; 1hr 5min; £6 single).

Thatcham and Newbury Racecourse both also have

stations on the same line; Thatcham station is less than two miles from the Nature Discovery Centre (35min walk).

BY BUS

National Express (ⓦ nationalexpress.com) operate a daily coach service from London Victoria to Newbury (6.30pm, 1hr 50min, £5.50), which also calls at Heathrow airport (1hr). This service continues on to Hungerford (15min

RIGHT, FROM TOP HIGHCLERE CASTLE; THE QUEENS AR

2

INTO HAMPSHIRE: THE BOMBAY SAPPHIRE DISTILLERY

Some 14 miles south of Newbury across the border into Hampshire, is the **Bombay Sapphire Distillery** at Laverstoke Mill (Apr–Oct daily 10am–8pm, Nov–Mar daily 11am–6pm, last admission 2hr before close, distillery.bombaysapphire.com, from £16, must be booked in advance). There has been a mill here since at least AD903 and a corn mill on this site appears in the Domesday Book of 1086. The current building is a 300-year-old paper mill with a stunning contemporary glasshouse at its front. This houses the botanicals that make up Bombay Sapphire's popular gin and can be explored – along with the rest of the distillery – on a self-guided or guided tour, which ends with a complementary drink in the Mill Bar.

---

further, £8.60). The return service departs Hungerford at 8.45am and Newbury at 9.10am. There is also a non-stop service from Newbury to Oxford (departs 9.45am and returns 5.45pm daily; 1hr 5min; £11 single).

West Berkshire Council (ⓦinfo.westberks.gov.uk) operate local bus services. Route 1 shuttles between Newbury and Reading (every 30min; 1hr 20min; £6/day), calling at Bourne Road in Thatcham, a short walk from the Nature Discovery Centre, while route 3 links Newbury and Hungerford (5 daily; 55min; £6/day) and route 5A runs from Newbury to Donnington Castle (3 daily; 15min; £6/day). To get to Highclere Castle take route 7 from Newbury to the Red House pub in Highclere (4 daily; 20min); from here it's a two-mile walk (40min).

There is also a bus service from Hungerford to Swindon (4–5 daily; 1hr 10min) which calls at the Bell in Ramsbury.

BY CAR

Newbury and Hungerford are both on the A4 and within easy reach of the M4 motorway – where Newbury is junction 13 and Hungerford 14. Newbury has plentiful parking, in car parks operated by the local council. The multi-storey car park at the Kennet Centre is a good bet (RG14 5BN; £3.90/3hr). The best car park in Hungerford is on Church Street (£1.70/3hr, free after 6pm & Sun).

A car is the best way to get around outside the towns, with most attractions not on the public transport network. All have free parking on-site.

BY BOAT

Newbury and Hungerford are both located on the Kennet & Avon Canal and mooring is permitted in most places along the towpath. Newbury's historic wharf is home to the Newbury branch of the Kennet & Avon Canal Trust; you'll find a teashop and information centre here (ⓣ01635 522609, ⓦkatrust.org.uk).

BY BIKE

It's easy to travel this part of the Great West Way by bike, with Sustrans (ⓦsustrans.org.uk) National Cycle Route 4 running through Newbury and Hungerford along the Kennet & Avon Canal towpath. It is about 9 miles between the two towns.

ACCOMMODATION

Donnington Grove Grove Rd, Newbury, RG14 2LA, ⓣ01635 581000, ⓦdonnington-grove.com; map p.58. Country house hotel set in 500 acres of grounds that includes an 18-hole golf course. Classic rooms in the main house are simple three-star en suites, those in the lodges around the grounds have a shared patio area. **£85**

The Queens Arms East Garston, RG17 7ET, ⓣ01488 648757, ⓦqueensarmseastgarston.co.uk; map p.58. Twelve en suite bedrooms in a traditional country pub, all styled individually. The suite has a separate sitting room with a sofa that can convert into a bed to make a family room. Downstairs the bar has a roaring fire and there's a large enclosed garden. **£105**

The Royal Oak The Square, Yattendon, RG18 0UF, ⓣ01635 201325, ⓦroyaloakyattendon.co.uk; map p.58. Upscale countryside inn with ten beautiful bedrooms spread throughout the main house and a separate cottage.

Dogs are welcome (£15 extra) and there are Z beds for children. **£99**

The Vineyard Stockcross, Newbury, RG20 8JU ⓣ01635 538770, ⓦthe-vineyard.co.uk; map p.58. Luxury hotel with 49 elegant rooms. Even the smallest rooms are spacious, with generous bathrooms, and there's a spa with a circular indoor pool with massage jets. **£255**

Warner's Littlecote House Hotel Hungerford, RG17 0SU, ⓣ01488 682509, ⓦwarnerleisurehotels.co.uk; map p.58. Grade I listed Tudor manor turned adults only hotel. Rooms are contemporary and there are two restaurants to choose from, as well as acitivies such as archery, bowls, shooting and nightly live entertainment. Packages include 3-course dinner in The Popham. Two-night min stay. **£145**pp

EATING AND DRINKING

Cobbs Farm Shop & Kitchen Bath Rd, Hungerford, RG17 0SP, ☎01488 686770, ⓦcobbsfarmshop.co.uk; map p.58. A 55-acre farm surrounds this excellent farm shop, which has a butcher, delicatessen, fishmonger and café. Breakfast is served until 11.30am and includes a full farmer's breakfast (£10), while lunch features homemade quiche of the day and Wiltshire cured ham and eggs (both £10). Mon–Sat 9am–5pm, Mon–Sun 10am–4pm.

The Lock Stock & Barrel 104 Northbrook St, Newbury, RG14 1AA, ☎01635 580550, ⓦlockstockandbarrel newbury.co.uk; map p.58. Riverside pub with roof terrace and heated patio serving modern pub meals such as chicken, smoked ham and ale pie (£13) and blackened salmon (£15). Mon–Thurs 11am–11pm, Fri & Sat 11am–midnight, Sun noon–10.30pm, food served Mon–Sat noon–9pm, Sun noon–8pm.

The Newbury 137 Bartholomew St, RG14 5HB, ☎01635 49000, ⓦthenewburypub.co.uk; map p.58. This nineteenth-century pub has been reimagined as a modern gastropub, complete with local beers, a roaring fire and a menu of hearty dishes. There's also a roof terrace with its own bar and a pizza oven. Sun–Wed noon–11.30pm, Thurs noon–12.30am, Fri noon–1pm, Sat 10am–2am.

★**The Royal Oak**, RG18 0UF, ☎01635 201325, ⓦroyaloakyattendon.co.uk; map p.58. Chef Nick MacGregor serves up refined dishes using local produce at chunky oak tables in the dining room of this welcoming country pub. Dishes include Keralan spiced crab croquettes (£10), rosemary roasted pork chop (£18.50) and 12hr slow roast lamb shoulder (£50 for two people). Local West Berkshire Brewery beers are on tap and there are log fires in winter and a sunny garden complete with boules pitch for the summer. Mon–Sat 11am–11pm, Sun noon–10.30pm, food served Mon–Fri noon–2.30pm & 6–9.30pm, Sat noon–3pm & 6–9.30pm, Sun noon–3.30pm & 6–9pm.

★**The Tutti Pole** 3 High St, Hungerford, RG17 0DN, ☎01488 682515, ⓦthetuttipole.co.uk; map p.58. Proper English tearooms serving everything from a full cooked breakfast (£7.15, served all day) to a luxury afternoon tea with homemade scone, cakes and Prosecco. Snacks on the menu include crumpets and toasted teacakes, while lunch runs the gamut from chicken kiev to a seafood platter (£9.65). Mon–Fri 9am–5.30pm, Sat & Sun 9am–6pm.

West Berkshire Brewery The Old Dairy, Yattendon, RG18 0XT, ☎01635 767090, ⓦwbbrew.com; map p.58. The ultra-modern Taproom at this independent brewery serves the full range of WBB beers alongside homemade pizzas (from £9) and burgers cooked on a Josper charcoal grill (from £11). Kitchen open Tues–Sun noon–3pm & Wed–Sat 6–9pm.

SHOPPING

Coco & Co 13 Bridge St, Hungerford, ☎01488 686319, ⓦcoco-co.co.uk; map p.58. Brand new and second hand designer clothing and a gorgeous selection of fine Italian leather bags. Mon–Sat 10.30am–5pm.

The Emporium 112 High St, Hungerford, ☎01488 686959, ⓦemporium-hungerford.co.uk; map p.58. Well laid out three-storey antiques shop in a seventeenth-century beamed building. Mon–Fri 10am–5pm, Sat 9.30am–5pm, Sun & hols 10am–4pm.

★**Hungerford Arcade Antiques & Collectibles** 26-27 High St, Hungerford ☎01488 683701, ⓦhungerfordarcade.com; map p.58. More than a hundred antiques dealers under one roof. Mon–Fri 9.15am–5.30pm, Sat 9.15am–6pm, Sun 11am–5pm.

Parkway Shopping Centre Park Way, Newbury, RG14 1AY, ☎01635 889070, ⓦshopatparkway.com; map p.58. Modern shopping centre with top high street brands including Jack Wills, Topshop and Superdry plus Marks & Spencer, John Lewis and Debenhams department stores.

ACTIVITIES AND ENTERTAINMENT

Clay pigeon shooting Donnington Grove, Grove Road, Newbury, RG14 2LA, ☎01635 581000, ⓦdonnington -grove.co.uk. Learn to aim a rifle at flying clay discs on a beginners lesson with Sean. £80 one on one, from £35 for groups (min 3 people).

Golf Donnington Grove, Grove Road, Newbury, RG14 2LA, ☎01635 581000, ⓦdonnington-grove.co.uk. Lovely 18-hole golf course flanked by Donnington Castle on one side and the River Lambourn on the other. The front nine is on high ground with views of Newbury while the back nine is a challenging parkland course with plenty of trees and water hazards. £15.

K&A Canal Trust Boat Trips ☎01380 721279, ⓦkatrust .org.uk. Short cruises on the Kennet & Avon, aboard the thirty-seater MV *Jubilee* narrowboat through Newbury or the fifty-seater *Rose of Hungerford*. £6.

The Watermill Theatre Bagnor, Newbury, RG20 8AE, ☎01635 46044, ⓦwatermill.org.uk; map p.58. Professional repertory theatre in a converted watermill, producing a range of highly regarded shows.

OXFORD

When visitors think of **OXFORD**, they almost always imagine its university, revered as one of the world's great academic institutions, inhabiting honey-coloured stone buildings set around ivy-clad quadrangles. The image is accurate enough, but although the university dominates central Oxford both physically and spiritually, the wider city has an entirely different character, its economy built chiefly on the factories of Cowley, south of the centre, where Britain's first mass-produced cars were made in the 1920s.

OXFORD'S COLLEGES

So where, exactly, is **Oxford University**? Everywhere – and nowhere. The university itself is nothing more than an administrative body, setting examinations and awarding degrees. What draws all the attention are the university's **colleges** – 38 of them (plus six religious foundations known as Permanent Private Halls), most occupying **historic buildings** scattered throughout the city centre. It is these that hold the eight hundred-year-old history of the university and exemplify its spirit.

There are common architectural features among the colleges, with the students' rooms and most of the communal areas – chapels, halls (dining rooms) and libraries – arranged around **quadrangles** (quads). Each, however, has its own character and collegiate rivalries are long established, usually revolving around sports.

CHRIST CHURCH COLLEGE

St Aldate's, OX1 1DP · Mon–Sat 10am–5pm, Sun 2–5pm; last entry 45min before closing · July & Aug £10, rest of year £8 · ☎ 01865 276492, ⓦ chch.ox.ac.uk

Stretching along the east side of St Aldate's is the main facade of **Christ Church College**, whose distinctive Tom Tower was added by **Christopher Wren** in 1681 to house the weighty "Great Tom" bell. The tower lords it over the main entrance of what is Oxford's largest and arguably most prestigious college, but visitors have to enter from the south, a signed five-minute walk away. This is the most touristy of all the Oxford Colleges, particularly popular thanks to its *Harry Potter* connections: many scenes from the films were shot here, while a studio recreation of the college's hall provided the set of **Hogwarts' Great Hall**.

From the entrance it's a few steps to the striking **Tom Quad**, the largest quad in Oxford, so large that the Royalists penned up their mobile larder of cattle here during the English Civil War. Guarded by Tom Tower, the quad's soft, honey-coloured stone makes a harmonious whole, but it was actually built in two main phases, with the southern side dating back to Wolsey, and the north finally finished in the 1660s. A wide stone staircase in the southeast corner beneath a stupendous fan-vaulted ceiling leads up to the Hall, the grandest **refectory** in Oxford, with its fanciful hammer-beam roof and a set of stern portraits of past scholars by a roll call of famous **artists**, including Reynolds, Gainsborough and Millais. As well as Albert Einstein, William Gladstone and no fewer than twelve other British **prime ministers** were educated here.

MERTON COLLEGE

Merton St, OX1 4JD · Mon–Fri 2–5pm, Sat & Sun 10am–5pm, last entry 30min before closing · £3 · ☎ 01865 276310, ⓦ merton .ox.ac.uk

Merton College is historically the city's most important. Balliol and University colleges may have been founded earlier, but it was Merton – opened in 1264 – which set the model for colleges in both Oxford and Cambridge, being the first to gather its students and tutors together in one place. Furthermore, unlike the other two, Merton retains some of its original **medieval** buildings, with the best of the thirteenth-century architecture clustered around **Mob Quad**, a charming courtyard with mullioned windows and **Gothic** doorways to the right of the Front Quad. From the Mob Quad, an archway leads through to the **Chapel**, dating from 1290, inside which you'll find the funerary plaque of Thomas Bodley, founder of Oxford's famous **Bodleian Library**.

MAGDALEN COLLEGE

High St, OX1 4AU · Daily: late June–late Sept 10am–7pm or dusk if earlier; Oct–June 1–6pm or dusk · £6 · ☎ 01865 276000, ⓦ magd.ox.ac.uk

At the east end of the High Street stands **Magdalen College** (pronounced "maudlin"), whose gaggle of stone buildings is overshadowed by its chunky medieval **bell tower**. Steer right from the entrance and you reach the chapel, which has a handsome reredos, though you have to admire it through the windows of an ungainly stone screen. The adjacent cloisters are adorned by standing figures, some biblical and others folkloric, most notably a tribe of grotesques. Magdalen also boasts better grounds than most other colleges, with a bridge at the back of the cloisters spanning the River Cherwell to join **Addison's Walk**. You can rent **punts** from beneath Magdalen Bridge, beside the college.

BRIDGE OF SIGHS

Spanning New College Lane a few paces off Catte Street, you can't miss the iconic **Bridge of Sighs**, an archway completed in 1914 to link two buildings of **Hertford College**. In truth it bears little resemblance to its Venetian namesake, but nonetheless has a certain Italianate elegance. It was designed, so the story goes, to give residents of Hertford's older buildings to the south a way to reach the newfangled flushing toilets being installed across the road without having to venture outdoors.

BODLEIAN LIBRARY

Broad St, OX1 3BG · Tours 4–6 Daily, 30min or 60min; £6–£9 · ☎ 01865 287400, ⓦ bodleian.ox.ac.uk

Christopher Wren's pupil **Nicholas Hawksmoor** designed the **Clarendon Building**, a domineering, solidly symmetrical edifice at the east end of Broad Street, completed in 1713. It now forms part of the **Bodleian Library**. Founded by scholar Sir Thomas Bodley in 1602, the Bodleian is the UK's largest library after the British Library in London, with an estimated 117 miles of shelving. It includes the Modernist 1930s Weston Library (formerly known as the New Bodleian) directly opposite the Clarendon, designed by Sir Giles Gilbert Scott and linked to the main building by tunnels. As one of the UK and Ireland's six copyright libraries, the Bodleian must find room for a copy of every book, pamphlet, magazine and newspaper published in Britain.

ASHMOLEAN MUSEUM

Beaumont St, OX1 2PH · Tues–Sun 10am–5pm, until 8pm last Fri of the month · Free · ☎ 01865 278000, ⓦ ashmolean.org

Occupying a mammoth neoclassical building, the Ashmolean grew from the collections of the magpie-like John Tradescant, gardener to Charles I and an energetic traveller. Today it possesses a vast and far-reaching collection covering everything from Minoan vases to Stradivarius violins. Light and airy modern galleries cover four floors (pick up a plan at reception). The "orientation" gallery in the basement provides a thematic overview of the museum, while the ground floor houses the museum's "ancient world" exhibits, including its superb Egyptology collection and an imposing room full of Greek sculptures. Floor 1 is dedicated to Mediterranean, Indian and Islamic artefacts (Hindu bronzes, Iranian pottery and so on) while floor 2 is mainly European, including the museum's wide-ranging collection of Dutch, Flemish and Italian paintings. Floor 3 focuses on European art since 1800, including works by the Pre-Raphaelites.

EATING

The Head of the River Folly Bridge, OX1 4LB, T01865 721600, ⓦ headoftheriveroxford.co.uk; map p.58. Thameside pub with a menu of modern pub classics such as burgers (£13.50) and roasted guinea fowl (£15). The huge riverside terrace is perpetually packed.

ACTIVITIES

Salter's Steamers Folly Bridge, OX1 4LA, T01865 243421, ⓦ salterssteamers.co.uk. Short cruises down the Thames from Folly Bridge to Iffley Lock (£8) plus punts and rowing boats for hire (£20/hr).

Oxford River Cruises Folly Bridge, OX1 4LA, T01865 987147, ⓦ oxfordrivercruises.com. Sightseeing cruises past Christ Church college and meadows and the university rowing houses (£12) plus picnic and afternoon tea cruises (from £39).

ALTON BARNES

Wiltshire

Wiltshire is packed with attractions from the world-famous Neolithic sites of Stonehenge and Avebury right through to delightfully unknown towns that have hosted weekly markets for centuries in their cobbled squares or along their ancient streets.

HIGHLIGHTS

❶ **Avebury stone circle** You can touch the stones at this prehistoric stone circle, and even sit in one: the Devil's Chair. **See p.87**

❷ **Marlborough** Check out Wiltshire's best boutique shopping along this ancient market town's lively High Street. Visit on Wednesday or Saturday for the weekly market. **See p.89**

❸ **Crofton Beam Engines** Have a go at working two ancient steam engines, used for pumping water up to the Kennet & Avon Canal's highest point. **See p.90**

❹ **Lacock** Step into the shoes of Harry Potter, Elizabeth Bennet or Lady Mary Crawley on a stroll around Lacock village and the stately Abbey – the backdrop to numerous films and TV shows. **See p.104**

❺ **Longleat Safari Park** There be lions in Wiltshire, reclining under the trees at Longleat, where the drive-through safari park offers the chance to see everything from big cats to towering giraffes. The cheeky monkeys are the highlight though – they love to clamber over visitors' cars. **See p.111**

❻ **Stonehenge** Get up early (and book ahead) for a Stone Circle Access tour, which allows you – and a small group – to stand among the stones before Stonehenge opens for the day. No touching, but you will get some incredible photographs. **See p.110**

❼ **Salisbury Cathedral** Just off the Great West Way, Salisbury is worth a detour to climb its cathedral spire – the tallest in England. The cathedral is also home to a (very rare) copy of the Magna Carta. **See p.113**

3

Avebury is the lesser-known of Wiltshire's two Neolithic big-hitters, but it is one of the largest prehistoric stone circles in the world and deserves to be at the very top of your must-visit list. The quite staggeringly beautiful market town of Marlborough should not be far behind, and there are numerous other small but vibrant towns and villages that are well worth calling in to – chief among them Devizes, Lacock and Bradford on Avon. In the north of the county Swindon is the largest town, and home to the engaging STEAM: Museum of the Great Western Railway, while in the south are several enticing attractions, including Longleat, England's first drive-through safari park, and Stourhead, one of the country's most engaging gardens – plus, of course, Stonehenge, without which no trip along the Great West Way would be complete.

Avebury and around

The village of **AVEBURY** stands in the midst of a stone circle that rivals Stonehenge; the individual stones are generally smaller, but the circle itself is much wider and more complex. It presumably had a similar ritual or religious function to Stonehenge and forms part of the same UNESCO World Heritage Site, a **Neolithic** and **Bronze Age** landscape that is best explored on foot – and with time to stand back and wonder.

An illuminating exhibition that explains what we know about the stone circle is housed in the **Alexander Keiller Museum** in the village, while the sixteenth-century **Avebury Manor** has been recently reinvigorated and is now an interactive museum of English life, its rooms reflecting various periods in local history from the Tudor era to the twentieth century.

WILTSHIRE CYCLEWAY

The waymarked **Wiltshire Cycleway** circles the county for 160 miles. It is split into 16 sections and there are useful downloadable maps of the route, which also detail where National Cycle Routes join it and detours you can make (ⓦ wiltshire.gov.uk/leisure-wiltshire-cycle-ways).

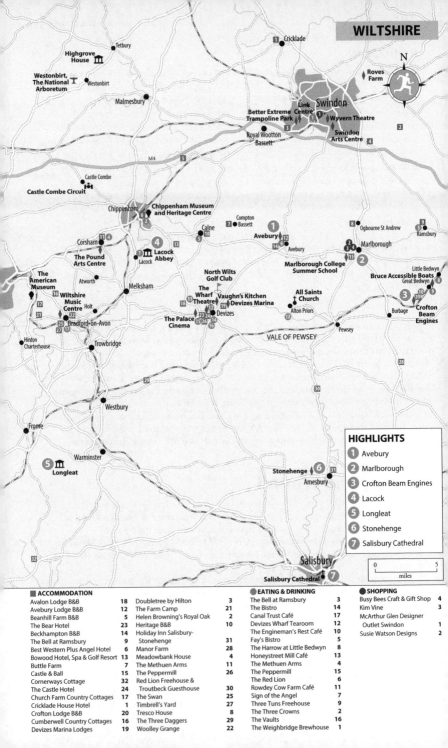

WILTSHIRE

N

Tetbury

Highgrove House

Westonbirt, The National Arboretum Westonbirt

Malmesbury

Cricklade 1

Roves Farm

Swindon

Better Extreme Trampoline Park

Link Centre

Wyvern Theatre

Royal Wootton Bassett

Swindon Arts Centre 4

2

M4

5

Castle Combe

Castle Combe Circuit

Chippenham

Chippenham Museum and Heritage Centre

Calne 10

Compton Bassett 7

Avebury 1

14 17

Avebury

Ogbourne St Andrew 8

Ramsbury 9 3

Corsham 11 4

The Pound Arts Centre

4 **Lacock Abbey**

Lacock

13

2 3 4 **Marlborough** 15

2

Marlborough College Summer School

Little Bedwyn

Bruce Accessible Boats Great Bedwyn 8

3 **The American Museum**

Atworth

Wiltshire Music Centre 10

Holt

Melksham

North Wilts Golf Club

The Wharf Theatre 11

Vaughn's Kitchen **Devizes Marina**

Devizes

All Saints Church

3 **Crofton Beam Engines** 10 20 9

Burbage

17 21

25 22

Bradford-on-Avon 27 17

The Palace Cinema 18

19 23 24 16

Alton Priors 13

Pewsey

VALE OF PEWSEY

Hinton Charterhouse

Trowbridge

29

28

Westbury

30

Frome

Warminster

5 **Longleat**

Stonehenge 6 31

Amesbury

32

Salisbury

Salisbury Cathedral 7

HIGHLIGHTS

1 Avebury
2 Marlborough
3 Crofton Beam Engines
4 Lacock
5 Longleat
6 Stonehenge
7 Salisbury Cathedral

0   5
miles

ACCOMMODATION

Avalon Lodge B&B	18	Doubletree by Hilton	3
Avebury Lodge B&B	12	The Farm Camp	21
Beanhill Farm B&B	5	Helen Browning's Royal Oak	2
The Bear Hotel	23	Heritage B&B	10
Beckhampton B&B	14	Holiday Inn Salisbury-	
The Bell at Ramsbury	9	Stonehenge	31
Best Western Plus Angel Hotel	6	Manor Farm	28
Bowood Hotel, Spa & Golf Resort	13	Meadowbank House	4
Buttle Farm	7	The Methuen Arms	11
Castle & Ball	15	The Peppermill	26
Cornerways Cottage	32	Red Lion Freehouse &	
The Castle Hotel	24	Troutbeck Guesthouse	30
Church Farm Country Cottages	17	The Swan	25
Cricklade House Hotel	1	Timbrell's Yard	27
Crofton Lodge B&B	20	Tresco House	8
Cumberwell Country Cottages	16	The Three Daggers	29
Devizes Marina Lodges	19	Woolley Grange	22

EATING & DRINKING

The Bell at Ramsbury	3
The Bistro	14
Canal Trust Café	17
Devizes Wharf Tearoom	12
The Engineman's Rest Café	10
Fay's Bistro	5
The Harrow at Little Bedwyn	8
Honeystreet Mill Café	13
The Methuen Arms	4
The Peppermill	15
The Red Lion	6
Rowdey Cow Farm Café	11
Sign of the Angel	7
Three Tuns Freehouse	9
The Three Crowns	2
The Vaults	16
The Weighbridge Brewhouse	1

SHOPPING

Busy Bees Craft & Gift Shop	4
Kim Vine	3
McArthur Glen Designer	
Outlet Swindon	1
Susie Watson Designs	2

Close by are the prehistoric burial chamber of **West Kennet Long Barrow** and the mysterious mound of **Silbury Hill**, a pyramid-like hump whose story remains untold; while a few miles to the west is a far more recent addition to the landscape, a late eighteenth-century **chalk horse** carved into the hillside at **Cherhill Down**.

Avebury stone circle

Avebury, SN8 1RF • Daylight hours • Free • ☎ 01672 539250, ⓦ nationaltrust.org.uk/avebury

Far larger than Stonehenge, **Avebury stone circle** is in fact a series of three circles – one large outer ring that was once made up of around a hundred stones and two smaller inner circles. The whole thing is encircled by a 20ft high man-made henge bank and ditch some three quarters of a mile in circumference and built using only stone and bone. This is approached by four causeways across the inner ditch, two of them leading into wide avenues stretching over a mile beyond the circle. This is one of the **largest prehistoric stone circles** in the world and was built (and much altered) during the **Neolithic** period, between about 2850BC and 2200BC.

The joy of Avebury is in the freedom to roam. Here there are no restrictions on touching the stones and much of the original site remains. In recent years geophysical research has uncovered a square-shaped stone **monument** which is believed to be the earliest feature at the site.

3

The Alexander Keiller Museum

Avebury, SN8 1RF • Daily 10am–6pm • £4.90; free for National Trust and English Heritage members • ☎ 01672 539250, ⓦ nationaltrust
.org.uk/avebury

The Alexander Keiller Museum provides an excellent overview of the Avebury stones and their significance, plus information about the role of Keiller himself. A Scottish **archaeologist** and heir to a marmalade fortune, Keiller was responsible for restoring the stones and excavating the surrounding site. The museum is housed in two separate buildings: the **Stables Gallery** houses some of Keiller's original finds, while the seventeenth-century **Barn Gallery** has exhibits on local archaeology, interactive displays plus activities for children.

WALK: AN ARCHAEOLOGICAL WALK AROUND AVEBURY, SILBURY HILL AND WEST KENNET LONG BARROW

Avebury stone circle is simply one feature in an extensive prehistoric landscape, which is easiest explored on a **loop walk** from Avebury village. From the stone circle's southern edge (where the main Beckhampton road turns at a right angle) follow a line of standing stones referred to as **The Avenue** across the field to a gate crossing the road. From here a footpath runs along the fence line, passing a far smaller stone circle called **Faulkner's Circle** before reaching the crossroads of a byway and a farm track.

Here take the byway uphill passing clumps of beech trees which stand on top of **Bronze Age** round barrows. More of these barrows can be seen as you turn right (southwards) along the **Ridgeway** to reach the A4 main road at **The Sanctuary**. This was once the site of several timber circles and later a double stone circle, though today only low concrete markers, which set out what was once here, can be seen.

From here it's a short walk along the A4 to reach the path to **West Kennet Long Barrow**, a short diversion that leads up to the ancient burial chamber. Back at the main road take the footpath that runs along the River Kennet northwards alongside Silbury Hill and up Waden Hill for an excellent view of the mound. The footpath from here leads back to the end of the Avenue of stones, your return path to Avebury village.

Avebury Manor and Garden

High St, Avebury, SN8 1RF • Daily 11am–5pm • Manor and gardens £11.60, free for National Trust members • ☎ 01672 539250, ⓦ nationaltrust.org.uk/avebury

Built on the site of a former priory, the pretty sixteenth-century **Avebury Manor** was refurbished in 2011. Little of the house's original decoration remained, and almost all the furnishings here have been re-created in Tudor, Queen Anne, Georgian or Victorian style. As you wander round the house, you can lie on the beds, sit on the sofas and even play billiards in the Billiards Room. The **gardens** have been replanted too, with topiary and walled gardens, and there's a vintage-style tearoom in the former West Library.

Silbury Hill

Car parking on A4 • 24 hours • Free

Just outside Avebury, the neat green mound of **Silbury Hill** is disregarded by the majority of drivers whizzing by on the A4. At 130ft it's no great height, but when you realize that it's the largest **prehistoric** artificial mound in Europe, and was made using nothing more than primitive spades, it commands more respect. It was probably constructed around 2600 BC, and though no one knows quite what it was for, the likelihood is that it was a **burial mound**. You can't actually walk on the hill but it's worth stopping in the car park to admire it close up.

West Kennet Long Barrow

Car parking on A4 • 24 hours • Free

You can walk right down inside this **Neolithic chambered tomb** built in roughly 3650BC and in use for around a thousand years. Large **sarsen stones** stand sentry over the entrance but pass behind this curtain of rock and you can delve into a 42ft passage divided into chambers. Nearly 50 people were buried here and it's an atmospheric, if not somewhat spooky, place to explore.

ARRIVAL AND INFORMATION

AVEBURY AND AROUND

BY TRAIN
Great Western Railway trains from London to Bristol call at Swindon, where you can pick up the bus to Avebury (every 30min; 1hr from London, from £27.90 single; 45min from Bristol, from £15.90 single; ⓦ gwr.com).

BY BUS
Avebury is served by Stagecoach bus 49 (hourly; £3 single, £5.10 return; ⓦ stagecoachbus.com) which runs from

Swindon to Devizes and Thamesdown Transport bus 42 (every 1hr 15min; from £2 single; ☎ 01793 428428, ⓦ thamesdown-transport.co.uk) from Calne to Marlborough.

BY CAR
Avebury is just off the A4, a 12min drive from Marlborough. The best place to park for the stone circle, museum and manor house is the car park just outside the village (£7/

WILTSHIRE'S WHITE HORSES

There were once thirteen **white horses** carved into the chalk hills of Wiltshire and although today only eight remain, this is the county for spotting these eye-catching beasts. The origins of this practice are unknown, though we know that England's oldest white horse in Uffington, Oxfordshire dates back as far as the **Bronze Age** and is therefore several thousand years old.

Wiltshire's horses are far younger, mostly dating from the last three hundred or so years. The best for a visit are **Westbury White Horse** and **Cherhill White Horse**, both just a few miles from Avebury. Westbury's White Horse (Bratton Rd, BA13 3EP, daylight hours, free, ⓦ english-heritage.org.uk) is thought to date from the late 1600s and is carved into the hillside next to an **Iron Age hillfort**. Cherhill White Horse (SN11 8XY, daylight hours, free, ⓦ nationaltrust.org.uk) was cut in 1780, allegedly with a Dr Christopher Alsop of Calne giving instructions via megaphone. It stands next to **Oldbury Castle** Iron Age hillfort.

day, £4 after 3pm, National Trust and English Heritage members free). Parking at Silbury Hill is free but there is very little parking at West Kennet Long Barrow.

BY BIKE

National Cycle Network trail 403 (ⓦsustrans.org.uk) passes through Avebury on its way from Marlborough to Calne. There are bike racks near the Barn Gallery.

ON FOOT

The Ridgeway National Trail (ⓦnationaltrail.co.uk/ridgeway) ends at Avebury. The southern section of this 87-mile trail is on the Great West Way, crossing the Chilterns and the North Wessex Downs, both designated Areas of Outstanding Natural Beauty.

INFORMATION AND TOURS

National Trust hub Old Farmyard, Avebury, ☏01672 539250, ⓦnationaltrust.org.uk/avebury. Visitor centre for Avebury, with information, toilets and a picnic area. Volunteer guides run regular tours of the stone circle from here, lasting between 45min and 1hr. Check the board for timings. £3.

Oldbury Tours ☏07947 488665, ⓦoldburytours .co.uk. Bespoke private guided tours of Avebury and Stonehenge including pick up from hotels in Wiltshire or Bath and entrance fees. Half day from £57pp, whole day from £75pp, based on a group of six.

ACCOMMODATION

Avebury Lodge B&B High St, Avebury ☏01672 539023, ⓦaveburylodge.co.uk; map p.76. Vegetarian bed and breakfast inside the stone circle at Avebury. The two bedrooms both overlook the stones and have king-size beds. **£195**.

Beckhampton B&B Isobel Cottage, Beckhampton, SN8 1QJ, ☏01672 539534, ⓦaveburyworld.co.uk; map p.76. One en suite double, one double and one single room in a friendly home from home. A local breakfast is included and cream teas can be served in the garden. **£79**.

EATING AND DRINKING

The Red Lion High St, Avebury, SN8 1RF, ☏01672 539266, ⓦgreeneking-pubs.co.uk; map p.76. Straightforward pub with a unique location – inside the stone circle at Avebury. Local ales in the bar, simple meals

in the dining room. Expect the likes of scampi and chips (£9.49) and beef and ale pie (£9.99). Mon–Sat 10am–11pm, Sun 10am–10.30pm.

Marlborough and around

It's not just the attractive market town of **MARLBOROUGH** that makes this part of Wiltshire an enticing place to spend a day or two. Just outside the town is ancient **Savernake Forest**, home to some truly awe-inspiring great oaks, while 6 miles to the east is the idyllic village of **Great Bedwyn**.

Marlborough

Few towns are as appealing as **Marlborough** and it is immediately obvious that this market town has long been a place of prosperity. The town was devastated by a fire in 1653, after which the High Street was widened; it is now the UK's second widest (after Stockton) and is lined with elegant Georgian buildings, many with colonnades. It's an extremely pleasant place to shop, stroll and soak up country life – with some of the best **boutique shopping** in Wiltshire. There's also a vibrant **local market** on the High Street on Wednesdays and Saturdays.

At the west end of the High Street is the fifteenth-century St Peter's Church, now a vibrant **arts centre**, while just outside the town centre is Marlborough College, a gorgeous red-brick private school, best known these days for its alumnus **Kate Middleton**, now Duchess of Cambridge.

The Merchant's House

132 High St, Marlborough SN8 1HN • Tours: April–Oct Tues, Fri & Sat 10.30am, noon, 1.30 & 3pm; Mon 10.30am • £7.50 • ☏ 01672 511491, ⓦ themerchantshouse.co.uk

The most commanding house on the High Street was the house of wealthy silk merchant Thomas Bayly, built in 1653 after the **Great Fire of Marlborough**. Although Bayly was a Puritan, the house reflects the fact that this did not mean no fun was to be had – check out the brightly painted, striped walls in the Dining Room and the Great Staircase with its painted fictive balustrading.

Today there are often **musical performances** in the house and downstairs is a **shop** selling all manner of gifts and knick-knacks.

Savernake Forest

Between Marlborough and Great Bedwyn, off the A346 • Daylight hours • Free • ⓦ forestry.gov.uk/savernake

The ancient woodland of **Savernake Forest** extends for 2750 acres south of Marlborough between the A4 and A346 main roads and is a designated **Site of Special Scientific Interest** for its many old trees.

Many of the largest oak trees here date from the **medieval** period, when Forest Law protected the timber rights of the king and the deer that lived here. The largest oak tree is the **Big Bellied Oak**, with a circumference of more than 32ft – it can be seen from the A346 road just south of Cadley. Far better though to explore on two feet, **walking** the marked trails along avenues of beech, oak and sweet chestnut trees. **Cycling** is also permitted on the trails and there's parking, toilets and a picnic site just off the A346.

Great Bedwyn

Great Bedwyn may be small – and almost entirely unknown to the outside world – but it's a pleasant place to wander awhile and enjoy **village life**. The Grade I listed Church of St Mary's is home to a memorial to Sir John Seymour, father of King Henry VIII's wife Jane Seymour, and there's a traditional English **pub** and village **shop**.

Crofton Beam Engines

Crofton, SN8 3DW • Week before Easter–end Sept Thurs–Tues 10.30am–4.30pm • From £4.50 • ⓦ croftonbeamengines.org

Just two miles south of Great Bedwyn is the hamlet of **Crofton**, home to a unique – and living – piece of the Great West Way's **steam history**. The **Crofton Beam Engines** are the world's oldest working beam engines, fed by a hand-stoked coal-fired boiler and still plugging away at the same job they were designed to do more than two hundred years ago – pumping water up to the highest point of the **Kennet & Avon Canal**. No journey on the canal would be possible today without these incredible engines.

The two engines, one of which is an original two hundred-year-old Boulton & Watt, stand in the red-brick Engine House, a slender chimney off to one side, and the whole thing – right down to the leafy countryside around it – looks much as it would have done when it was built in 1807. **Steam Experiences** are also available, where you can go behind the scenes and take control of the engines.

Wilton Windmill

Off the A338, SN8 3SW • Tours: Easter–end Sept; Sun & hols 2–5pm • £5 • ☏ 01672 870594, ⓦ wiltonwindmill.co.uk

A mile or so east of the Crofton Beam Engines – and within easy walking distance – is another piece of industrial heritage, the nineteenth-century **Wilton Windmill**. This is the only operating windmill in the area and it still produces wholemeal, stone-ground flour. The short guided tour is illuminating, but the site is open daily year-round if you

CROP CIRCLES

Are aliens particularly partial to Wiltshire? You might think so, if the theories around the **crop circles** that frequently appear in local fields are to be believed. Modern crop circles – strange, circular patterns of flattened crops – have been materializing across Wiltshire since the 1970s and there is no doubt that they are real. Although crop circles appear around the world, it is Wiltshire where you are most likely to find one, and some of the most famous have appeared here over the years.

The question is, who is making them and why? One favoured theory is that they are the impressions left behind by **alien spacecraft**, and the speed with which they sometimes appear overnight has done much to galvanise support for this theory. There are even some who believe they are messages left for us by human time travellers communicating back from the future. More often than not though the cause is determined to be the same – **hoaxers**. Very committed hoaxers, who presumably have plenty of time on their hands.

just want a look from the outside. It's a lovely spot too, at a high point in the **North Wessex Downs AONB** with views out over the surrounding unspoilt countryside.

3

Ramsbury Brewery and Distillery

132 High St SN8 1HN • Tours: Wed & Fri 11am • £15 • ☎ 01672 541407, ⊕ ramsbury.com

Running from northeast Wiltshire into West Berkshire and North Hampshire, the **Ramsbury Estate** is responsible for more than 19,000 acres of beautiful **farmland** in the heart of the North Wessex Downs.

In 2004 the estate began brewing ale and craft beer, using water and barley from their own land and more recently a vodka and a gin have been added to the line-up. Tours of the modern, sustainably managed **brewery** and **distillery** include tastings of the beer and single estate spirits. Look out for them in local pubs too.

Wiltshire Wildlife Trust Jones's Mill

Dursden Lane, Pewsey SN9 5JN• 24hr • Free • ⊕ wiltshirewildlife.org

The **Wiltshire Wildlife Trust** looks after Jones's Mill wetland on the outskirts of the **Vale of Pewsey**. This area of fenland is made up of wet woodland (alder carr), ponds and wet grassland and is an excellent habitat for **wildlife** including water voles, water shrew, dragonflies and birdlife such as heron, snipe and kingfisher. A herd of belted Galloway cattle graze on the land.

A **footpath** and **boardwalk** loops around the reserve, criss-crossing the River Avon. Dogs are welcome but the paths are not suitable for wheelchairs or pushchairs.

ARRIVAL AND DEPARTURE

MARLBOROUGH AND AROUND

BY TRAIN

Bedwyn is on the Great Western Railway (⊕ gwr.com) line to London, with services calling at Newbury (15min), Reading (50min) and ultimately London Paddington (hourly, 1hr 15min, from £9 single). From Bedwyn it is possible to walk to the Crofton Beam Engines and Wilton Windmill and there are buses to Marlborough.

Pewsey is on the same line as Bedwyn but is served by different trains, with very few calling at both stations. Services from Pewsey run via Newbury (20min) and Reading (35min) to London Paddington (approx. 8 daily; 1hr; from £14.50 single). Jones's Mill is an easy 20min walk from Pewsey.

BY BUS

National Express (⊕ nationalexpress.com) operate daily coach services from Marlborough to London calling at Hungerford (15min), Newbury (25min), Heathrow airport (1hr 40min), and London Victoria (departs 8.30am; 2hr 45min; from £5.50 single). The return journey departs London Victoria at 6.30pm and Heathrow airport at 7.15pm, arriving in Marlborough at 8.55pm.

Thamesdown (☎ 01793 428428, ⊕ thamesdown -transport.co.uk) buses 20 and 22 link Marlborough with Great Bedwyn and its train station (7 daily; 30min; £2.30 single). Some services continue on to Hungerford (£3) and there is a bus stop close to Savernake Forest on the A4.

3

Thamesdown buses 46 and 48 run from Swindon to Marlborough (6 daily; 1hr 10min; £3.50 single).

Salisbury Reds (W salisburyreds.co.uk) bus X5 runs from Swindon to Pewsey (Mon–Sat hourly; 50min) and on to Salisbury (1hr, £6 single).

BY CAR

Marlborough has parking along the centre of the High Street (daily except Wed & Sat, 2hr/£1.90). There are also bays along either side of the street, which are free for 30min and operate daily. All other sites listed here have on-site parking.

BY BOAT

Narrowboats can moor at Great Bedwyn Wharf on the Kennet & Avon Canal, operated by the Canal and River Trust (W watersidemooring.com). There are 22 mooring sites here, above and below Church Lock.

BY BIKE

National Cycle Network (W sustrans.org.uk) route 4 runs through Great Bedwyn where it joins NCN route 403, which continues to Marlborough. The Wiltshire Cycleway (W wiltshire.gov.uk) runs from Marlborough to Ramsbury and on to Great Bedwyn and Wilton.

ACCOMMODATION

The Bell at Ramsbury The Square, High St, Ramsbury, SN8 2PE, ☎01672 520230, W thebellramsbury.com; map p.76. Nine luxurious en suite rooms arranged throughout the inn and its coach house. There's underfloor heating, Hypnos mattresses and White Company toiletries; some rooms have views of the Square at Ramsbury's centre. **£110**.

Bruce Accessible Boats Great Bedwyn, ☎01380 721279, W bruce.katrust.org.uk; map p.76. Accessible narrowboats, for hire either Friday–Friday or Saturday–Saturday from Great Bedwyn. The fleet of four boats are specially adapted for those with accessibility issues, including for wheelchair use. From **£970**.

Castle & Ball High St, Marlborough, SN8 1LZ, ☎01672 515201, W oldenglishinns.co.uk; map p.76. Traditional inn dating from the fifteenth century in an unbeatable location on the High Street. Rooms are classically stylish and when booked in advance guests can get 25 percent off in the restaurant. **£87.50**

Crofton Lodge B&B Crofton, SN8 3DW, ☎01672 870328, W croftonlodge.co.uk; map p.76. Located 1.5 miles outside Great Bedwyn and next to the Kennet & Avon Canal, this B&B offers a country escape with easy access to local attractions. There are just three rooms – a double, a twin and a single – but surprisingly extensive facilities: the house has a tennis court and heated swimming pool. **£90**.

Manor Farm B&B Collingbourne Kingston, SN8 3SD, ☎01264 850859, W manorfm.co.uk; map p.76. Bijou bed and breakfast in a beautiful Grade II listed farmhouse. The three rooms each have their own bathrooms (two are en suite) and there's a hearty cooked breakfast each morning, with vegetarian and vegans catered for. **£84**.

Tresco House Ogborne St Andrew, SN8 1RZ, ☎07823 886695, W trescohouse.com; map p.76. Two double en suite bedrooms in the main house plus two self-contained self-catering cottages with private gardens, all decorated to a high standard. The Courtyard Cottage sleeps two adults, the Coach House sleeps up to four. **£99**.

EATING AND DRINKING

The Bell at Ramsbury The Square, High St, Ramsbury, SN8 2PE, ☎01672 520230, W thebellramsbury.com; map p.76. Part of the Ramsbury Estate this three hundred-year-old coaching inn serves produce from the estate and the kitchen garden. The menu changes seasonally – expect the likes of haddock battered with Ramsbury Brewery's own beer (£14) and homemade burgers (£15). Mon–Sat noon–11pm, Sun noon–10pm.

The Engineman's Rest Café Crofton, SN8 3DW W enginemansrest.co.uk; map p.76. Located at the Crofton Beam Engines this friendly café serves a range of sandwiches (£5.95) and light meals (Ploughmans £8.95). Daily 10.30am–4.30pm.

★**The Harrow at Little Bedwyn** High St, Little Bedwyn, SN8 3JP, ☎01672 870871, W theharrowat littlebedwyn.com; map p.76. Sue and Roger Jones celebrated the twentieth anniversary of running this Michelin-stared restaurant in 2018. The wine list runs to 900 bins while the menu changes daily and depends on what's in season. There's a five-course set lunch menu (£40), while in the evenings your choice is for six (£60) or eight courses (£85). The eight-course gourmet menu is also available for vegetarians and vegans and wine pairing is offered with each menu. Wed–Sat lunch until 4pm & dinner until midnight.

★**Three Tuns Freehouse** 1 High St, Great Bedwyn, SN8 3NU, ☎01672 870280, W tunsfreehouse.com; map p.76. This authentic village pub serves ales and ciders from local producers plus small batch spirits from around the southwest. On weekends the food menu changes according to what's in season – roasted hake with tabbouleh (£17) or cola-cooked ham (£19) perhaps. Out back you'll find a dog-friendly beer garden with boules pitch. Tues–Thurs 10am–3pm & 6–11pm, Fri & Sat 10am–11pm, Sun 10am–6pm.

SHOPPING

Busy Bees Craft & Gift Shop St Peter's Church, Marlborough, SN8 1HQ, ☎01672 511453, ⓦstpeters marlborough.com/craft-shop; map p.76. Locally sourced handmade crafts. Mon–Sat 10am–4.30pm, Sun 10am–3pm.

Kim Vine 92 High St, Marlborough, SN8 1HD ☎01672 519937, ⓦkimvine.com; map p.76. Ladies designer fashion and occasion wear in a boutique with excellent customer service. Mon–Sat 10am–5.30pm.

Susie Watson Designs 114 High St, Marlborough, SN8 1LT, ☎01672 514542, ⓦsusiewatsondesigns.co.uk; map p.76. Hand-finished furniture, homewares and ceramics plus an excellent selection of fabrics. Mon–Sat 9am–5.30pm.

ACTIVITIES

Marlborough College Summer School Marlborough, SN8 1PA, ☎01672 892388, ⓦsummerschool.co.uk; map p.76. Annual summer school offering courses in everything from music and theatre to art history and creative writing for all ages from three upwards. Mid–July to mid–August.

Swindon and around

3

SWINDON was a small market town until the arrival of the Great Western Railway in 1840. The original town is still visible in the **Old Town**, at the top of the hill, though very little remains and today the town is more of a service centre, home to the headquarters of the **National Trust**, the **English Heritage National Monument Record Centre** and the offices of several large international companies. There is also an increasingly lively arts scene and a cluster of interesting **museums**.

STEAM: Museum of the Great Western Railway

Fire Fly Avenue, SN2 2EY • Mon–Sat 10am–5pm, Sun 10am–4pm, last admission 1hr before closing • £9.35 • ☎01793 466646, ⓦsteam-museum.org.uk

Located in a Grade II listed railway building in the heart of what was once the Swindon railway works, **STEAM: Museum of the Great Western Railway** tells the story of the train line that changed Swindon – and many other places hereabouts – forever. There are famous **locomotives** from throughout the railway's history, plus the opportunity to drive a **train simulator** and work the signals in the interactive GWR signal box.

Museum of Computing

6-7 Theatre Square, SN1 1QN • Fri 10am–4pm, Sat 9.30am–4pm, last admission 3.30pm • £2 • ⓦmuseumofcomputing.org.uk

The UK's first museum dedicated to the history of **computing** is run by enthusiastic volunteers and is not-for-profit. There is a mixture of permanent and temporary displays, including plenty of memory-inducing computing ephemera and **artefacts**.

Swindon Museum & Art Gallery

Bath Road, SN1 4BA • Tues–Sat 11am–4.30pm • Free • ☎01793 466566, ⓦswindonmuseumandartgallery.org.uk

Although **Swindon Museum** started life in 1919 as a place for Charles Gore to display his extensive geological collection, today it focuses more on **local history** and has a collection of objects from prehistory to the present, which tell the story of the Swindon area and its people. The large collection of **photography** is fascinating for anyone with an interest in English social history and there is also a wonderful **local art** collection featuring paintings, drawings and prints both of the Swindon area and by local artists.

There remains a sizeable **Natural World Gallery**, home to the personal collections of Gore and William Morris (founder of the *Swindon Advertiser*) which run the gamut from palaeontology to botany.

Lydiard House and Park

Lydiard Tregoze, SN5 3PA · Park: 7.30am–dusk; **House**: Wed–Sun & hols 11am–4pm, last admission 3.30pm; **Walled garden**: daily 11am–4pm; **Park**: free; house and walled garden: £6.50; walled garden only: £4; parking: £2/2hr or £4/day · ☎ 01793 466664, ⓦ lydiardpark.org.uk

The historic **Lydiard estate** on the western edge of Swindon is much beloved of local families for its free-to-access 260 acres of **parkland**. **Cycling** is encouraged along the grand avenues and there are plenty of places for a picnic, with barbecues available for hire in the summer. The warmer nights also see occasional open-air **theatre** performances and **cinema** screenings.

The house itself is a Palladian mansion with some interesting ornate plasterwork, furnishings and Elizabethan-era portraits but the real attraction here is the outdoors and it's well worth paying the entry fee to the **Walled Garden**, a restored Georgian fruit and flower garden that has dazzling floral and topiary displays throughout the warmer months.

Studley Grange Garden & Leisure Park

Hay Lane, Wroughton, SN4 9QT · Late March–Oct Mon–Sat 10am–5.45pm, last admission 4.30pm; late Oct–March Mon–Sun 10am–4.45pm, last admission 3.30pm · **Craft village**: free; **Butterfly World**, **Zoo** and **Farm Park**: £7.45 (£6.45 in winter) · ☎ 01793 852400, ⓦ studleygrange.co.uk

There are two main attractions at **Studley Grange**: a **craft village** with more than a dozen shops where you can watch artists making their wares, and the more popular **Butterfly World** and **Farm Park**.

One combined ticket gets you into the Butterfly World and Farm Park. Here you'll find the Butterfly House, home to hundreds of colourful butterflies, flying freely among the tropical plants and ponds. The main season is March to October and this is when you'll see the most activity. In the Farm Park you'll find all the farmyard favourites, from rabbits and guinea pigs to goats, sheep and cows. In the summer, trailer rides take visitors out around the fields to see the animals. There's also a **Zoo Area**, stocked with more exotic animals including meerkats, wallabies and reptiles. Zookeeper experiences are available here too, when you can get behind the scenes and have a go at husbandry tasks, including feeding.

Wiltshire Wildlife Trust Blakehill Farm

Cricklade, SN6 6RA · 24hr · Free · ⓦ wiltshirewildlife.org

At **Blakehill Farm** the Wiltshire Wildlife Trust are returning a former military airfield that once saw **World War II** Dakotas taking off for the battlefields of Europe to its original hay meadow habitat.

The local **wildlife** loves this development, and there are significant numbers of dragonflies, bullfinches and lapwings here. In the summer the reserve comes alive with wildflowers, including oxeye daisies and ladies bedstraw, and butterflies are seen in large numbers as well as birds including partridges, barn owls and tawny owls.

The five meadows at **Stoke Common Meadows** are also part of this reserve and feature an impressive bluebell display beneath the century-old oak trees every May.

There are paths suitable for **wheelchairs** and pushchairs at this reserve.

Wiltshire Wildlife Trust Lower Moor

Cricklade, SN16 9TW · 24hr · Free · ⓦ wiltshirewildlife.org

Lower Moor Farm acts as a gateway into a complex of Wiltshire Wildlife Trust (WWT) reserves, all within walking distance of each other. Three manmade **lakes** form the core and are home to large populations of wildfowl including great crested grebe, goosander and shoveler duck. At Swallow Pool and Cottage Lake there are **bird hides**; the one at Cottage Lake is accessible to wheelchairs and pushchairs.

RIGHT, FROM TOP CAEN HILL LOCKS; WADWORTH BREWERY, DEVIZES

3

> **WALK: THE RIDGEWAY**
>
> **The Ridgeway** (ⓦnationaltrail.co.uk/ridgeway) could be said to be England's oldest road, with a history of being used by soldiers, shepherds and travellers as long ago as the prehistoric era. The 87-mile **trail** over the high ground of southern central England remains entirely in protected **Areas of Outstanding Natural Beauty** (AONBs): the **North Wessex Downs** and the **Chilterns**, with its southern section part of the Great West Way. The ancient landscapes here are some of the country's best preserved and walking through them yields precious views of rolling chalk downland that are unchanged for centuries.
>
> It is the River Thames that forms the border between the two AONBs. To its south and west, the North Wessex Downs section of the route begins in Avebury and features numerous **archaeological monuments** including Stone Age long barrows, Bronze Age round barrows and Iron Age forts as well as the famous Wiltshire **white horses**. East and north of the river the trail runs through the **Chilterns** before ending at the Iron Age hill fort of **Ivinghoe Beacon**.

Lower Moor Farm leads on to **Clattinger Farm**, the UK's finest remaining example of enclosed lowland grassland. This is a Site of Special Scientific Interest and a haven for wildlife – look out for teal, lapwing and snipe foraging in the winter and enjoy the extensive wildflower displays in summer.

At **Sandpool** you'll find a wet woodland popular with bees and birds; visit at dusk for the chance to spot barn owls and bats. The bird hide here is the best place to watch herons raising their chicks (January–June).

Swindon and Cricklade Railway

Blunsdon Station, Tadpole Lane, SN25 2DA • March–Dec selected dates 10.30am–3.30pm • Steam-hauled trains: £8 all day; diesel trains: £6 all day • ☏01793 771615, ⓦ swindon-cricklade-railway.org

The **Swindon and Cricklade Railway** is Wiltshire's only standard gauge heritage railway. Both steam and diesel trains, all restored and run by volunteers, ride this old branch line from Taw Valley Holt to Blunsdon Station, Hayes Knoll and South Meadow Lane, a distance of a little over 2 miles.

Blunsdon Station is the railway's main visitor centre and is home to two **museums**, one of railway memorabilia, the other a Wartime Museum focusing on World War II. There is also a café, picnic area, toilets and free parking here. All major facilities are accessible via ramps and one of the carriages is **wheelchair accessible**. At Halloween there are special "Ghost Trains" and in December a timetable of "Santa Specials".

Roves Farm

Sevenhampton, SN6 7QG • Daily Jan 2–Dec 23 9am–5pm • £9.50 • ☏01793 763939, ⓦ rovesfarm.co.uk

Roves Farm is perfect for families, even on rainy days. In Pets Corner you can meet and feed the animals, and there are different activities every day, from animal grooming to crafts. You can also take tractor rides and inside the heated activity barn is a play area with giant slides and ball ponds.

ARRIVAL AND INFORMATION   SWINDON AND AROUND

BY TRAIN

Swindon is a major stop on the Great Western Railway (ⓦgwr .com), both for trains traveling east-west on the London to Bristol line and for those travelling north-south. Trains to London (every 15min) call at Reading (30min) and London Paddington (1hr, from £11.50 single); trains to Bristol (every 30min) call at Chippenham (15min), Bath Spa (30min) and Bristol Temple Meads (45min, from £15.90 single). There are

also trains through Wiltshire (9 daily) calling at Chippenham (15min) before arriving in Salisbury (1hr 40min, from £6.50 single); and trains to the Cotswolds, calling at Kemble (hourly, 15min, from £6.80 single).

BY BUS

National Express (ⓦnationalexpress.com) operate buses from London Victoria to Swindon, which also call at

Heathrow Airport (every 90min, 2hr 20min, from £4 single). There is also a daily bus (10.35am) to Bristol calling at Chippenham (30min), Corsham (45min), Bath (1hr 10min) and Bristol (2hr).

Local buses are operated by Thamesdown Transport (ⓦthamesdown-transport.co.uk) and include numerous routes around the town. The most useful is route 1, which links the town centre with the McArthurGlen Designer Outlet Centre and STEAM (every 10min, 10min, £1.60 single), the Link Centre (every 10min, 15min, £2.10 single) and Lydiard Park (get off at Hampton Drive, every 20min, 20min, £2.10 single). For the Swindon and Cricklade Railway, take route 15 to the Tawny Owl pub for Taw Valley Holt station (Mon–Sat every 2hr, 40min, £2.10 single). Routes 46 and 48 run from Swindon to Marlborough (6 daily; 1hr 10min; £3.50 single).

BY CAR

Swindon is a good place to pick up a rental car, with several of the large providers having offices here. Try Europcar (ⓦeuropcar.co.uk), Enterprise (ⓦenterprise.co.uk) or Budget (ⓦbudget.co.uk).

Swindon is a reasonably car friendly town and is located just off the M4 motorway (junctions 15 and 16). You can have a unique driving experience here – navigating the Magic Roundabout, a central roundabout surrounded by five smaller ones.

There is plenty of parking in town and most attractions listed above have free parking. Note that for STEAM the parking is at the McArthurGlen Designer Outlet: either the North car park on Kemble Drive or the West on Penzance Drive. If you need a car park in the town centre the central Fleming Way Multi-Storey is a good bet, with 654 spaces and 24hr parking (Islington St, SN1 2HG, £1.30/hr for first 4hrs, £8.50/6hr, or £1/2hrs after 6pm).

BY BIKE

National Cycle Route 45 (ⓦsustrans.org.uk) passes through Swindon. To the north it links the town with the Swindon and Cricklade Railway, while to the south it crosses the M4 to join the old railway path to Chiseldon before turning right along the Ridgeway to Avebury.

In the town centre there is secure bike parking on the ground floor at Fleming way car park, accessed from Gordon Gardens. You'll need to register for an access card online (ⓦswindontravelchoices.co.uk, £10) but once registered parking is free.

3

ACCOMMODATION AND EATING

★**Cricklade House Hotel** Common Hill, Cricklade, SN6 6HA, ☏01793 750751, ⓦcrickladehotel.co.uk; map p.76. With views over the Vale of Cricklade on the edge of the Cotswolds this luxury hotel feels a million miles away from Swindon. The 45 en suite bedrooms are modern and there's a swimming pool, jacuzzi, tennis court, gym and billiards room for guests to use free of charge. There's also a 9-hole golf course (£10). £109.

Doubletree by Hilton Lydiard Fields, Great Western Way, SN5 8UZ, ☏01793 881777, ⓦdoubletree3.hilton.com; map p.76. Large modern hotel just off junction 16 of the M4. The contemporary rooms have a soothing soft grey décor, and there's a gym, a simple restaurant and a Starbucks in the lobby. Self-parking £3/night; breakfast extra charge. £139.

★**Helen Browning's Royal Oak** Cues Lane, Bishopstone, SN6 8PP, ☏01793 790481; map p.76. All of the twelve rooms here have their own door off a sunny courtyard and are named after a field on the farm. There's a luxury feel; two rooms are dog-friendly. The restaurant focuses on local organic food, serving generous portions of their own pork, lamb and beef. Roast pork belly is £16, fillet of beef £25. Bar Mon–Sat noon–11pm, Sun noon–2.30pm; food served Mon–Fri 7–10am, noon–2.30pm & 6–9pm, Sat 8–10am, noon–2.30pm & 6–9pm, Sun 8–10am, noon–3pm & 6–9pm.

Meadowbank House Medbourne Lane, Liddington, SN4 0EY, ☏01793 791401, ⓦmeadowbankhouse.com; map p.76. Welcoming B&B in a small village four miles east of Swindon town centre and close to junction 15 of the M4. There are three simple double bedrooms (one en suite) and a lovely lounge overlooking the gardens and a terrace. There's also a log fire for cooler nights. £75.

The Weighbridge Brewhouse Penzance Drive, SN5 7JL, ☏01793 881500, ⓦweighbridgebrewhouse.co.uk; map p.76. Once the weighing bridge for trains, this large pub-style restaurant is close to STEAM and the McArthurGlen Designer Outlet Centre. The menu features classic pub meals with a modern twist, from a starter of gin and juniper cured trout with baby beetroot salad (£8) to a main of rosemary crusted rack of lamb with mint and garlic yoghurt (£26.50). Drinks include beers brewed in the on-site microbrewery. Mon–Sat noon–late, Sun noon–10pm; food served Mon–Sat noon–2pm & 6–9.30pm, Sun noon–8pm.

ENTERTAINMENT AND ACTIVITIES

Better Extreme Trampoline Park Link Centre, Whitehill Way, SN5 7DL, ☏01793 877323, ⓦextreme.better.org.uk; map p.76. Trampoline park where adults and kids can bounce in a huge arena and try acrobatic tricks on the performance walls. There are also foam pits, basketball and dodgeball. From £7.95.

Ice Skating Link Centre, Whitehill Way, SN5 7DL, ☏01793 877323, ⓦbetter.org.uk; map p.76. Large indoor ice skating rink for public skating sessions and lessons. £7.20.

Swindon Arts Centre Devizes Rd, Old Town, SN1 4BJ, ☏ 01793 524481, ⓦ swindontheatres.co.uk; map p.76. Eclectic range of theatre, comedy and music performances in a two hundred-seat space.

Wyvern Theatre Theatre Square, SN1 1QN, ☏ 01793 524481, ⓦ swindontheatres.co.uk; map p.76. One of Wiltshire's leading large theatres, the Wyvern Theatre hosts classic and contemporary performances including an annual pantomime.

SHOPPING

McArthurGlen Designer Outlet Swindon Kemble Drive, SN2 2DY, ☏ 01793 507600, ⓦ mcarthurglen. com; map p.76. Located in the restored Great Western Railway works, this undercover upmarket shopping centre brings together stores from more than a hundred designer brands (Calvin Klein, Jack Wills, Levi's) offering discounts of up to 60 percent. In a nod to the building's history, there's a steam locomotive on display in the restaurant area, where you'll find well-known brands *Starbucks*, *Carluccio's* and *Wagamama*. Mon–Fri 9am–8pm, Sat 9am–7pm, Sun 10am–6pm.

3 Devizes and around

The heart of Wiltshire is an agricultural one, far from motorways and train lines and with traffic that frequent pootles along at tractor pace. The area around the pleasant market town of **DEVIZES** epitomises this and though it may seem not much is going on, there is a surprising amount to detain you for a day or two, including the wonderful red-brick **Wadworth Brewery**, a world-class **museum**, Wiltshire's largest **vineyard** and the chance to tackle the longest lock flight on the Kennet & Avon Canal, **Caen Hill**.

Devizes

The town of **Devizes** might feel small, but this is the largest community for miles around and the **market** at its centre has brought people from the surrounding villages together every Thursday for centuries.

Today, though, there is far more to Devizes than just its weekly market and the town is an engaging place to spend a few hours. The Market Place itself is the place to start, with a pretty collection of historic buildings arranged around a large cobbled square, while the Brittox and Little Brittox pedestrianised **shopping streets** are home to independent shops and cafes. Don't miss the bijou **St John's Alley** off St John's Street, an atmospheric historic alleyway that feels like something out of *Harry Potter*, and be sure to take a stroll up Long Street, lined with Georgian houses and home to the **Wiltshire Museum**.

Wiltshire Museum

41 Long St, SN10 1NS · Mon–Sat 10am–5pm, Sun noon–4pm · £6 · ☏ 01380 727369, ⓦ wiltshiremuseum.org.uk

Touting itself – correctly – as being midway between Stonehenge and Avebury, this diminutive museum punches well above its weight for **prehistoric artefacts**. It has an

---

THE CONFETTI BATTLE

As far as anyone can tell, Devizes is the only town to have one particular tradition – an annual **Confetti Battle**. Although the origins of the battle are unknown it has certainly been happening since at least 1913, when onlookers used to throw confetti and rose petals at performers in the town's carnival procession. Around 1955 this evolved into a full-on battle, and now every **carnival week** one night (usually the last Wednesday in August) sees several thousand complete strangers flinging handfuls of confetti at each other in a mad half hour of sheer joy. The event traditionally ends with a fireworks display.

For more information on all Devizes' **events**, including the **Carnival Parade**, visit the Devizes Outdoor Celebratory Arts website (ⓦ docadevizes.org.uk).

especially interesting collection of gold from the time of Stonehenge, which includes jewellery that would have been worn at the time of its building, some 4,500 years ago, and for the human dimension it adds to the county's prehistoric sites, is worth visiting before heading for the stone circles themselves.

There are also engaging **modern galleries** focused on the history of Wiltshire and a Saxon gallery which tells the story of how the Kingdom of Wessex (the ancient name for the area south and west of here) came to be.

Wadworth Brewery

41-45 Northgate St, SN10 1JW • Mon–Sat 9am–5pm; Tours: Mon–Sat 11am & 2pm • Visitor centre: free; Tours: £12 • ☎ 01380 723361, Ⓦ wadworth.co.uk

The red-brick Victorian **Wadworth Brewery** stands sentry over the town centre, proudly signalling its importance to Devizes. Beer has been brewed here since 1885 when the Wadworth family built the brewery and today Wadworth's bestselling 6X real ale can be found on hand pumps and in bottles around the country.

The story here though is not all about the beer. Wadworth is also home to three **Shire horses**, who can be seen in the stables across the road from the brewery. For more than 125 years Wadworth has delivered beer locally using Shire horses and they can still be seen on weekdays clip-clopping around the town pulling a cart and delivering to local pubs. There is also a full-time sign writer on-site, working in a dedicated studio to produce handwritten pub signs – the only UK brewer to do so. The **visitor centre** has a shop and a bar for tastings and there are informative two-hour tours around the brewery, detailing the beermaking process.

Caen Hill Lock Flight

The **Kennet & Avon Canal** runs through Devizes and as the town is atop a hill the water must rise more than 200ft in the process. The Caen Hill (pronounced "cane") lock flight is what brings it up here, a set of 29 locks that rises 237ft over 2 miles. This is one of the longest continuous lock flights in the country and takes around half a day to tackle in a **narrowboat**. This is one of the great challenges of a trip along the canal and as the water reaches the town itself narrowboaters can expect an audience – a favourite local walk is a stroll along the towpath from **Devizes Wharf** to see the lock gates being opened and closed to let the boats pass through. This is an unmissable experience for those travelling the Great West Way by water.

a'Beckett's Vineyard

High St, Littleton Panell, SN10 4EN • Wed–Sat 11am–4.30pm • Free • ☎ 01380 816669, Ⓦ abecketts.co.uk

Just 4 miles south of Devizes in the village of Littleton Panell, **a'Beckett's Vineyard** was first planted in 2001. The first vintage was produced in 2003 and today the vines extend over more than 11 acres. The two primary grape varieties here are **pinot noir** and **chardonnay** and the estate produces white, rose and sparkling wines plus an award-winning pinot noir. The **shop** is open for tastings and purchases, while **tours** are offered for groups (10–30 people, from £9pp).

All Saints' Church

Alton Priors, SN8 4LB • Daily • Free • Ⓦ visitchurches.org.uk

Eight miles east of Devizes in the village of Alton Priors, **All Saints' Church** is a medieval church standing tall above the surrounding fields. The churchyard is shaded by the building's Perpendicular tower and a yew tree said to be 1700 years old. Inside you'll find Jacobean choir stalls and a trapdoor that conceals a buried Sarsen stone.

CYCLE: THE KENNET & AVON CYCLE ROUTE

One of the best long-distance cycling trails in England is the 85-mile **Kennet & Avon Cycle Route**, also known as National Cycle Route 4 (Ⓦsustrans.org.uk), which follows the towpath of the eponymous canal from Bath to Reading.

The surface along the route is compacted stone and the path is wide and smooth, making it a straightforward cycle ride for all **abilities**. Most of the route is traffic free but pedestrians (and plenty of fishermen) also use this path so care must be taken.

Highlights include the Caen Hill lock flight, the impressive limestone aqueducts of Dundas and Avoncliff between Bath and Bradford on Avon, and the Vale of Pewsey (Ⓦvisitpewseyvale .co.uk), where you'll see the Pewsey White Horse.

The Vale of Pewsey

The Vale of Pewsey stretches to the east of Devizes, a bucolic area of low-lying countryside that divides Salisbury Plain to the south from the Marlborough Downs to the north. It is part of the North Wessex Downs AONB and is a wonderful place for a walk, or to pootle along the Kennet & Avon Canal on a narrowboat.

ARRIVAL AND INFORMATION | DEVIZES AND AROUND

BY TRAIN

Devizes has no train station of its own and is best served by either Chippenham, 11 miles away, or Swindon, 20 miles away, both on the Great Western Railway (Ⓦgwr.com) main line between London and Bristol and both connected to Devizes by bus.

BY BUS

National Express (Ⓦnationalexpress.com) operate daily coach services from Devizes to London calling at Marlborough (30min), Hungerford (50min), Newbury (1hr 15min), Heathrow airport (2hr 15min) and London Victoria (departs 7.55am; 3hr 20min; from £7.80 single). The return journey departs London Victoria at 6.30pm and Heathrow airport at 7.15pm, arriving in Devizes at 9.20pm.

Stagecoach (Ⓦstagecoachbus.com) bus 49 runs from Swindon, including the train station, to Devizes (hourly; 1hr; £3 single, £5.10 return). Faresaver (Ⓟ01249 444444, Ⓦfaresaver.co.uk) bus X33 links Devizes to Chippenham, including the train station (hourly; 30min; £7.50/day), while bus X72 runs from Devizes to Bath (hourly; 1hr; £7.50/day).

BY CAR

Devizes is at the junction of several major roads and there is plenty of parking in the town. The Market Place (SN10 1JG) offers 30min free parking, while the streets around the town offer either one hour or two for free, though spaces can be hard to come by. The Central car park is the best option for visitors, located off Maryport Street (SN10 1DW) and offering 162 spaces for a maximum three-hour stay (80p/1hr, £2.30/3hrs).

BY BOAT

Devizes is a major stop on the Kennet & Avon Canal and there are numerous places to moor in and around the town. At the top of Caen Hill local flight is Devizes Flight Moorings operated by the Canal & River Trust (Ⓦwatersidemooring .com), which can accommodate fifteen narrowboats and is a 10min walk from the town centre. There are further visitor moorings at Devizes Wharf in the town centre, which is the home base of the Kennet & Avon Canal Trust. The Trust operates a tearoom, shop and small museum here (Ⓦkatrust.org.uk).

At Devizes Marina Village (Ⓟ01380 725300, Ⓦdevizes marina.co.uk), just over a mile along the canal from the wharf, there are further moorings as well as a self-drive day boat for hire. This can accommodate 8 people and has a galley and toilet facilities.

Honey Street Boats (Ⓟ01672 851166, Ⓦhoney streetboats.co.uk) are based 8 miles east of Devizes in the village of Honey Street and offer narrowboat rental from £450 for either a weekend (Fri–Mon) or week's (Mon–Fri) rent and £699 for a week (Fri–Fri). Boats sleep up to 6.

BY BIKE

The Kennet & Avon Cycle Route, also known as National Cycle Route 4 (Ⓦsustrans.org.uk), follows the towpath of the eponymous canal from Bath to Reading over 85 miles, passing through Devizes.

The Wiltshire Museum allows visitors to leave their bikes just inside the staff car park, though this closes at 5pm daily.

3

ACCOMMODATION

Avalon Lodge B&B ☎01380 728189, ⊛bed-breakfast-devizes.co.uk; map p.76. Nick and Jenny make every guest feel at home in their welcoming modern B&B within walking distance of Devizes town centre. Three of the four rooms have private balconies; all are en suite. **£88**.

The Bear Hotel ☎01380 722444, ⊛thebearhotel devizes.co.uk; map p.76. Ancient coaching inn that is one of the lynchpins of the Market Place. Some of the 25 bedrooms are a little tired but there's free parking for guests and an unbeatable location, plus a friendly bar downstairs. Two of the rooms have four-poster beds. **£70**.

The Castle Hotel ☎01380 727981, ⊛castlehotel devizes.co.uk; map p.76. Simple rooms spread over two floors above an eighteenth-century coaching inn that is

one of the town's most handsome buildings. In summer there's a roof terrace overlooking the adjacent St Mary's Church. **£75**.

Devizes Marina Lodges ☎0345 498 6060, ⊛hoseasons.co.uk; map p.76. Brand new lodges with views over the marina and private outdoor hot tubs. Each has 2 bedrooms and can sleep 4. From **£473**/wk.

★**The Peppermill** 40 St John's St, SN10 1BL, ☎01380 887961, ⊛peppermilldevizes.co.uk; map p.76. Boutique hotel located just off the Market Place with 7 stylish contemporary rooms and one of the town's best restaurants downstairs (see below). Owner Phil can't do enough for guests and breakfast is served in the bistro. There's also a guest lounge with Netflix. **£115**.

EATING AND DRINKING

★**The Bistro** 7 Little Brittox, SN10 1AR, ☎01380 720043, ⊛thebistrodevizes.co.uk; map p.76. Chef Peter Vaughan opened this creative restaurant in 2003 and changed the way Devizes thought about food. In summer he sets up a street food stall outside, while all year round his naturally balanced dishes change with the seasons and feature produce from local suppliers. There is also a catch of the day, brought in from Cornwall daily (two courses £23.50). Tues–Sat 11am–2pm & 6.30pm–late.

Devizes Wharf Tearoom 5 Couch Lane, SN10 1EB, ☎01380 721279; map p.76. Warm and welcoming small tearoom next to the Kennet & Avon Canal Museum at Devizes Wharf. Serves a great bacon sandwich (£3.50) and jacket potatoes (£5.95) plus daily specials.

Honey Street Mill Café Honeystreet, Pewsey Vale, SN9 5PS, ☎01672 851155, ⊛honeystreetmillcafe.co.uk; map p.76. Laidback canalside café serving a cooked breakfast of local produce (£7.99), lunches such as Ploughman's with Wiltshire ham (£6.99) and afternoon tea. Daily 9am–5pm.

The Peppermill 40 St John's St, SN10 1BL, ☎01380 887961, ⊛peppermilldevizes.co.uk; map p.76. Bistro-style restaurant that draws a local crowd. Mains change

with the seasons but there are always burgers (from £13) and cracking steaks (from £18), while the wine list is extensive. The bar area at the front of the restaurant can get a little rowdy on weekend evenings. Mon–Fri 9.30am–3pm & 5pm–late, Sat 9am–late.

Rowdey Cow Farm Café Lower Farm, Devizes Rd, Rowde, SN10 2LX, ☎01380 829666, ⊛rowdeycow.co.uk; map p.76. Just outside Devizes in the village of Rowde (hence the name) this family-friendly café and ice cream parlour makes its own ice cream from the milk of its very own cows. There are various farmyard animals you can see too, as well as a children's play area. Lunches include ham, egg and chips (£9.25) and a pulled pork burger (£10.50). Mon–Sat 9am–5pm, Sun 9am–4pm, lunch served 11.45am–4pm.

★**The Vaults** 28a St John's St, SN10 1BN, ☎01380 721443, ⊛thevaultsdevizes.com; map p.76. Tucked away behind the Town Hall, this friendly beer-focused bar is a must for real ale aficionados with an ever-changing array available on tap – the widest selection in town. Staff will let you have a taste before committing so this is your chance to try something new. There are also pies from Lovett Pies, near Bristol (£4). Mon–Thurs 5–9pm, Fri–Sun noon–9pm.

ENTERTAINMENT AND ACTIVITIES

Boat trips ☎01380 721279, ⊛katrust.org.uk. The Kennet & Avon Canal Trust operate trips along the canal on the 45-seat *Kenavon Venture* three or four times a week between April and October. £6.

Ghost Walk ☎01380 725018, ⊛devizestours.co.uk. Spooky walks led by local historian John Girvan. Tours visit thirteen haunted locations including the site of the town's old gallows. Evenings only.

North Wilts Golf Club Bishops Cannings, SN10 2LP, ☎01380 860330, ⊛northwiltsgolf.com; map p.76. Downland 18-hole golf course that welcomes visitors seven days a week, though call to check availability in advance. Green fees from £15.

The Palace Cinema 19-20 Market Place, SN10 1JQ, ☎01380 722971, ⊛palacedevizes.co.uk, map p.76. Small, one-screen cinema showing all the latest releases.

Vaughan's Kitchen 8 White Horse Business Centre, SN10 2HJ, ☎01380 530203, ⊛vaughanskitchen.co.uk; map p.76. Peter Vaughan of The Bistro runs courses on everything from pasta making to Thai cookery here. There are classes for children, mostly on weekends and evenings. From £30.

The Wharf Theatre Wharf St, SN10 1EB, ☎0333 666 3366, ⊛wharftheatre.co.uk; map p.76. Small theatre on the canalside with an eclectic roster of drama, comedy and musical performances on the bill.

Chippenham and around

The sizeable market town of **CHIPPENHAM** makes a useful hub (complete with a train station) and sits amid a patchwork of fields and farms replete with attractive small towns and villages. Seven miles to the town's east is **Calne**, the original home of Wiltshire ham, while 5 miles west is **Corsham**, a historic town that has been seen on screen and is home to a herd of wild peacocks, often seen roaming the High Street.

The best-known village hereabouts is **Lacock**, which you may never have heard of but will almost certainly have seen on screen – in the likes of *Downton Abbey* and *Harry Potter*. No visit to Wiltshire would be truly complete without at least calling in to this picture-perfect English idyll, 4 miles south of Chippenham.

Chippenham

Although most appealing as a base for touring the surrounding area, **Chippenham**, 20 miles east of Bristol, has a pleasant ancient heart that is worthy of a short visit. You'll find a historic cobbled marketplace here, host to a lively **market** every Friday and Saturday, as well as the Grade I listed **Yelde Hall**, a medieval timber-framed building that dates from the mid fifteenth century. The High Street and surrounding streets of Emery Gate and Borough Parade form a useful **shopping** centre too.

Chippenham Museum and Heritage Centre

9-10 Market Place, SN15 3HF • Mon–Sat 10am–4pm • Free • ☎ 01249 705020, ⓦ chippenham.gov.uk

Chippenham Museum and Heritage Centre tells the story of Chippenham, including the town's links to the river, road and rail connections that now make up the Great West Way. It is housed in an eighteenth century townhouse and also hosts temporary exhibitions, often focused on local themes.

Lacock Abbey and the Fox Talbot Museum

Lacock, SN15 2LG • Abbey Jan Sat & Sun 11am–5pm, Feb–Dec daily 11am–5pm; museum, cloisters and grounds Feb–Dec daily 10.30am–5.30pm • £14.80; National Trust members free • ☎ 01249 730459, ⓦ nationaltrust.org.uk/lacock

Lacock Abbey is a quirky house built on the foundations of a former nunnery. The cloisters are the most atmospheric part of this historic building and there are several rooms here that have appeared on screen in the *Harry Potter* films.

Apart from its more recent on-screen fame, the Abbey is best known for the work of William Henry Fox Talbot, the first person to produce a photographic negative. **The Fox Talbot Museum**, in a sixteenth-century barn by the gates of the Abbey, captures something of the excitement he must have experienced as the dim outline of an oriel window in the abbey imprinted itself on a piece of silver nitrate paper. The museum also houses the **Fenton Collection**, featuring photographs and cameras from the birth of photography to the 1980s, which was donated by the **British Film Institute**.

Bowood House and Gardens

SN11 0LZ • End March–early Nov 11am–5.30pm • £12.75 • ☎ 01249 812102, ⓦ bowood.org

The Grade I listed **Bowood House** stands amid some of the region's most beautiful **gardens**, landscaped by **Lancelot "Capability" Brown** (see p.105) in the late eighteenth century. The estate is home to the Lansdowne family, holders of the title Marquis of Lansdowne since 1784 when William Petty, Prime Minister from 1782–3, was awarded the title for negotiating peace with America after the **War of Independence**.

The house itself is a Georgian masterpiece, with interiors by Scottish neoclassical architect and designer Robert Adam and a wonderful range of **art** and **antiques**. You can also see the former laboratory of Joseph Priestley, who discovered oxygen in 1774.

3

THE WORLD'S MOST FAMOUS VILLAGE?

You've almost certainly seen **Lacock** before – on screen in one of the numerous TV shows and films to have used its historic streets and glorious Abbey as a backdrop.

The village recently appeared in the final series of the hugely successful ITV series *Downton Abbey*, when Church Street hosted the 1920s fatstock show where Mrs Drewe kidnaps Marigold.

Other TV shows to use Lacock for filming include the BBC period drama *Cranford*, when the village stood in for the Cheshire village of Knutsford, and the BBC's hugely successful *Pride and Prejudice* 1995 TV series, which used Lacock to represent Meryton – you can almost hear the Bennett sisters gossiping in their bonnets as you stand in front of the shop windows here.

Lacock has also appeared in several of the *Harry Potter* films, with the ancient Abbey being the focus of the film crew's attention. Wander through the fifteenth-century cloister and you can almost see Hedwig stretching her wings in the grassy central courtyard, while in the sacristy you can feel the force of Professor Snape, bursting through the door to teach Harry's very first Potions class.

Make time for a moment of reflection in the **Chapter House**, where Harry finds the Mirror of Erised in *The Philosopher's Stone* and sees his parents, his heart's true desire. This vaulted medieval room, with its slender columns and fluted archways, also appeared as Professor McGonagall's classroom. A more inspiring place to learn is hard to imagine.

Finally, don't miss the **Warming Room**, aka Professor Quirrell's Defence Against the Dark Arts classroom. The cauldron used in these scenes remains here at Lacock, having had a platform built around it for the film. Quirrell is seen standing here when McGonagall interrupts the class to, "borrow Oliver Wood for a moment", introducing him to Harry, the Gryffindor Quidditch team's new seeker.

The National Trust website has a downloadable **map** highlighting film **locations** in and around the village (⍵ nationaltrust.org.uk).

The gardens though are the main draw, running to a hundred acres and considered to be one of the finest examples of Capability Brown's work. The **Terrace Gardens** were grown into an Italian-inspired landscape, where stone balustrades divide each row of burgeoning and brightly coloured plants from the next, while the **parkland** that extends out from the house flows in a series of sweeping lawns down to a huge mile-long **lake**. There's plenty to explore here, including a dramatically-cascading waterfall, a Doric temple and a hermit's cave, as well as one of the country's best **adventure playgrounds**, complete with pirate ship and "death slide". Don't miss Brown's **arboretum**, which displays more than seven hundred different species of tree including 11 "champion trees" – the tallest or largest of their kind in Britain.

The Woodland Gardens

Devizes Road, SN11 9PG · Late April–early June 11am–6pm · £6 · ☎ 01249 812102, ⍵ bowood.org

Separate from the main gardens, **Bowood's Woodland Gardens** are only open for six weeks during flowering season. They surround the family mausoleum, a classical building designed in 1761 by Robert Adam, and feature a dazzling display of brightly coloured rhododendrons and other plants, some of which were planted by the 3rd Marquis of Lansdowne back in 1854.

Calne

CALNE is most celebrated for the **Wiltshire cure**, a method of curing ham and bacon that was invented here by the Harris family in the eighteenth century. Today this small town is worth a visit chiefly for its wonderful **motor museum**, as well as being the jumping off point for **Bowood**, just 4 miles away.

Atwell-Wilson Motor Museum

36 Stockley Lane, SN11 0LJ • Mon–Sat 9am–5pm; Tours: Mon–Sat 11am & 2pm • Visitor centre: free; Tours: £12 • ☎ 01249 813119, ⓦ atwellwilson.org.uk

Wiltshire's only **motor museum** has a small but spectacular collection of vintage motor cars, most of them from the 1920s onwards – highlights include a 1952 Austin Sheerline and an Issigonis Mini 9x gearless prototype. There is also a fascinating array of **motorcycles** and **bicycles** as well as a Jack Spittle Model Lorry collection and a reconstructed 1930s garage complete with vehicles.

Corsham

CORSHAM is an enticing alternative to Lacock when the crowds there get too much. This historic village has also appeared on screen – in the first series of BBC drama *Poldark* – and there is a photogenic line-up of historic buildings here, including the seventeenth century **Hungerford Almshouses** along Pound Pill. You're also almost certain to see a cluster of brightly coloured peacocks roaming the streets here – they live at **Corsham Court** but are free to roam around the village and are rather confident about it too.

3

Corsham Court

Church St, SN13 0BZ (parking in Church Sq) • Oct, Nov & Jan–late March Sat & Sun 2–4.30pm; late March–Sept Tues–Thurs, Sat & Sun 2–4.30pm, last admission 30min before closing • £10; gardens only £5 • ☎ 01249 712214, ⓦ corsham-court.co.uk

There has been a great house at **Corsham Court** since the late tenth century, when it was home to the kings of Wessex, and it remained in royal possession until Elizabeth I granted a lease to Thomas Smyth, who built an **Elizabethan mansion** on the site in 1582. This forms the core of the house you see today, one of the finest stately homes in the area.

In 1745 the house was acquired by Paul Methuen, who transformed the interior into a venerable setting for his collection of Italian and Flemish **paintings**. He also redeveloped the **gardens**, contracting Capability Brown to design the Picture Gallery on the extended east wing and add a Great Walk a mile long and planted with trees, as well as a "haha" to divide the pleasure grounds from the park beyond. Today much of Brown's work remains and the grounds, with their areas of **woodland** and 13-acre **lake**, are a pleasant place for a stroll – as well as being home to Corsham's peacock population.

CAPABILITY BROWN

The Great West Way is home to several gardens landscaped by highly regarded English gardener **Lancelot "Capability" Brown**. Brown is said to have changed the face of eighteenth-century England, partly because he was unafraid of performing larger redevelopments, such as moving hills and altering the courses of rivers, in order to achieve the look he desired. Brown believed that the landscape should work for the house it surrounded, and he pioneered the use of the "haha", a sunken fence that was used to divide one separately managed piece of land from the next without disrupting the flow of the view.

One of the finest examples of Brown's work is **Bowood** where more than 100 acres of beautifully landscaped parkland display his signature style, while **Highclere Castle** in Berkshire has extensive grounds planned by Brown in 1770. Brown also landscaped the grounds of **Corsham Court** and redesigned the house's picture gallery. **Lacock Abbey** is also thought to have benefited from Brown's work, though the surviving receipts for the amount he was paid do not show exactly what he did – it is thought that he may have designed the field landscape in the south park. **Longleat** was landscaped by Brown and has perhaps been put to the strangest use of any of his work – as England's first drive-through safari park.

Sutton Lane Meadows

Sutton Lane, Sutton Benger, SN15 4LW • Daylight hours • Free • ☎ 01672 539920, ⓦ nationaltrust.org.uk

One of Wiltshire's most unspoiled areas of ancient meadow, **Sutton Lane Meadows** is a series of three fields rich in wildlife and managed as traditional English hay meadows. Two of the fields are designated **Sites of Special Scientific Interest** and there is an extensive population of green-winged and southern marsh orchids.

REME Museum

Prince Philip Barracks, MoD Lyneham, SN15 4PZ • Tues–Sat 10am–4.30pm • £7 • ☎ 01249 894869, ⓦ rememuseum.org.uk

REME Museum focuses on the history of REME, the **Royal Electrical and Mechanical Engineers**, who were formed in 1942 "to keep the punch in the Army's fist".

The collection here includes more than a hundred thousand items, ranging from large World War II vehicles to more than a thousand medals awarded to REME soldiers. There is also an extensive **weapons collection** and an early prototype of the CARRV (Challenger Armoured Repair and Recovery Vehicle), a recovery vehicle still in use by the British Army.

ARRIVAL AND INFORMATION

CHIPPENHAM AND AROUND

BY TRAIN

Chippenham is a major station on the London–Bristol line of the Great Western Railway (ⓦ gwr.com). Trains to London (every 15min) call at Swindon (15min), Reading (45min) and London Paddington (1hr 15min, from £16 single); trains to Bristol (every 30min) call at Bath Spa (15min) and Bristol Temple Meads (30min, from £8.90 single). There are also trains to Salisbury (1hr 20min, from £11 single) on the TransWilts line, run by the TransWilts Community Rail Partnership (ⓦ transwilts.org).

BY BUS

Faresaver (☎ 01249 444444, ⓦ faresaver.co.uk) operate buses from Chippenham bus station to Lacock (X34; every 30min; 15min; £7.50/day), Calne (33 and X33; Mon–Sat up to 10 Daily; 15min; £7.50/day) and Corsham (X31; Mon–Fri every 20min, Sat every 30min; 30min; £7.50/day). For Bowood take the X33 and get off at the stop in Derry Hill village for the 1.5-mile walk to the entrance. For Sutton Lane Meadows take the 91 to Sutton Benger, a mile's walk from the entrance.

Stagecoach (ⓦ stagecoachbus.com) operate a service linking Chippenham railway and bus stations with Calne (15min, £2.10 single), MoD Lyneham for REME (35min;

£3.60 single) and Swindon (1hr 20min; £4.20 single; Mon–Sat every 20min, Sun every 30min).

BY CAR

Wiltshire council operate car parks in Chippenham (Bath Road, SN15 2SA; £1.60/2hr; £8.40/day), Calne (Church St, SN10 0HY; 80p/2hr, £4.50/day) and Corsham (High St, SN10 0HB; £1.20/2hr; £2.20/3hr; 3hr max stay); all are free after 6pm and all day Sun.

The National Trust operate a large pay and display car park for Lacock on Hither Way (SN15 2LW); there is no parking for visitors in the village itself.

There is limited free parking in lay-bys near Sutton Lane Meadows; Bowood House and REME have plentiful free parking on-site.

BY BIKE

National Cycle Route 403 (ⓦ sustrans.org.uk) starts in Great Bedwyn and runs west through Marlborough and Avebury to reach Calne and Chippenham, passing close to Bowood House before turning south through Lacock to join NCN Route 4. There are bike racks at Chippenham train station and Pound Arts in Corsham.

ACCOMMODATION

Beanhill Farm B&B Christian Malford, SN15 4BS, ☎ 01249 720672, ⓦ beanhillfarm.net; map p. 76. Farmhouse B&B with one double and one twin room, both en suite. Breakfast includes eggs freshly laid by the farm's chickens and there's a pub in the village. __£75__.

Best Western Plus Angel Hotel 8 Market Place, Chippenham, SN15 3HD, ☎ 01249 652615, ⓦ best western.co.uk; map p.76. This seventeenth-century

coaching inn is now a 3-star hotel, right in the centre of Chippenham and overlooking the Market Place. Rooms are modern and spacious and there's a gym and heated indoor pool. Free parking, off Gladstone Road (SN15 3BW). __£125__.

★**Bowood Hotel, Spa & Golf Resort** Derry Hill, Calne, SN11 9PQ, ☎ 01249 822228, ⓦ bowood.org; map p.76. Luxury hotel on the Bowood Estate, surrounded by parkland and with an extensive range of leisure facilities including a spa and championship 18-hole golf course. The rooms were designed by the Marchioness of Lansdowne and are elegant and contemporary; some have balconies with lovely parkland views. **£280**.

★ **Buttle Farm** Compton Bassett, SN11 8RE, ☎ 01249 814918, ⓦ buttlefarm.co.uk; map p.76. High quality self-catering accommodation in a barn conversion on a working farm. There's a spacious feel throughout the four bedrooms, which have vaulted ceilings and super-king beds and there's a large sitting room and light-filled kitchen-diner complete with microwave, dishwasher and washing machine. Two of the bedrooms are in the main house, the other two are across the yard. Minimum stay two nights; main house bookable separately. **£1008**/2 nights, sleeps 8.

Heritage B&B 1 Kerry Crescent, New Road, Calne, SN11 0JH, ☎ 07770 770004, ⓦ heritagebandb.co.uk; map p.76. Ellie and Gillian's friendly adults-only bed and breakfast has three comfortable en suite rooms: one double, one king-size and one single. There's a shared guest lounge on the first floor too, and a pretty courtyard garden that guests can use. Breakfast is top quality, with plenty of local organic produce. **£115**

The Methuen Arms 2 High St, Corsham, SN13 0HB, ☎ 01249 717060, ⓦ themethuenarms.com; map p.76. Beautifully designed rooms with exposed beams and large Georgian windows, above a popular local inn. All fourteen rooms are en suite and the breakfasts, served in the restaurant downstairs, are superb. **£140**.

EATING AND DRINKING

Fay's Bistro 3 Beach Terrace, Calne, SN11 0RD, ☎ 01249 812508, ⓦ faysbistro.co.uk; map p.76. Bistro staples made with wonderfully fresh produce – the fish is bought in fresh to make the fish fingers, the steak sandwich (£9.55) is made with a 4oz sirloin steak. Fay's special lasagne (£8.95) is a hit too. Mon–Sat 9am–5pm, Sun 9.30am–3.30pm.

The Methuen Arms 2 High St, Corsham, SN13 0HB, ☎ 01249 717060, ⓦ themethuenarms.com; map p.76. Right next door to Corsham Court and in an elegant Georgian house, this upscale English pub/restaurant serves high quality, creative dishes such as crispy duck egg with chargrilled asparagus (£17) and fillet of stone bass with tempura prawns and crab bisque (£23). Local produce stars and afternoon teas and a Sunday roast are also served. Mon–Sat 8am–midnight, Sun 8am–11pm.

★ **Sign of the Angel** 6 Church St, Lacock, SN15 2LB, ☎ 01249 730230, ⓦ signoftheangel.co.uk; map p.76. Beautiful fifteenth-century coaching inn serving the best food in the local area – awarded two AA rosettes. The menu is seasonal and local wherever possible. The dinner menu features English classics such as pork tenderloin (£20) and lamb rump (£21.50) and there are vegan, vegetarian and gluten-free menus too. Tues–Sat 10am–11pm, Sun noon–3pm.

The Three Crowns 18 The Causeway, Chippenham, SN15 3DB, ☎ 01249 449029, ⓦ threecrownschippenham .co.uk; map p.76. Proper local pub serving a good range of real ales and ciders as well as a decent wine list. Pork pies from local butcher Walter Rose available on weekends. Mon–Wed 5pm–midnight, Thurs–Sun noon–midnight.

ENTERTAINMENT AND ACTIVITIES

Bowood Hotel, Spa & Golf Resort Derry Hill, Calne, SN11 9PQ, ☎ 01249 823881, ⓦ bowood.org; map p.76. Championship 18-hole golf course that is arguably the best in Wiltshire. Green fees from £35.

The Pound Arts Centre Pound Pill, Corsham, SN13 9HX, ☎ 01249 701628, ⓦ poundarts.org.uk; map p.76. Local arts centre with a year-round line-up of performances, workshops and exhibition.

Bradford on Avon and around

With its buildings of auburn stone and lovely river and canalside walks, **BRADFORD ON AVON** is a handsome town. Sheltering against a steep wooded slope, it takes its name from its "broad ford" across the **River Avon**, though the original fording place was replaced by a bridge dating mainly from the seventeenth century. The domed structure at one end is a quaint old jail converted from a chapel.

The local industry, based on **textiles**, was revolutionized with the arrival of Flemish weavers in 1659 and many of the town's buildings reflect the prosperity of this period. Yet Bradford's most significant building is the tiny **Church of St Laurence** on Church Street, an outstanding example of Saxon church architecture dating from AD 700. Its distinctive feature is the carved angels over the chancel arch.

Bradford on Avon Tithe Barn

Pound Lane, BA15 1LF · Daily 10.30am–4pm · Free · Ⓦ english-heritage.org.uk

Just outside the town centre between the River Avon and the Kennet & Avon Canal, stands a spectacular **Tithe Barn** dating from the fourteenth century. The barn is cared for by English Heritage and is free to access, its 167ft-long timber cruck roof is a staggering piece of historic carpentry that is well worth seeing.

Iford Manor Gardens

Bradford on Avon, BA15 2BA · April–Sep Wed–Sun, hols 11am–4pm; last admission 3.30pm · £6 · ☎ 01225 863146, Ⓦ ifordmanor.co.uk

Iford Manor stands in the eponymous valley, a steep-sided indent in the landscape 2 miles west of Bradford that has been occupied since Roman times. Although medieval in origin, the current classical façade was added in the eighteenth century and the Italianate garden designed by architect and landscape gardener **Harold Ainsworth Peto** during his time living here (1899–1933).

The house is built into the hillside and so the gardens is terraced, organised into different sections including a loggia and the beautiful cloisters, used in the summer for **operas** and recitals. There are wonderful views out over the valley too.

Great Chalfield Manor

Great Chalfield, SN12 8NH · Sun & Tues–Thurs; Garden: 11am–5pm; Manor: by guided tour Tues–Thurs 11am, noon, 2pm, 3pm & 4pm, Sun 2pm, 3pm & 4pm · £6.20; National Trust members free · ☎ 01225 782239, Ⓦ nationaltrust.org.uk

The charming manor house at **Great Chalfield**, 3 miles northeast of Bradford, dates from the fifteenth century, when it was commissioned by Wiltshire landowner Thomas Tropenell. Lovingly restored in 1905 by Major Robert Fuller, whose family still live here, today it appears much as it would have done in its earliest days. At its heart is the **Hall**, flanked with beautiful oriel windows and atop its roof are soldiers, griffons and monkeys cast in stone. The 7-acre **gardens** are also delightful.

The Courts Garden

Holt, BA14 6RR (park in village hall car park) · Thurs–Tues April–Oct 11am–5.30pm · £8.80; National Trust members free · ☎ 01225 782875, Ⓦ nationaltrust.org.uk

This English country garden in the village of **Holt** is a peaceful place to visit, with water gardens and colourful herbaceous borders as well as some beautifully shaped topiary and an arboretum. A small **museum** in the Orchard Room tells the history of the gardens, the previous owners and the cloth mill that once stood here.

ARRIVAL AND INFORMATION	BRADFORD ON AVON AND AROUND

BY TRAIN

Bradford on Avon is on the Great Western Railway with services to Bath (2–3 hourly; 15min; £4.60) and Salisbury (1–3 hourly; 45min; £13.40).

BY BUS

Zig Zag bus 69 (Ⓦ connectingwiltshire.co.uk) runs from Bradford on Avon to Holt (6min) and on to Corsham (40min; Mon–Sat 4-5 daily; £2 single). First Group (Ⓦ firstgroup.com) operate buses between Bradford on Avon and Bath (Mon–Sat every 30min, Sun hourly; 40min; £6/day).

BY CAR

The local council operates several car parks in Bradford, including the central St Margaret's car park (BA15 1DE; £2.30/3hr; max stay 3hr; free Mon–Sat after 8pm & all day Sun). Iford Manor has free parking on-site; Great Chalfield has free parking outside the manor gates. Parking for the Courts is in the free village hall car park.

BY BOAT

The Canal & River Trust (Ⓦ watersidemooring.com) operate five towpath moorings at Avoncliffe Aqueduct, which is easily accessible, just 3 miles outside Bradford on Avon.

Sally Narrowboats (☎01225 864923, ⓦsallynarrowboats
.co.uk) is based at Bradford on Avon Marina and has
narrowboats for hire from £585/4 nights. They also have
canoes for hire from £12/hr or £45/day.

BY BIKE
National Cycle Network Route 254 (ⓦsustrans.org.uk) is

part of the Wiltshire Cycleway and runs through Bradford
on Avon and past Great Chalfield.

ON FOOT
It's a pleasant one-mile walk on a public footpath between
Great Chalfield and the Courts.

ACCOMMODATION, EATING AND DRINKING

Canal Trust Café 15 Frome Rd, BA15 1LE, ☎01225
868683, ⓦcanaltrustcafe.co.uk; map p.76. Tarkan and
Victoria run this friendly café in the old lock keepers
cottage. Inside is cosy but the garden outside is the main
draw, with seating overlooking the canal. A full English is
served for breakfast, while the lunch menu includes dishes
such as burgers (£8.95) and a range of sandwiches. Daily
10am–4pm.
★**Church Farm Country Cottages** Winsley, BA15
2JH, ☎01225 722246, ⓦchurchfarmcottages.com;
map p.76. Located on the edge of Winsley village, with its
pub and shop, Church Farm has a range of self-contained
cottages as well as an indoor pool and a games room. The
cottages sleep two to twelve people and all come with
their own patio with outdoor seating and a cream tea on
arrival. The farm also operates the Farm Camp, with its bell
tents, wood burning stoves and proper beds, plus a well-
equipped camp kitchen and hot showers. £395/week for a
2-person cottage.
Cumberwell Country Cottages Great Cumberwell
Farm, BA15 2PQ, ☎01225 869230, ⓦcumberwell
countrycottages.com; map p.76. Seven light and
spacious cottages in a converted tythe barn a mile from
Bradford on Avon and just 5 miles from Bath. Cottages
can sleep up to 4 and have all en suite bedrooms, a fully
equipped kitchen and patio. There are two golf courses on
site. From £370/week for a two-person cottage.

The Swan 1 Church St, BA15 1LN, ☎01225 868686,
ⓦtheswanbradford.co.uk; map p.76. Grade II listed
building with twelve en suite bedrooms, all of them
different. The pub and restaurant downstairs serve Thai
dishes and pub classics such as Wiltshire ham, egg and
chips (£9.95) and there's also regular live music. £120
Timbrell's Yard 49 St Margaret's St, BA15 1DE,
☎01225 869492, ⓦtimbrellsyard.com; map p.76.
Contemporary rooms, from teeny doubles through to
large rooms with separate bathtubs and river views. The
restaurant serves modern English dishes such as chicken
with courgette fries (£16.50) and a beef burger with
smoked bacon ketchup (£13.50). There's a great range of
West Country cheeses too, and the bar serves local beers
and ciders. £85.
★**Woolley Grange** Woolley Green, BA15 1TX,
☎01225 864705, ⓦwoolleygrange.hotel.co.uk; map
p.76. Parents will love Woolley Grange, a luxury hotel
where all the family get to relax – thanks to two hours'
free childcare every day, a free baby-listening system
and in-house babysitters. There's tons for kids to do, too,
from swimming lessons to egg-collecting from the
ducks and chickens, plus indoor and outdoor swimming
pools and a spa (for grownups). Rooms are stylish and
spacious, and all baby paraphernalia can be organised in
advance, including cots and nappy bins. £145.

ACTIVITIES AND ENTERTAINMENT

Boat trips ☎01380 721279, ⓦkatrust.org.uk. The
Kennet & Avon Canal Trust operate trips along the canal on
the forty-seat *Barbara McLellan* three times a week
between Easter and October. Most cruises go to the
Avoncliffe Aqueduct. £8.

Wiltshire Music Centre Ashley Rd, BA15 1DZ, ☎01225
860100, ⓦwiltshiremusic.org.uk; map p.76. Concert hall
with three hundred seats, offering a lineup of jazz, classical,
folk and world music as well as workshops and family
events. The centre is also home to the Wiltshire Youth Jazz
Orchestra.

Trowbridge

TROWBRIDGE is Wiltshire's county town and has a rich history as part of the local
textile industry. The free **Trowbridge Museum** (☎01225 751339, ⓦtrowbridgemuseum
.co.uk, reopens 2020) tells the tale. Every Wednesday there's a lively market on Fore
Street, where you can buy excellent local produce, and the park at the rear of the Town
Hall is a pleasant place for a stroll.

ACTIVITIES AND ENTERTAINMENT

The Civic St Stephen's Place, BA14 8AH ☎01225 765072, ⊚thecivictrowbridge.co.uk. Modern auditorium hosting comedy and theatre acts by British household names. The Café has open mic nights.

Trowbridge Arts Town Hall, BA14 8EQ, ☎01225 774306, ⊚trowbridgearts.com. Trowbridge Town Hall is the venue for theatre, music, dance and comedy performances, plus art exhibitions and workshops.

Southern Wiltshire

Southern Wiltshire is home to some of the county's most famous attractions, including the UNESCO World Heritage-listed **Stonehenge**. In this area you'll also find **Longleat**, England's first drive-through safari park, and **Stourhead**, one of the most beautiful gardens in the country.

Stonehenge

3

Off the A360, SP4 7DE • Daily: mid-March to May & Sept to mid-Oct 9.30am–7pm; June–Aug 9am–8pm; mid-Oct to mid-March 9.30am–5pm; last entry 2hr before closing; advance booking of timed tickets essential • £19.30 in advance, £21.50 on arrival; English Heritage & National Trust members free • ☎0370 333 1181, ⊚english-heritage.org.uk/visit/places/stonehenge • Shuttle buses to the site (every 10min; 10min) leave from the visitor centre

HISTORY OF STONEHENGE

Some people may find **Stonehenge** underwhelming – it is a lot smaller than many assume – but understanding a little of its history and ancient significance gives an insight into its mystical appeal. What exists today is only a small part of the original prehistoric complex, as many of the outlying stones were probably plundered by medieval and later farmers for building materials. The construction of Stonehenge is thought to have taken place in several stages. In about 3000 BC the outer circular bank and ditch were built, with a ring of 56 pits dug inside this and which at a later date were filled with a mixture of earth and human ash. Around 2500 BC the first stones were raised within the earthworks, comprising approximately forty great blocks of dolerite (bluestone), whose ultimate source was **Preseli** in Wales. Some archeologists have suggested that these monoliths were found lying on **Salisbury Plain**, having been borne down from the Welsh mountains by a glacier in the last Ice Age, but the lack of any other glacial debris on the plain would seem to disprove this theory. The most likely explanation is that the stones were cut from quarries in Preseli and dragged or floated here on rafts, a prodigious task that has defeated recent attempts to emulate it.

The crucial phase in the creation of the site came during the next six hundred years, when the incomplete bluestone circle was transformed by the construction of a circle of 25 **trilithons** (two uprights crossed by a lintel) and an inner horseshoe formation of five trilithons. Hewn from Marlborough Downs sandstone, these colossal stones (called **sarsens**), ranging from 13ft to 21ft in height and weighing up to thirty tons, were carefully dressed and worked – for example, to compensate for perspectival distortion the uprights have a slight swelling in the middle, the same trick as the builders of the Parthenon were to employ hundreds of years later. More bluestones were arranged in various patterns within the outer circle over this period. The purpose of all this work remains baffling, however. The symmetry and location of the site (a slight rise in a flat valley with even views of the horizon in all directions) as well as its alignment towards the points of **sunrise** and **sunset** on the summer and winter solstices tend to support the supposition that it was some sort of **observatory** or time-measuring device. The site ceased to be used at around 1600 BC, and by the Middle Ages it had become a "landmark". Recent excavations have revealed the existence of a much larger settlement here than had previously been thought (the most substantial **Neolithic village** of this period to be found on the British mainland, in fact), covering a wide area.

CAN YOU TOUCH THE STONES?

In a word, no. It is never permitted to touch the stones at Stonehenge, and even if you book one of the **Stone Circle Access** visits security guards will be on hand to make sure you don't.

This is not to say that these tours are not worth joining. It is a real privilege to enter the interior of the stone circle and the fact that this is usually early in the morning before the site opens makes the experience all the more special. To request a Stone Circle Access tour (£38.50) fill in the form on the English Heritage website (ⓦ english-heritage.org.uk).

No ancient structure in England arouses more controversy than **Stonehenge**, a mysterious ring of monoliths. While archaeologists argue over whether it was a place of ritual sacrifice and sun-worship, an astronomical calculator or a royal palace, the guardians of the site have struggled for years to accommodate its enormous visitor numbers, particularly during the **summer solstice**, when crowds of 35,000 or more gather to watch the sunrise. The stones are part of a more extensive landscape looked after by the National Trust (ⓦ nationaltrust.org.uk/stonehenge-landscape). Access to the stones is via a shuttle-bus service from a sleek **visitor centre** that opened in 2013, after years of debate and planning. This low-rise, environmentally sensitive pair of buildings includes a shop, café and **exhibition space** combining archaeological remains from the area with high-tech interactive displays explaining the significance and history of it all. Outside, you can look round a cluster of re-created **Neolithic** houses, and try your hand at pulling a life-size Preseli bluestone. Perhaps a more fitting way to approach the site, however, is on foot – it's a pleasant, way-marked 30-minute **walk** from the visitor centre across fields to the stones.

3

Longleat

Warminster, BA12 7JS • Opening hours and closing days vary throughout the season, but are generally 10am–5pm, 6pm or 7pm; check website for exact times and days • **House and grounds** only £18.95, or £17.05 online in advance, all attractions £34.95 or £29.70 online in advance; with **Cheddar Gorge** £46.65 or £41.98 online in advance • ☎ 01985 844400, ⓦ longleat.co.uk

The African savanna intrudes into the bucolic Wiltshire countryside at **Longleat Safari Park**. In 1946 the 6th Marquess of Bath became the first stately-home owner to open his house to the paying public on a regular basis, and in 1966 he caused even more amazement when Longleat's Capability Brown landscapes were turned into England's first drive-through safari park, with lions, tigers, giraffes and rhinos on show, plus monkeys clambering all over your car. Other attractions followed, including boat trips on a **lake** full of sea lions, a large hedge **maze**, various **exhibitions**, and high-tech simulators. Beyond the razzmatazz, there's an exquisitely furnished **Elizabethan house**, with an enormous library and a fine collection of pictures, including Titian's *Holy Family*.

Stourhead

Near Mere, BA12 6QD • **House** Mid-Feb to mid-March Sat & Sun 11am–3pm; mid-March to Oct daily 11am–4.30pm; first two weeks of Nov & Dec daily 11am–3.30pm • **Gardens** Daily: mid-April to Oct 9am–6pm; Nov to mid-April 9am–5pm • House and gardens £18.30, National Trust members free • **King Alfred's Tower** Aug daily noon–4pm • £4.40, National Trust members free • ☎ 01747 841152, ⓦ nationaltrust.org.uk/stourhead

Landscape gardening was a favoured mode of display among the grandest eighteenth-century landowners, and **Stourhead** is one of the most accomplished examples of the genre. The estate was bought in 1717 by Henry Hoare, who commissioned the Scottish architect Colen Campbell to build a new villa in the **Palladian** style. Hoare's heir, another Henry, returned from his Grand Tour in 1741 and dammed the River Stour to create a lake, then surrounded it with blocks of trees, domed temples, stone

3

bridges, grottoes and statues. At the entrance, you can pick up a map detailing a lovely 2-mile walk around the **lake**. The estate itself includes a pub, a church and a **farm shop**, plus **King Alfred's Tower**, 3 miles or so from the main entrance. Built in 1772, it is one of England's oldest follies, and you can climb the two hundred or so steps up to the top for fine views across the estate and into neighbouring counties.

ARRIVAL AND INFORMATION

BY TRAIN

The closest train station to Stonehenge is Salisbury, which is served by direct South Western Railway trains from London Waterloo (2 hourly; 1hr 30min; from £9.10 single; ⓦ southwesternrailway.com) as well as Great Western Railway (ⓦ gwr.com) services from Bristol (1hr 5min, £11 single), Bath (50min, from £11 single) and Bradford on Avon (40min, from £13.40 single). There are buses from Salisbury to Stonehenge.

Frome is the closest station to Longleat and is served by direct South Western Railway trains from London Waterloo (3 daily; 2hr 15min; from £11.60 single). The only way to get to Longleat from the station is by taxi (Tony's Cabs, ⓣ 01373 469898, around £25).

Gillingham (in Dorset) is the best train station for Stourhead, with direct services from Salisbury (hourly; 30min; from £7 single) and London Waterloo (hourly; 2hr; from £11.60 single). There is a bus from here to Zeals, just over a mile from the entrance.

BY BUS

The Stonehenge Tour (ⓦ thestonehengetour.info) operates buses from Salisbury to Stonehenge (every 30min; 30min; £15 excluding admission; £36.50 with admission to Stonehenge, Old Sarum and Salisbury Cathedral).

Stourhead is just over a mile from the nearest bus stop at Zeals; Salisbury Reds bus 25 runs from Gillingham train station Mon–Fri at 9.08am and back at 2.40pm (10min; £8.80 return).

BY CAR

Stonehenge, Longleat and Stourhead all have plenty of dedicated visitor parking. At Stonehenge and Longleat there is no extra charge; at Stourhead non-National Trust members must pay £4/day.

BY BIKE

National Cycle Network Route 45 (ⓦ sustrans.org.uk) runs from Salisbury to Stonehenge. Routes 24 and 25 meet at Longleat, with 25 heading north to Frome and 24 running east–west between Salisbury and Bath. The Wiltshire Cycle Way links Longleat and Stourhead before looping through Salisbury and up to Stonehenge.

TOURS

Salisbury, Stonehenge & Sarum Tours ⓣ 01722 421777, ⓦ salisburystonehengetours.co.uk. Specialist in shore excursions and transfers for cruise passengers disembarking in Southampton. Tours include Stonehenge, Old Sarum and Salisbury Cathedral and can also include Runnymede. From £300 for two people.

ACCOMMODATION AND EATING

Cornerways Cottage Longcross, Zeals, BA12 6LL, ⓣ 01747 840477, ⓦ cornerwayscottage.co.uk; map p.76. Small, comfortable bed and breakfast in the village of Zeals, just 1.5 miles from Stourhead and a 10min drive from Longleat (for which they can also arrange discounts). One of the rooms has a four-poster bed. **£70**.

★**Red Lion Freehouse & Troutbeck Guesthouse** East Chisenbury, SN9 6AQ, ⓣ 01980 671124, ⓦ redlionfreehouse.com; map p.76. Excellent pub awarded a Michelin star for its high-quality menu of local produce. Fixed price menu available Wed–Fri lunch and Wed & Thurs dinner. Across the road is a boutique guesthouse with five rooms, with a private deck overlooking the River Avon. Wed–Sat noon–2.30pm & 6–9pm, Sun noon–2pm. Rooms from **£160**.

The Three Daggers 47 Westbury Rd, Edington, BA13 4PG, ⓣ 01380 830940, ⓦ threedaggers.co.uk; map p.76. Recently revamped village pub with its own microbrewery. There's a two-course lunch menu of dishes such as pie of the day and fish and chips (£14.95); dinner mains are fancier. There are three contemporary rooms upstairs and a separate six-bedroom cottage for private hire. Mon–Sat 10am–11pm, Sun 10am–10.30pm; food served Mon–Fri noon–2.30pm & 6–9pm, Sat noon–2.30pm & 6–9.30pm, Sun noon–8pm. Rooms from **£85**, cottage from **£125**pp.

SALISBURY

SALISBURY, huddled below Wiltshire's chalky plain in the converging valleys of the Avon and Nadder, sprang into existence in the early thirteenth century, when the bishopric was moved from nearby Old Sarum. Today, it looks from a distance very much as it did when **Constable** painted his celebrated view of it, and this prosperous and well-kept city is designed on a pleasantly human scale, with no sprawling suburbs or high-rise buildings to challenge the supremacy of the cathedral's immense spire. The city's inspiring silhouette is best admired by taking a twenty-minute walk through the water meadows southwest of the centre to the suburb of Harnham.

SALISBURY CATHEDRAL

The Close, SP1 2EL · **Cathedral** daily Mon–Sat 9am–5pm, Sun noon–4pm; **chapter house** April–Oct Mon–Sat 9.30am–5pm & Sun 11am–4pm, Nov–March Mon–Sat 10am–4.30pm & Sun 11am–4pm · £7.50 suggested donation · **Tower tours** 1–6 daily; 1hr 45min; book ahead · £13.50 · ☎ 01722 555120, ⓦ salisburycathedral.org.uk

Begun in 1220, **Salisbury Cathedral** was mostly completed within forty years and is thus unusually consistent in its style, with one prominent exception – the **spire**, which was added a century later and, at 404ft, is the highest in England. Its survival is something of a miracle – the foundations penetrate only 6ft into marshy ground and when **Christopher Wren** surveyed it he found the spire to be leaning almost 2.5ft out of true. He added tie rods, which finally arrested the movement.

The interior is austere, but there's an amazing sense of space and light in its high nave, despite the sombre pillars of grey Purbeck marble, which are visibly bowing beneath the weight they bear. Monuments and carved tombs line the walls. Don't miss the octagonal **chapter house**, which displays a rare original copy of the **Magna Carta**, and whose walls are decorated with a frieze of scenes from the Old Testament.

THE CATHEDRAL CLOSE

Surrounding the Cathedral is the **Cathedral Close**, a peaceful precinct of lawns and mellow old buildings. Most of the houses have beautiful Georgian facades, though some – like the Bishop's Palace and the deanery – date from as early as the thirteenth century.

MOMPESSON HOUSE

The Close, SP1 2EL · mid-March–Oct daily 11am–5pm; £7.70, garden only £1, National Trust members free; ☎ 01722 335659, ⓦ nationaltrust.org.uk/mompesson-house.

Built by a wealthy merchant in 1701, Mompesson House contains some beautifully furnished eighteenth-century rooms and a superbly-carved staircase. You might recognize it from the 1995 film *Sense and Sensibility*.

Also in the Cathedral Close is the **King's House**, home to the **Salisbury and South Wiltshire Museum** (Oct–late May Mon–Sat 10am–5pm; late May–Sep Mon–Sat 10am–5pm & Sun noon–5pm; £7.50; ☎ 01722 332151, ⓦ salisburymuseum.org.uk). The History of Salisbury Gallery offers an absorbing account of local history while the Wessex Gallery winds back time to the earliest evidence of human occupation in the area to tell the story of the ancient kingdom of Wessex, including treasures from Old Sarum and Stonehenge. There are also interesting displays of ceramics and Wiltshire fashion from the 1750s onward.

AROUND THE MARKET SQUARE

The Close's **North Gate** opens onto the centre's older streets, where narrow pedestrianized alleyways bear names like Fish Row and Salt Lane, indicative of their trading origin. Many half-timbered houses and inns have survived, and the last of four market crosses, Poultry Cross, stands on stilts in Silver Street, near the **Market Square**. The market, held on Tuesdays and Saturdays, still serves a large agricultural area, as it did in earlier times when the city grew wealthy on wool. Nearby, the **Church of St Thomas** – named after Thomas Becket – is worth a look inside for its carved timber roof and "Doom painting" over the chancel arch, depicting Christ presiding over the Last Judgement. Dating from 1475, it's the largest of its kind in England.

OLD SARUM

Castle Rd, SP1 3SD, 2 miles north of Salisbury · Daily: Mar–Sept 10am–6pm; Oct 10am–5pm; Nov–April 10am–4pm · £5.80; English Heritage members free · ☎ 01722 335398, ⓦ english-heritage.org.uk/visit/places/old-sarum

The ruins of **Old Sarum** occupy a bleak hilltop site. Possibly occupied up to five thousand years ago, then developed as an Iron Age **fort** whose double protective ditches remain, it was settled by Romans and Saxons before the

Norman bishopric of **Sherborne** was moved here in the 1070s. Within a couple of decades a new **cathedral** had been consecrated at Old Sarum, and a large religious community was living alongside the soldiers in the central castle. Old Sarum was an uncomfortable place, parched and windswept, and in 1220 the dissatisfied clergy – additionally at loggerheads with the castle's occupants – appealed to the pope for permission to decamp to **Salisbury** (still known officially as New Sarum). When permission was granted, the stone from the cathedral was commandeered for Salisbury's gateways, and once the church had gone the population waned. By the nineteenth century Old Sarum was deserted, and today the dominant features of the site are huge earthworks, banks and ditches, with a broad trench encircling the rudimentary remains of the Norman palace, castle and cathedral.

WILTON HOUSE

Wilton, SP2 0BJ, 5 miles west of Salisbury · **House** Easter & May–Aug Sun–Thurs & hols Sat 11.30am–5pm · £15.50 (includes grounds) · **Grounds** May to mid-Sept Sun–Thurs & hols Sat 11am–5.30pm · £6.50 · ☎ 01722 746714, ⓦ wiltonhouse.co.uk

The splendid **Wilton House** dominates the village of Wilton, renowned for its carpet industry. The original Tudor house, built for the first earl of Pembroke on the site of a dissolved Benedictine abbey, was ruined by fire in 1647 and rebuilt by **Inigo Jones**, whose hallmarks can be seen in the sumptuous Single Cube and Double Cube rooms, so called because of their precise dimensions.

The easel **paintings** are what makes Wilton really special, however – the collection includes works by Van Dyck, Rembrandt, two of the Brueghel family, Poussin, Andrea del Sarto and Tintoretto. In the grounds, the famous **Palladian Bridge** has been joined by various attractions including an adventure playground.

ARRIVAL AND INFORMATION SALISBURY

BY TRAIN

Salisbury is served by South Western Railway trains from London Waterloo (2 hourly; 1hr 30min; from £9.10 single; ⓦ southwesternrailway.com) as well as Great Western Railway (ⓦ gwr.com) services from Bristol (1hr 5min, £11 single) and Bath (50min, from £11 single).

BY BUS

Salisbury Reds (ⓦ salisburyreds.co.uk) buses operates services around Salisbury, the most useful of which are route 2 to Devizes (Mon–Sat roughly hourly; 1hr 10min) and route X5 to Marlborough and Swindon (Mon–Sat hourly; 1hr 25min to Marlborough, 1hr 50min to Swindon). Day rover tickets on all services in Wiltshire cost £8.50.

BY CAR

Salisbury has numerous car parks operated by the local council. Central car park on Mill Stream Approach (SPA 1HE) has no max stay (£1.50/1hr, £8.90/day, £1.90 Sun).

ACCOMMODATION AND EATING

Holiday Inn Salisbury-Stonehenge Mid Summer Park, Solstice Place, Amesbury, SP4 7SQ, ☎ 0345 241 3535, ⓦ hisalisbury-stonehenge.co.uk; map p.76. Funky modern rooms close to Stonehenge and with a bar and grill on-site. £88.

The southern and Wiltshire Cotswolds

Beginning in Bath and stretching northwards, the Cotswolds Area of Outstanding Natural Beauty is the sort of place visitors find themselves falling head over heels for – think quintessentially English villages presided over by stately stone churches, verdant rolling hills in brilliant green and neat fields divided by crumbling drystone walls.

HIGHLIGHTS

❶ Castle Combe village Quintessential English village that has banned cars – all the better for exploring on two feet. Some great places for afternoon tea too. **See p.117**

❷ Dyrham Park Extensive ancient parkland ripe for discovery, with walks, wild cooking, a kids' playground and al fresco Shakespeare, plus a seventeenth-century mansion at its core. **See p.117**

❸ Westonbirt, The National Arboretum The national arboretum has 17 miles of

walking trails to get you out among the ancient specimens on display here, plus an elevated walkway into the tree canopy that is accessible to all. **See p.121**

❹ Highgrove Royal Gardens HRH Prince Charles started this leading organic garden some forty years ago and today it offers fascinating tours that take in everything from the Cottage Garden to the Wildflower Meadow. The shop has some wonderful local produce you can buy too. **See p.121**

The Cotswolds is the largest of the 46 AONBs of England, Wales and Northern Ireland and extends over 790 square miles and into six counties. It is the second largest area of protected landscape in England, after the Lake District.

On the Great West Way (🌐 GreatWestWay.co.uk) are the southern landscapes of the Cotswolds, some of the least visited and consequently most pleasant areas of the AONB to explore. This is a landscape that whispers its beauty quietly rather than splashing it about with drama, a place where the hills are rolling, the fields jade green and the villages sleepily

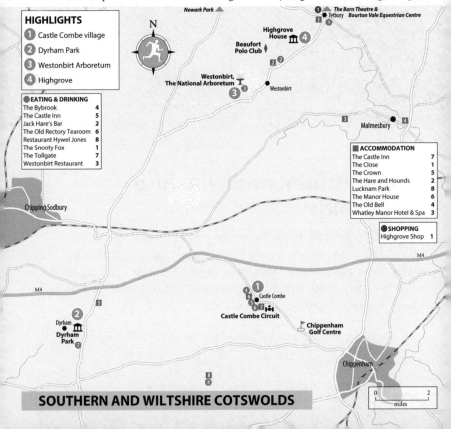

SOUTHERN AND WILTSHIRE COTSWOLDS

cast in Bath stone. The whole area stands on oolitic limestone, a bedrock that has dictated where villages and agriculture may occur and which has directly contributed to the Cotswolds' homogenous architecture, being used in the building of everything from churches to barns for centuries. A more perfect landscape would be hard to imagine.

Castle Combe and around

For many visitors, **CASTLE COMBE** is the perfect English village. Here you'll find cottages of honey-coloured Bath stone lined up in a picturesque village scene that has, unsurprisingly, been used on screen to represent various iterations of "Ye Olde England".

Just under a mile from the village is the renowned **Castle Combe Circuit**, one of the best places in the country to get behind the wheel of a race car, while the spectacular seventeenth century mansion and gardens at **Dyrham Park**, 8 miles west of the village, have an altogether slower pace.

Castle Combe village

There are dozens of cute villages in the Cotswolds but perhaps the prettiest is **Castle Combe**, an idyllic car-free spot that is perpetually packed with visitors snapping pictures of this quintessentially English scene. Pick of the postcard-worthy shots is a few yards along the By Brook looking towards the arched stone of the packhorse bridge, the thirteenth century church tower and a line-up of cute cottages in the background.

The village is kept car-free and a visit at quiet times (early mornings and evenings) is rewarded with a feeling of calm and tranquillity, the locals unobtrusively selling homemade cakes and home-grown flowers from their cottages as the church bells toll in the background.

Castle Combe has appeared on screen numerous times, including in the original *Dr Doolittle* film (1966) and more recently in *Stardust and the Wolf Man.*

4

Castle Combe Circuit

Castle Combe, SN14 7EY, ☎ 01249 782417, ⓦ castlecombecircuit.co.uk

A very different soundtrack fills the air at **Castle Combe Circuit**, just outside the village. Here sports car and race car engines roar, a calendar of **race meetings**, **track days** and **driving experiences** keeping petrolheads happy here throughout the year.

The circuit is based on what was once the perimeter track of RAF Castle Combe, a former World War II airfield and base for Polish airmen. The circuit opened in 1950 and is approximately 1.85 miles in length.

Dyrham Park

Dyrham, SN14 8HY • Daily 11am–5pm (last admission 1hr before closing) • £13.80; free to National Trust members • ☎ 0117 937 2501, ⓦ nationaltrust.org.uk

The seventeenth-century Baroque mansion house at **Dyrham** stands in a vast area of beautifully kept gardens and is more worth a visit for what you'll find around it than for what you can see inside.

The house was once home to the Blathwayt family and is packed with artwork, ceramics and furniture including a particularly notable collection of Dutch **delftware**. The highlights are displayed in "Mr Blaythwayt's Apartment" where visitors can snoop on seventeenth century life, harpsicord music, smelling pouches and all.

Outside a herd of fallow deer roams freely around the 270 acres of ancient **parkland** and so can you. Be sure to check out the West Garden, currently being transformed into a 21st century version of the seventeenth century original, inspired by a 1712 engraving of Dyrham Park as well as Versailles in France and Het Loo in the Netherlands. The spring display of tulips is especially memorable.

If you're travelling with **children**, Dyrham Park is a great place to tire them out. Younger ones (under 10) will love the Old Lodge playground with its ride on diggers and full-size tractor to clamber on, while older children can build a den at Hollow Ways. During school holidays there are numerous **activities** for families on offer, from wild cooking to dry stone walling (some require booking in advance, check the website). Summer also sees al fresco **Shakespeare** performed in the grounds – bring a picnic.

ARRIVAL AND INFORMATION   CASTLE COMBE AND AROUND

BY TRAIN
The closest train station to Castle Combe is Chippenham, located on the main London-Bristol line of the Great Western Railway (W gwr.com).

BY BUS
Faresaver bus (T 01249 444444, W faresaver.co.uk) number 35 runs to Castle Combe from Chippenham town centre and train station (20–25min; Mon–Fri five daily, Sat 3 daily; £3.50 return).

BY CAR
No cars are allowed into Castle Combe but there is a large car park on Dunns Lane a few minutes' walk outside the village centre (SN14 7HU, free, open 24hrs). There is plenty of parking at Castle Combe Circuit and Dyrham Park.

ON FOOT
The Cross Cotswold Pathway, part of the Macmillan Way Association, passes through Castle Combe en route from Banbury to Bath (W macmillanway.org).

ACCOMMODATION

The Castle Inn Castle Combe SN14 7HN T 01249 783030, W thecastleinn.co.uk; map p.105. Simple, classic rooms above a pub in the centre of Castle Combe village. All twelve rooms are en suite, some have views of the ancient Market Cross in the village centre. £145.

The Crown Tolldown, Dyrham SN14 8HZ T 01225 891166, W thecrowntolldown.co.uk; map p.105. Nine comfortably cosy double en suite rooms in a self-contained building out the back of a traditional English pub. You're surrounded by countryside here and just a mile from Dyrham Park. £75.

★**Lucknam Park Hotel & Spa** Colerne SN14 8AZ T 01225 742777, W lucknampark.co.uk; map p.105. This five-star hotel is a 10min drive from Castle Combe is the sort of hotel you mean to use as a base for exploring

but end up barely leaving. From classes at the cookery school and horse riding around the 500-acre estate to hydrotherapy in the spa, there's loads going on, plus rooms in the Palladian mansion are supremely comfortable. £295

The Manor House Castle Combe SN14 7HX T 01249 782206, W exclusive.co.uk/the-manor-house; map p.105. Five-star hotel with individually designed rooms, just outside Castle Combe village. The style here is classic opulence, with large beds, stuffed armchairs and heavy drapes in the bedrooms and heavy stone walls and fireplaces in the common areas. Margaret Thatcher wrote her memoirs in the oak-panelled Full Glass bar. The grounds run to 365 acres and include a river for fly fishing, a croquet lawn and the Manor House Golf Club. £202.

EATING AND DRINKING

The Bybrook Castle Combe SN14 7HX T 01249 782206, W exclusive.co.uk/the-manor-house/restaurants-bars/ the-bybrook; map p.105. Michelin-starred restaurant at the Manor House hotel serving a seasonal menu including produce from the kitchen garden – think Salisbury Plain venison, with parsnip puree and sloe gin sauce. A six-course tasting menu is available (£95). Sun–Thurs 6.30–9.00pm, Fri & Sat 6.30–9.30pm.

The Castle Inn Castle Combe SN14 7HN T 01249 783030, W thecastleinn.co.uk; map p.105. Proper English pub with twelfth-century origins in the heart of Castle Combe village. The all-day menu has the likes of a Ploughmans sharing board (£12), sandwiches from £7 and pie and mash (£16) as well as cream teas served in the

afternoons. Daily 11am–1pm; kitchen noon–9pm.

The Old Rectory Tearoom The Street, Castle Combe, SN14 7HU, T 01249 782366, W castlecombetearooms .co.uk; map p.105. Quaint tearoom serving homemade two-course lunches and afternoon teas. Reservations always required. Afternoon tea £22, lunch £40 for two. Daily from noon.

Restaurant Hywel Jones Lucknam Park Hotel & Spa Colerne SN14 8AZ T 01225 742777, W lucknampark .co.uk; map p.105. The signature tasting menu from the eponymous chef has Loch Duart salmon, braised halibut and pork from nearby Roundway Hill. There's a vegetarian tasting menu and wine matching to boot. It has held a Michelin star since 2006. Wed–Sun 6.30–10pm, Sun also 12.30–2.30pm.

The Tollgate Dyrham, SN14 8LF ☎01225 891585, ⓦthetollgate.co; map p.105 Once the turnpike for the main road (now the A46) this friendly tearoom serves simple lunches such as ham and cheese rarebit (£7.50) and Wiltshire ham, egg and chips (£8) as well as cooked breakfasts (from £6) and afternoon tea. The cosy tearoom with its wood burning stove is the best place to sit on chilly days; in summer arrive early to nab a table in the front or rear garden, with views across Bristol and the Severn into Wales. Daily 9am–5pm.

ACTIVITIES

Andy Cook Cycling 01249 783399, ⓦandycookcycling.com. Tuesday night cycling at Castle Combe Circuit (5.30-8pm). £2/yr membership fee, £3 entry fee.

Castle Combe Circuit Castle Combe, SN14 7EY, ☎01249 782417, ⓦcastlecombecircuit.co.uk; map p.105. Experience the thrill of driving a race car such as a Ford Fiesta Zetec S or Lotus Elise or pretending to be an F1 driver in a single seater, all on a proper track on a Driving Experience course. From £110/2hr. There are also regular car (£170) and bike (£130) track days for you to let your wheels loose on the track (driving licence and own vehicle required).

Chippenham Golf Centre Tiddleywink, Chippenham SN14 7BY ☎01249 783121, ⓦchippenhamgolfcentre.co.uk; map p.105. Par three golf course (£7) that challenges the short game of intermediate and advanced golfers, plus a 300-yard driving range (£4.20/50 balls) and 18-hole putting green. Mon–Thurs 10am–9pm, Fri 10am–8pm, Sat & Sun 9am–6.30pm.

Manor House Golf Club Castle Combe SN14 7JW ☎01249 782206, ⓦexclusive.co.uk/the-manor-house; map p.105. Starting from the fortifications of the original castle from which the village gets its name, this 6500yd 18-hole course challenges golfers with water hazards (from the By Brook) and plenty of mature trees. Green fees from £35.

Malmesbury and around

Just on the eastern fringes of the Cotswolds, the ancient town of **MALMESBURY** is the gateway to the rest of the southern Cotswolds, to the north of the M4 motorway and in the very far north of Wiltshire. This is a well-to-do area, home to plenty of attractive towns, luxurious places to stay and cosy pubs that happen to also serve some very fine food indeed. It is also home to **Westonbirt, The National Arboretum**, and to Prince Charles and Camilla, Duchess of Cornwall, who make their home here at **Highgrove**, just outside the appealing town of **Tetbury**.

Malmesbury

This charming **market town** is at the heart of England's oldest borough. Its origins date back as far as the middle of the sixth century, when the Saxons took control from the Britons, and **Malmesbury** was first given a charter by Alfred the Great as early as c.880.

Although Malmesbury once had an Abbey with a spire higher than that of Salisbury Cathedral today it languishes in relative obscurity, its main draw to most being its position at the edge of the Cotswolds AONB. Most visitors passing through do make time though for the **Norman Abbey**, and a lengthier stay is rewarded with the chance to discover a thriving town with plenty of independent retailers and a weekly farmers' and artisans' market (Fridays).

Malmesbury Abbey

Gloucester St SN16 9BA · Daily 9am–5pm (4pm in winter) · Free · ☎01666 826666, ⓦmalmesburyabbey.com

Malmesbury's twelfth-century **abbey** stands at its heart, towering over the town below in all its Gothic splendour. It is a calming and reflective place to visit and is also home to the tomb of King Athelstan and an interesting fifteenth-century illuminated Bible.

The gravestone of a local girl, Hannah Twynnoy, who was killed by a tiger in the garden of the White Lion pub in 1703 (allegedly the first person this happened to in Britain), can also be seen in the graveyard here.

Abbey House Gardens

The Abbey House SN16 9AS • April–Sep 11am–5.30pm • £8 • ☎ 01666 827650, ⓦ abbeyhousegardens.co.uk

The **Abbey House** was first built after the arrival at the Abbey of Abbot William of Colerne in 1260 and used as his official lodging; what you see today is a sixteenth-century building whose foundations have been built onto the original house.

Chief draw, though, is the spectacular **garden**, which runs to five acres and straddles the River Avon. You'll find something in bloom here most of the year, with a vast collection of roses and tulips as well as ten thousand different plants. Paths and yew hedging in the upper garden have been laid out to the exact footprint of the missing parts of the ancient Abbey, much of which collapsed around 1500, including a spire that is six times the height of the arch now left behind. **Dogs** welcome on a short lead.

Westonbirt, The National Arboretum

3 miles southwest of Tetbury, GL8 8QS • Daily 9am–5pm (last admission Dec–Feb 4pm, March–Nov 4.30pm) • £10 or £7 if arriving by bike or public transport (Dec–Feb £7 or £5) • **Guided walks** March–Oct Mon, Wed & Fri 11am, Sat & Sun 11am & 2pm; 2hr • Free with admission • ☎ 0300 067 4890, ⓦ forestry.gov.uk/westonbirt

Originally planted by the Holfords, a wealthy Victorian family, **The National Arboretum** is the protector of some of the oldest, biggest and rarest trees in the world. There are seventeen miles of paths to roam here across six hundred acres, divided into the larger, wilder **Silk Wood** and the more ornamental **Old Arboretum**.

Every season (if not every day) here is different, with **maps** printed and **trails** laid out according to what's in season. There is also an award-winning STIHL **Treetop Walkway**, which winds its way slowly upwards into the tree canopy for a closer look – with level access it's accessible to all and there are interactive information panels every few yards. There's also a **bird viewing** shelter and **activity trails** each season for kids. Make a day of it – there's plenty to see, as well as a very good restaurant (see page 123).

Dogs are permitted only in Silk Wood; the Old Arboretum is a dog-free zone.

4

Tetbury

TETBURY is the second largest town in the Cotswolds (after Cirencester further north) and is home to one of the most attractive **high streets** in the area. This is a town that has been wealthy since the fifteenth century wool trade and it shows in the line-up of historic architecture along its streets. Look out especially for the **Market House** – though you can't really miss it, its yellow paintwork and columned frontage presiding over the town as it has done since 1655. Shoppers should allow plenty of time in Tetbury, this is one of the best boutique **shopping** destinations on the Great West Way.

Highgrove Royal Gardens

Doughton, GL8 8TQ • Garden tours April–Oct selected days & times; 2hr • From £27.50 • Booking essential: ☎ 0303 123 7310, ⓦ highgrovegardens.com

Highgrove is the home of Prince Charles and Camilla, Duchess of Cornwall, but is perhaps best known for its innovative **organic gardens**, which have been more than 35 years in the making – a impressive achievement from the days when they were just lawns.

Tours of the gardens – led, needless to say, by a guide rather than Prince Charles himself – operate in the summer, with stories that evoke each setting, from the mighty Thyme Walk to the calm of the Cottage Garden, Stumpery and aromatic Kitchen Garden. There's a waiting list of several weeks, so ensure you book ahead. Photo ID is required on entry and mobile phones and cameras are not permitted.

Newark Park

Ozleworth, Wotton-Under-Edge, GL12 7PZ • Feb daily 11am–4pm, March–end Oct daily 11am–5pm, Nov–mid Dec Sat & Sun 11am–4pm • £9.50, gardens only £6.90; free to National Trust members • ☎ 01453 842644, ⓦ nationaltrust.org.uk

Newark Park stands atop the Cotswold escarpment – whichever way you look out from here there is hardly a sign of modern life in sight. The grounds are ripe for a stroll, with views across the Cotswold countryside and lovely gardens that are known for their end of winter snowdrops.

The house here was built in 1550 by one of Henry VIII's courtiers, Nicholas Poyntz, as a hunting lodge and after a period of decline was restored by a Texan architect in the 1970s and 80s. The result is an eclectic mix of styles from the past five centuries.

ARRIVAL AND INFORMATION

BY TRAIN

The nearest train station to Malmesbury is at Chippenham, on the Great Western Railway mainline that runs from London to Bristol (ⓦ gwr.com).

There is also a station at Kemble, just to the east of the Cotswolds AONB about eight miles northeast of Tetbury. The Great Western Railway runs services from Kemble to Swindon (15min) and on through Reading (45min) to London Paddington (every 1hr, 1hr 15min, from £24 single). There are also services through Wiltshire to Southampton, calling at Swindon (20min), Chippenham (40min) and Westbury (1hr 10min) en route (two daily, 2hr 20min, from £33 single).

BY BUS

Coachstyle (☎ 01249 782224, ⓦ coachstyle.ltd.uk) operates buses from Chippenham bus station to Malmesbury (Mon–Sat every 1hr, 50min; £4.50 return). They also run regular buses from Swindon to Malmesbury (Mon–Sat every 1hr, 1hr; £5 return) and a weekly service from Malmesbury to Castle Combe and on to Bath (Wed 9.30am, 30min to Castle Combe, 1hr 20min to Bath).

Stagecoach (ⓦ stagecoachbus.com) run buses from Tetbury to Westonbirt (Mon–Sat four daily; 6min; from £1.90 single).

Pulhams Coaches (☎ 01451 820369, ⓦ pulhamscoaches .com) operate services between Kemble station and

MALMESBURY AND AROUND

Tetbury, timed to coordinate well with arriving and departing London trains (Mon–Fri six daily, Sat three daily; 20min; from £2.70 single).

BY CAR

Malmesbury has two main car parks. The car park at Burnham Road (SN16 0BQ) is located on the edge of the town centre and is free (open 24hrs). Alternatively, there is a car park on Station Road (SN16 9JT) Mon–Sat 8am–6pm (£2.20/3hr, £4.50/day) and there are steep steps to reach the town centre.

Tetbury has four car parks. The Old Railyard car park (GL8 8EY) is free at all times; the others (at Church St & West St, both GL8 8LL and at The Chipping GL8 8EU) are only free after 3pm and on Sundays.

There is plenty of free parking at Westonbirt and Highgrove. Note that the postcode for Highgrove will not lead you to the main entrance – set Doughton as your destination.

BY BIKE

Arrive at Westonbirt by bike and you'll get a discount; no cycling is permitted in the arboretum but there are plenty of bike racks in the car park.

Bainton Bikes (☎ 01865 311610, ⓦ baintonbikes.com) offer bike hire in Tetbury as well as in Cirencester, the Cotswold Water Park and Oxford.

ACCOMMODATION

The Close Long St, Tetbury, GL8 8AQ ☎ 01666 502272, ⓦ cotswold-inns-hotels.co.uk; map p.105. A former sixteenth-century townhouse turned boutique country hotel in the heart of Tetbury. Just nineteen bedrooms, all with big beds – some four-poster. There's a traditional pub with a contemporary feel downstairs, too. **£220**.

The Hare and Hounds Bath Rd, Westonbirt, GL8 8QL ☎ 01666 881000, ⓦ cotswold-inns-hotels.co.uk; map p.105. Beautiful traditional hotel with 42 bedrooms spread across the Main House and around the extensive grounds. Plenty of communal space, including the cosy Library and the Drawing Room, stocked with board games. Rooms are classic with contemporary design

touches and divided into "Good" and "Very good", based on how spacious they are. **£140**.

★**The Old Bell** Abbey Row, Malmesbury, SN16 0BW ☎ 01666 822344, ⓦ oldbellhotel.co.uk; map p.105. This traditional hotel next to the twelfth-century Malmesbury Abbey claims to be England's oldest. There are Nespresso machines in rooms with four-poster beds and roll-top baths. The 34 bedrooms are spread throughout the main house and adjoining coach house, with those at the cheaper end in the latter. **£120**.

★**Whatley Manor Hotel & Spa** Easton Grey, Malmesbury, SN16 0RB, ☎ 01666 822888, ⓦ whatleymanor.com; map p.105. Whatley Manor is set in 16 acres of gardens near Malmesbury. The Dining Room here has a Michelin star and there's also a more low-key brasserie and, in the summer, tables on the terrace outside in the kitchen garden. The 23 bedrooms are individually styled but all share an elegant décor, with rich fabrics and earthy textures. The Aquarius Spa has an indoor/outdoor hydrotherapy pool and there's a cinema for private hire and Sunday screenings. No children under 12. **£260**.

EATING AND DRINKING

Jack Hare's Bar Bath Rd, Westonbirt, GL8 8QL ☎ 01666 881000, ⓦ cotswold-inns-hotels.co.uk; map p.105. Warm and welcoming pub with outdoor seating and a great range of ales on tap. The menu is a rundown of the best in contemporary English pub food, from simple burgers (from £17.50) to fancier tuna steak (£19). Full afternoon tea also served £17 or £26 with champagne). Mon–Sat 11am–11pm, Sun noon–10.30pm (food daily noon–2.30pm & 6.30–9.30pm.

The Snooty Fox Market Place, Tetbury GL8 8DD ☎ 01666 502436, ⓦ snooty-fox.co.uk; map p.105. Food is served all day; until 11.30am there are generous breakfasts, while at lunch and dinner a classic pub menu is served - think honey and mustard roasted ham (£11.50), mussels (£7) and steaks (from £17). Daily 9am–9pm.

Westonbirt Restaurant Westonbirt, The National Arboretum, GL8 8QS, ☎ 01666 880064, ⓦ forestry.gov .uk/Westonbirt-food; map p.105. Good refuelling stop in the heart of the arboretum. Main courses include haddock fishcakes and a chicken and chorizo salad (all around £8). Daily 9.30am–4pm.

SHOPPING

Highgrove Shop 10 Long St, Tetbury, GL8 8AQ, ☎ 0333 222 4555, ⓦ highgrovegardens.com; map p.105. A wide range of luxury products from stationery to jewellery is for sale at Highgrove's Tetbury shop. There is of course also food and drink, including chutneys, teas and chocolates. All profits go the Prince of Wales's Charitable Foundation. Mon–Sat 9.30am–5pm, Sun 10.30am–4.30pm.

ACTIVITIES AND ENTERTAINMENT

Beaufort Polo Club ☎ 01666 880510, ⓦ beaufort poloclub.com; map p.105. Matches at weekends and some weekdays throughout the summer season. Check the fixture list on the website or call for details.

Giffords Circus ☎ 01242 691181, ⓦ giffordscircus .com. Village green circus that tours England during the summer, with shows along the Great West Way. Expect plenty of acrobatics, both human and equestrian.

4

SIDE TRIP

THE REST OF THE COTSWOLDS

Further north the Cotswolds get busier and better known, with some of the AONB's most famous sights – and most photographed scenery – found around the northern reaches of the area, past **CIRENCESTER**. Cirencester is an attractive market town that styles itself as the "capital of the Cotswolds" but the main draw is the scenery that surrounds it, which is well worth exploring.

NORTHLEACH

Secluded in a shallow depression, **NORTHLEACH** is one of the most appealing and atmospheric villages in the Cotswolds – a great base to explore the area. Despite the fact that the A40 Oxford–Cheltenham road and A429 Fosse Way cross at a large roundabout nearby, virtually no tourist traffic makes its way into the centre and rows of immaculate late medieval cottages cluster around the **Market Place** and adjoining green.

Just off the High Street is the wonderful **Church of St Peter and St Paul** (ⓦ northleach .org), one of the finest of the Cotswolds "wool churches" and a classic example of the fifteenth-century **Perpendicular style**, with a soaring tower and beautifully proportioned nave lit by large windows. The floors of the aisles are inlaid with an exceptional collection of memorial brasses, marking the tombs of the merchants whose endowments paid for the church. On several, you can make out the woolsacks laid out beneath the owner's feet – a symbol of wealth and power that survives today in London's **House of Lords**, where a woolsack is placed on the Lord Chancellor's seat.

BOURTON-ON-THE-WATER

BOURTON-ON-THE-WATER is the epicentre of

Cotswold tourism. Beside the village green – flanked by photogenic Jacobean and Georgian facades in yellow Cotswold stone – five picturesque little **bridges** span the shallow **River Windrush**, dappled by shade from overhanging trees. It looks lovely, but its proximity to main roads means that it's invariably packed with people: tourist coaches cram in all summer long and the little **High Street** now concentrates on souvenirs and teashops.

LOWER SLAUGHTER

A mile outside Bourton-on-the-Water, **LOWER SLAUGHTER** has some of the most celebrated village scenery in the Cotswolds, as the **River Eye** snakes its way between immaculate honey-stone cottages. There is a small **museum** (and souvenir shop) signposted in a former mill, but the main attraction of the stroll through the village is to stop in for a little something at one of the grand **hotels** occupying gated mansions on both sides of the street.

STOW-ON-THE-WOLD

Ambling over a steep hill 700ft above sea level, **STOW-ON-THE-WOLD** is home to a beautiful old **marketplace** surrounded by pubs, shops selling antiques and souvenirs, and a huge number of **tearooms**. The narrow-walled alleyways, or "tchures", running into the square, which is itself dominated by an imposing Victorian hall, were designed for funnelling sheep into the market. **St Edward's Church** has a photogenic north porch, where two yew trees flanking the door appear to have grown into the stonework.

CHIPPING CAMPDEN

Situated on the northern edge of the Cotswolds, **CHIPPING CAMPDEN** gives a good idea of how a prosperous **wool town** might have looked in the Middle Ages. The elegant High Street is hemmed in by mostly Tudor and Jacobean facades. The evocative seventeenth-century **Market Hall**, where farmers once gathered to sell their produce has survived too.

Just off the High Street is the **Old Silk Mill** (ⓦhartsilversmiths.co.uk), where designer Charles Ashbee relocated the London Guild of Handicraft in 1902, introducing the **Arts and Crafts** movement to the Cotswolds. Today, as well as housing galleries of local art, the building rings with the noise of chisels from the resident stone carvers. Upstairs, you're free to wander into the workshop of Hart, a **silversmith** firm with metalworking tools strewn everywhere under low ceilings, and staff perched by the windows working by hand on

decorative pieces.

The history of the Guild of Handicraft, and its leading exponents, is explained at the superb **Court Barn Museum** (ⓦcourtbarn.org.uk). Sited opposite a magnificent row of seventeenth-century Cotswold stone almshouses, the museum displays the work of Charles Ashbee and eight Arts and Crafts cohorts, placing it all in context with informative displays and short videos. Featured works include the **bookbinding** of Katharine Adams, the **stained-glass** design of Paul Woodroffe and **furniture** by Gordon Russell.

EATING

Badgers Hall High St, Chipping Campden, GL55 6HB ☎01386 840839, ⓦbadgershall.com. This tearoom in an old stone house has won awards for its traditional English tea and cakes, all freshly made daily. Afternoon tea with a glass of prosecco is £24.95. Fri & Sat only for non-residents.

The Plough Inn Cold Aston, GL54 3BN ☎01451 822602, ⓦcoldastonplough.com. In the village of Cold Aston near Northleach is this recently relaunched country pub, which offers some of the best food in the area. The indoor charcoal oven cooks perfect whole fish and chargrilled steaks (from £18.50). Mon–Thurs noon–3pm & 6–9pm, Fri & Sat noon–3pm & 6–9.30pm, Sun noon–4pm & 6–9pm.

The Wheatsheaf Inn West End, Northleach, GL54 3EZ ☎01451 860244, ⓦtheluckyonion.com/property/the-wheatsheaf. This seventeenth-century coaching inn is the quintessential English inn – all plump sofas, fireplaces and warm hospitality. The menu features decadent dishes such as Cornish lobster tagliatelle (£29) and old spot pork chop (£17).

ACTIVITIES

The Barn Theatre 5 Beeches Rd, Cirencester, GL7 1BN, ☎01285 648255, ⓦbarntheatre.org.uk; map p.105. Top-class regional theatre showing an exciting line-up of professional productions in a state-of-the-art auditorium.

Bourton Vale Equestrian Centre Bourton on the Water, GL54 2HN, ☎07910 138465, ⓦbourtonvaleequestrian.co.uk; map p.105. Circular hacks around the villages of Lower and Upper Slaughter, suitable for all levels including beginners. £40/hr.

Cotswold Way ⓦnationaltrail.co.uk/cotswold-way. National Trail running for 102 miles along the Cotswold escarpment through picturesque villages and past abbeys, churches and historic houses. The route follows the western edge of the AONB, running from Bath Abbey northwards past Dyrham Park and Chipping Sodbury on the Great West Way, before continuing on to Chipping Campden. There are also several circular walks along the route – downloaded PDFs at ⓦcotswoldaonb.org.uk.

ROMAN BATHS

Bath

A graceful succession of urban set pieces, Bath is a visual feast: harmonious, compact and perfectly complemented by the softly undulating hills that surround it. The city's elegant crescents and Georgian buildings are studded with plaques naming Bath's eminent inhabitants from its heyday as a spa resort; it was here that Jane Austen set *Persuasion* and *Northanger Abbey*, and where Gainsborough established himself as a portraitist and landscape painter.

5

HIGHLIGHTS

❶ **Roman Baths** Iconic Roman bathing place that stands in testament to just how seriously the Romans took their baths. Visit on a summer evening to see the graceful columns and intricate stonework lit by torchlight. **See below**

❷ **Thermae Bath Spa** Modern iteration of a public bathing house, where you can take the natural thermal waters in the stunning rooftop pool – complete with unrivalled views of the Bath skyline. **See p.127**

❸ **Holburne Museum** The city's first public art gallery has works by Constable, Stubbs, Gainsborough and Angelika Kauffman as well as a classical facade that is a worthy highlight on its own. **See p.130**

❹ **The Royal Crescent** A more perfect terrace of homes would be hard to imagine. Take a stroll on the lawns of neighbouring Victoria Park and stand well back to fit all thirty Grade I listed Bath stone houses in your viewfinder. **See p.130**

❺ **Jane Austen Festival** Fan of *Pride and Prejudice*? You've found your tribe. Join the seriously dressed up legions of Jane fans on a parade through the city and at a Regency ball during this annual festival. **See p.136**

❻ **Shopping in Bath** Bath is the best place on the Great West Way for shopping, with independent boutiques lining its Georgian streets and the extensive SouthGate shopping centre, home to numerous British and international brands. **See p.137**

Bath owes its name and fame to its hot springs, the only ones in the country, which made it a place of reverence for the local Celtic population, though it took Roman technology to turn it into a fully-fledged bathing establishment. The baths fell into decline with the departure of the Romans, but the town later regained its importance under the Saxons, its abbey seeing the coronation of the first king of all England, Edgar, in 973. A new bathing complex was built in the sixteenth century, popularized by the visit of Elizabeth I in 1574.

The city reached its fashionable zenith in the eighteenth century. It was at this time, Bath's "Golden Age", that the city acquired its ranks of Palladian mansions and Regency townhouses, all of them built in the local Bath stone. The legacy is a city whose greatest enjoyment comes simply from wandering its streets, with their pale gold architecture and sweeping vistas.

The Roman Baths

Abbey Churchyard, BA1 1LZ • Daily: March to mid-June, Sept & Oct 9am–6pm; mid-June to Aug 9am–10pm; Nov–Feb 9.30am–6pm; last entry 1hr before closing • £16.50, £17.50 mid-June to Aug, £22.50 combined ticket with **Fashion Museum & Victoria Art Gallery** • Tours Daily, from 10am, on the hour; 1hr • Free • ☎ 01225 477785, ⓦ romanbaths.co.uk

There are hours of entertainment in **BATH'S** premier attraction, the **Roman Baths**, which comprises the baths themselves and an informative **museum** – highlights include the **Sacred Spring**, part of the temple of the local deity Sulis Minerva, where water still bubbles up at a constant 46.5ºC; the open-air (but originally covered) **Great Bath**, its vaporous waters surrounded by nineteenth-century pillars, terraces and statues of famous Romans; the **Circular Bath**, where bathers cooled off; and the **Norman King's Bath**, where people were taking a restorative dip right up until 1978. The free **audio guide** is excellent.

Among a quantity of coins, jewellery and sculpture exhibited are the bronze head of Sulis Minerva and a grand, Celtic-inspired gorgon's head from the temple's pediment. Models of the complex at its greatest extent give some idea of the awe which it must have inspired, while the graffiti salvaged from the Roman era – mainly curses and boasts – offer a personal slant on this antique leisure centre.

You can get a free glimpse into the baths from the next-door **Pump Room**, the social hub of the Georgian spa community and still redolent of that era, which houses a formal tearoom and restaurant.

Thermae Bath Spa

Hot Bath St, BA1 1SJ • **Baths** Daily: New Royal Bath 9am–9.30pm, last entry 7pm • £36 for 2hr (Sat & Sun £40), £10 per additional hour • **Cross Bath** 10am–8pm, last entry 6pm • Mon–Fri £18, Sat & Sun £20 • **Visitor centre** April–Sept Mon–Sat 10am–5pm, Sun 11am–4pm • Free • ☎ 01225 331234, ⓦ thermaebathspa.com

At the bottom of the elegantly colonnaded Bath Street, the **Thermae Bath Spa** allows you to take the waters in much the same way that visitors to Bath have done throughout the ages, but with state-of-the-art spa facilities. Heated by the city's thermal waters, the spa includes two open-air pools, one on the roof of its centrepiece, the **New Royal Bath**, Sir Nicholas Grimshaw's sleekly futuristic "glass cube". The other, larger pool is inside and has a series of relaxing hydrotherapy jets. There's also a new Wellness Suite, with two steam rooms, an infra-red sauna and ice chamber. There are also various spa treatments on offer, from classic massages to the wonderful **watsu** water massage.

The **Cross Bath** is a separate area, with a small al fresco pool and its own changing facilities. It can be hired for exclusive use. For those who don't want to swim, the small **visitor centre** has displays relating to Bath's thermal waters.

Bath Abbey

Abbey Churchyard, BA1 1LT • March–Oct Mon–Sat 10am–5.30pm, Nov–March Mon–Sat 10am–4.30pm • Free, but £4 donation requested • **Tower tours** From 10/11am: Mon–Fri on the hour, Sat every 30min; 45–50min • £8 • ☎ 01225 422462, ⓦ bathabbey.org

Although there has been a place of Christian worship on this site for well over a thousand years, **Bath Abbey** sat in ruins after the dissolution of the monasteries in 1539, until being repaired in 1616. The Bishop at the time, Oliver King, began work on the ruins of the previous **Norman** building, some of which were incorporated into the new church. The bishop was said to have been inspired by a vision of angels ascending and descending a ladder to heaven, which the present facade recalls on the turrets flanking the central window. The west front also features the founder's signature in the form of carvings of olive trees surmounted by crowns, a play on his name.

The interior was completely transformed in the 1860s and 1870s by Sir George Gilbert Scott in **Victorian Gothic** style and boasts splendid fan vaulting on the ceiling. The floor and walls are crammed with elaborate monuments and memorials, and traces of the grander Norman building are visible in the **Gethsemane Chapel**.

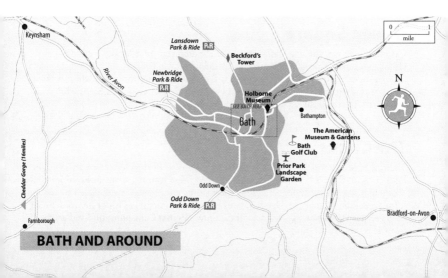

BATH AND AROUND

5

On most days, you can join a **tower tour** to see the massive bells, clock and bell-pulling machinery, and can enjoy a bird's-eye view of Bath – but be prepared for the 212 spiral steps.

Jane Austen Centre

40 Gay St, BA 1 2NT • March–early Nov Daily 9.45am–5.30pm, Nov–March Mon–Fri & Sun 11am–4pm, Sat 9.45am–5.30pm • £12 • ☎ 01225 443000, ⏚ janeausten.co.uk

The **Jane Austen Centre** provides an overview of the author's connections with Bath, illustrated by extracts from her writings, contemporary costumes, furnishings and household items. Visits start with a **talk** every twenty minutes and there's an opportunity to **dress up** in Regency costume and pose with a new waxwork of the author, as well as to have tea in the **Regency Tea Room**.

Austen herself, who wasn't entirely enamoured with the city, lived for a time just down the road at 25 Gay Street – though this was just one of a number of places she inhabited while in Bath.

Queen Square

Queen Square was the first Bath venture of the architect John Wood the Elder (1704–54), champion of **Neoclassical Palladianism**, who lived at no. 15 (not no. 24, as a tablet there asserts). East of the square is the wide shopping strand of Milsom Street, which was designed by Wood as the main thoroughfare of Georgian Bath, while Gay Street runs north to the Circus.

The Circus

The elder John Wood's masterpiece, **The Circus** consists of three crescents arranged in a tight circle of three-storey houses, with a carved frieze running around the entire circle. Wood died soon after laying the foundation stone, and the job was finished by his son, John Wood the Younger (1728–82), who was as instrumental as his father in defining Bath's elegant **Georgian** appearance. The painter **Thomas Gainsborough** lived at no. 17 from 1760 to 1774.

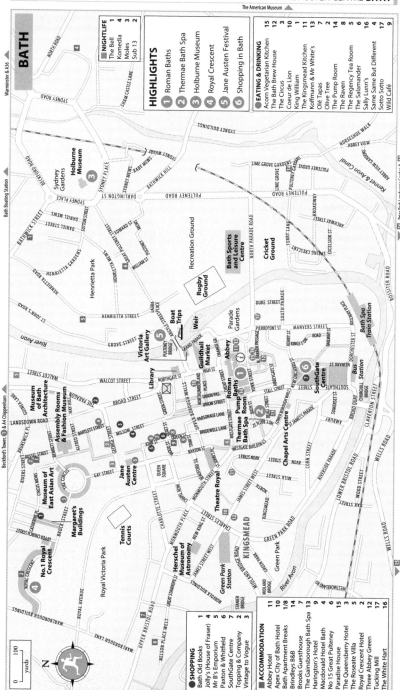

5

The Royal Crescent and Royal Victoria Park

No. 1 Royal Crescent BA1 2LR • Daily 10am–5pm • £10.30, or £16.80 with Museum of Bath Architecture, the Herschel Museum of Astronomy and Beckford's Tower • ☎ 01225 428126, Ⓦ no1royalcrescent.org.uk

The Royal Crescent is the grandest of Bath's crescents, begun by John Wood the Younger in 1767. The stately arc of thirty houses – said to be the country's first crescent – is set off by a spacious sloping lawn from which a magnificent vista extends to green hills and distant ribbons of honey-coloured stone. The interior of **No. 1 Royal Crescent**, on the corner with Brock Street, has been restored to reflect as nearly as possible its original Georgian appearance at the end of the eighteenth century.

At the bottom of the Crescent, Royal Avenue leads onto **Royal Victoria Park**, the city's largest open space, containing an aviary and nine acres of botanical gardens.

Pulteney Bridge

The River Avon is crossed by the graceful, shop-lined **Pulteney Bridge**, an Italianate structure designed by Robert Adam, from the other side of which a lengthy vista stretches along Great Pulteney Street to the imposing classical facade of the **Holburne Museum**.

The Holburne Museum

Great Pulteney St, BA2 4DB • Mon–Sat 10am–5pm, Sun & hols 11am–5pm • Free • ☎ 01225 388569, Ⓦ holburne.org

The classical style building of the **Holburne Museum** has a startlingly modern extension at the back and holds an impressive range of decorative and fine **art**, started by Sir William Holburne, 5th Baronet of Menstrie, in the nineteenth century. The collection is mostly furniture, silverware, porcelain and paintings, including several works by Gainsborough, notably the famous Byam Family, his largest portrait. Look out, too, for works by Constable, Stubbs and Angelika Kauffman.

The Fashion Museum

Assembly Rooms, Bennett St, BA1 2QH • Daily: March–Oct 10.30am–6pm; Nov–Feb 10.30am–5pm; last admission 1hr before closing • £9, or £22.50 with the Roman Baths & Victoria Art Gallery • ☎ 01225 477789, Ⓦ fashionmuseum.co.uk

The younger John Wood's **Assembly Rooms**, east of the Circus, were, with the Pump Room at the Roman Baths, the centre of Bath's **social scene**. The building was virtually destroyed by bombing during World War II, but it has since been perfectly restored and houses the **Fashion Museum**, an entertaining collection of clothing from the Stuart era to the latest designs.

The History of Fashion in 100 Objects exhibition celebrates the evolution of fashion over the last four hundred years and features embroidered coats from Bath's Georgian heyday, Regency fashion from the era of **Jane Austen** and ten shoe "moments" from Georgian silk shoes to Nike trainers. Kids will love the **children's trail**, which shows how children have been dressed throughout history.

Victoria Art Gallery

Bridge St, BA2 4AT • Daily 10.30am–5pm; last admission 20min before closing • Free • Temporary exhibitions £4.50, or £22.50 with the Roman Baths & Victoria Art Gallery • ☎ 01225 477233, Ⓦ victoriagal.co.uk

This council-run art museum holds the city's **art collection**, which is free to visit and includes painting, sculpture and decorative art across two rooms. The smaller space houses the decorative art collection, from British porcelain to a quirky collection of pottery dogs, while the main room has been restored to its Victorian splendour and features five hundred years of European art, including works by Gainsborough.

Herschel Museum of Astronomy

19 New King St, BA1 2BL • Sept–June Mon–Fri 1–5pm, Sat & Sun 10am–5pm; July & Aug Daily 11am–5pm • £6.50 or £16.80 with No. 1 Royal Crescent, Museum of Bath Architecture and Beckford's Tower • ☎ 01225 446865, ⊕ herschelmuseum.org.uk

The small **Herschel Museum of Astronomy** is the former home of the musician and astronomer Sir William Herschel and his sister Caroline, who together discovered the planet **Uranus** here in 1781. Among the furnishings, musical instruments and knick-knacks from the Herschels' era, you can see a replica of the telescope with which the planet was identified – a design of Sir Williams which helped to double the known size of the solar system.

Beckford's Tower

Lansdown Rd, BA1 9BH • March–Oct Sat, Sun & hols 10.30am–5pm, last admission 30min before closing • £4.50 or £16.80 with No. 1 Royal Crescent, Museum of Bath Architecture and Herschel Museum of Astronomy • ☎ 01225 422212, ⊕ beckfordstower.org.uk

This 120ft **Neoclassical tower** was completed in 1827 for writer, art collector and politician William Beckford (1760–1844). It was a sort of "garden shed" – a place to tinker with his collection, read his books and spend time alone with his thoughts. The rooms display furniture made for the tower, as well as paintings and objects illustrating Beckford's fascinating life – as the man once believed to be Europe's wealthiest, as well as one accused of having a homosexual affair with his cousin and murdering his wife Margaret.

A shapely spiral staircase leads to the Belvedere for panoramic **views** of Bath and the countryside around it – on a clear day it's possible to see across Wiltshire as far as **Salisbury Cathedral**, some 35 miles distant.

Museum of Bath Architecture

The Vineyards, The Paragon, BA1 5NA • Mid-Feb to Nov Mon–Fri 1–5pm, Sat & Sun 10am–5pm, last admission 30min before closing • £6.50, or £16.80 with No. 1 Royal Crescent, the Herschel Museum of Astronomy and Beckford's Tower • ☎ 01225 333895, ⊕ museumofbatharchitecture.org.uk

The Georgian-Gothic Countess of Huntingdon's Chapel houses the **Museum of Bath Architecture**, a fascinating exploration of the construction and architecture of the city and a great place to start your visit to the city. Everything is covered, from the kind of facades associated with the two John Woods, older and younger, to balustrades, door designs and such aspects of interior ornamentation as marbling, stencilling and japanning.

The American Museum & Gardens

Claverton Manor, BA2 7BD • March–Oct Tues–Sun 10am–5pm • £14 • ☎ 01225 460503, ⊕ americanmuseum.org

The only museum of **Americana** outside the US is brimming with **folk art** from across the pond. There are ancient maps, pictures and quilts as well as period rooms which show how people in America lived throughout history – there's a seventeenth-century Puritan home, an eighteenth-century tavern and a New Orleans bedroom from the eve of the **Civil War**, all with authentic artefacts and décor from America. The **garden**

5

features the largest collection of American horticulture in the UK, including a replica of George Washington's garden at Mount Vernon.

Prior Park Landscape Garden

Ralph Allen Drive, BA2 5AH • Mid–Feb to Nov daily 10am–5.30pm • £8.20; free to National Trust members • ☎ 01225 833977, Ⓦ nationaltrust.org.uk

Visiting **Prior Park Landscape Garden** is like stepping back into the eighteenth century. Set in a broad valley with views back to Bath, the park features a series of tranquil **lakes** and a centrepiece **Palladian bridge** that is one of only four of its type in the world. Local entrepreneur Ralph Allen created this masterpiece with advice from Capability Brown and today it is popular with local families, who come to see the grazing cows, stately swans and leaping carp.

Just 328yds away is the **Bath Skyline loop walk**, a six-mile trail through meadows, ancient woodland and secluded valleys, which runs in a circle around Bath. It has been clearly waymarked by the National Trust and requires only a moderate level of fitness and 3-4 hours.

ARRIVAL AND INFORMATION
BATH

BY TRAIN

Bath Spa station is a short walk south of the centre at the bottom of Manvers St.

There are regular direct trains to London Paddington on the Great Western Railway (every 30min, 1hr 30min; from £17.50 single; Ⓦ gwr.com), which stop at Great West Way gateways, Chippenham (15min), Swindon (30min) and Reading (1hr). There are also trains to Wiltshire which call at Bradford on Avon (15min), Trowbridge (20min) and Westbury (30min) en route to Salisbury (1hr) and Southampton (1hr 30min), England's main cruise ship port.

BY BUS

Bath's bus station lies next to the train station on Dorchester St. First Group (Ⓦ firstgroup.com) run local services and have an route-planning app. The most useful routes are the number 2, which runs to Prior Park and the number 31 which travels up to Lansdown Road Park & Ride past Beckford's Tower. Both destinations are in the Inner Bath zone (single journey £2.50).

National Express (Ⓦ nationalexpress.com) run direct coach services from Bath to London, calling at Earl's Court and Victoria coach station (daily every 1hr 15min, 3hr 15 min, from £1 one way). There is also a daily non-stop service to Bristol bus station (noon, 40min, from £3.30 one way).

Megabus (Ⓦ megabus.com) has direct non-stop services to London from Bond St, calling at Victoria coach station only (every hour throughout the day, 2hr 35min, from £1).

BY CAR

Park & Ride Bath is plagued by traffic problems and leaving the car outside the city centre is advisable. If you're visiting for the day the best place to park is in one of the Park & Ride car parks (Ⓦ travelwest.info). There are three: at Newbridge to the west (BA1 3NB), Lansdown to the north (BA1 9BJ) and Odd Down (BS4 5LR) to the south (BA2 8PA). Parking is free with no ticket needed; you just pay for the bus into the city (from £3 return). The last bus back is around 8.30pm and overnight parking is not permitted.

Parking If you decide to take your car into the city centre you can expect to pay around £10 for 12 hours or upwards of £17 overnight. The cheapest of the council-run car parks is Charlotte Street (BA1 2NE) which is just off Queen Square (£8.50/12hr, £17/2 days, £25.50/3 days). There are 1,056 spaces.

BY BIKE

The 13-mile Bristol & Bath Railway Path (Ⓦ bristolbath railwaypath.org.uk) connects the two cities along the route of a disused railway line and the River Avon.

Bike hire Nextbike (Ⓦ nextbike.co.uk) is a bike-sharing scheme with 100 bikes and 14 pick-up and drop-off stations around the city. Download the app and you'll receive a four-digit code to unlock the bike. There's no cost to register and hire costs £1/30min.

INFORMATION AND TOURS

★**Around and About Bath** ☎ 08000 747 949, Ⓦ aroundandaboutbath.com. One-day tours in and around Bath for 2-8 people. Itineraries include Bath's

Backstories and Backstreets (on foot, £39.95) and Medieval Marvels & Movies, which takes in Castle Combe and Lacock in neighbouring Wiltshire (by minibus, £149.95). A range of

RIGHT, FROM TOP THE ROYAL CRESCENT; KOFFMANN & MR WHITE'S

5

winter tours is also available including festive jaunts that take in Christmas markets.

Bath Bus Company ⊕ 01225 444102, ⊛ bathbus company.com. Open-top sightseeing bus that does a loop around the city. Use the City Tour route to hop on and off at sites such as the Roman Baths and Royal Crescent or stay onboard for a quick and easy 50min tour of the city, complete with audio commentary (available in 10 languages). The Skyline tour (45min) also takes in the American Museum, Prior Park and the train station. £15.50/24hrs. Tickets also get you discounted entry into many of the top attractions, including the Roman Baths and Jane Austen Centre.

iTours International ⊕ 07890118929, ⊛ itours international.com. Group tours around Bath and further afield (Stonehenge, Lacock) in a variety of languages,

including Spanish, French and German. £95–£295.

Mayor of Bath's Corps of Honorary Guides ⊛ bath guides.org.uk. Informative, free walks by voluntary guides (no tips accepted) around the city for individuals and groups of up to 11. The route is a leisurely two miles and includes all the key sights. No need to book; meet outside the Roman Baths. Sun–Fri 10.30am & 2pm, Sat 10.30am. Evening walks May–Aug Tues & Thurs 6pm.

★ **Savouring Bath** ⊛ savouringbath.com. Get straight to the best bites of Bath's food and drink scene on a 2-3hr tour of the city. Groups are a maximum of 10 and you'll generally get eight food and drink tastings. The Local Flavours tour (£40, Sat 9.30am) is a good introduction to the area's produce and starts at Bath Farmer's Market.

ACCOMMODATION

Abbey Hotel North Parade, BA1 1LF ⊕ 01225 805615, ⊛ abbeyhotelbath.co.uk; map p.117. Independent hotel across three Georgian townhouses, with classic meets contemporary style in the bedrooms and modern British cuisine in the restaurant. The bar serves afternoon tea and a range of mean G&Ts. Book online directly for 10 percent off in the restaurant. **£93**

Apex City of Bath Hotel James St West, BA1 2DA, ⊕ 0808 115 1411, ⊛ apexhotels.co.uk; map p.117. The largest hotel in the city centre has 177 contemporary bedrooms, all with walk-in showers and some with balconies. There's a decent-sized indoor pool too. **£89**

Bath Apartment Breaks 3 Herschel Place and 4 St George's House ⊕ 01225 852861, ⊛ bathapartment breaks.co.uk; map p.117. Two well-kept self-catering apartments, both have two double bedrooms, private parking and wifi. Each is around a 10min walk from the city centre. **£150**

Brindleys B&B 14 Pulteney Gardens, BA2 4HG ⊕ 01225 310444, ⊛ brindleysbath.co.uk; map p.117. Half a dozen light, airy, elegantly decorated rooms that have more than a hint of a French country manor house about them, a feeling that extends to the stylish communal areas. It's set in a quiet residential area just a 5min walk from the centre. **£115**

Brooks Guesthouse 1 Crescent Gardens, Upper Bristol Rd, BA1 2NA, ⊕ 01225 425543, ⊛ brooksguesthouse .com; map p.117. Stylish 22-bedroom guesthouse a few hundred metres from the Royal Crescent. Breakfast is included if you book direct and there's an honesty bar. **£59**

★ **The Gainsborough Bath Spa** Beau St, BA1 1QY ⊕ 01225 358888, ⊛ thegainsboroughbathspa.co.uk; map p.117. The only hotel in the UK with access to natural thermal waters. The hotel occupies two listed buildings, with Georgian and Victorian facades and sits in the heart of the city. Its rooms were custom-designed in 2015 and are understated, with neo-Georgian touches and a soothing

colour scheme. In some you can run a bath with the thermal waters. Book direct and you'll get 20 percent off spa treatments and a bottle of champagne. **£204**

★ **No 15 Great Pulteney** 15 Great Pulteney St, BA2 4BR ⊕ 01225 807422, ⊛ no15greatpulteney.co.uk; map p.117. Bath's grandest street is home to this contemporary luxury hotel, its forty rooms running from cosy loft rooms to massive suites looking out over Bath's best Georgian architecture. Rooms differ greatly – some feature bright murals, others fireplaces and chandeliers – but all are designed with brilliance and a dash of fun. **£122**

Harington's Hotel 8-10 Queen St, BA1 1HE ⊕ 01225 461728, ⊛ haringtonshotel.co.uk; map p.117. Central hotel in a converted townhouse with friendly service and thirteen well-equipped rooms with funky modern decor. There's a hot tub you can book for private relaxation (£7.50pp/60min) and dedicated off-site parking (£11/night). Breakfast is included if you book direct and features lots of local produce; a snack menu is also available throughout the day. **£84**

Macdonald Hotel Bath Sydney Rd, BA2 6NS ⊕ 0344 879 9106, ⊛ macdonaldhotels.co.uk; map p.117. Smart chain hotel in extensive grounds close to the city centre. The 131 rooms are classic in style and there's a pool, gym and thermal suite, plus plenty of private parking. **£140**.

Paradise House 86–88 Holloway, BA2 4PX ⊕ 01225 317723, ⊛ paradise-house.co.uk; map p.117. This seventeenth-century Georgian villa is an uphill trudge from the city centre but has wonderful views to compensate. Open fires in winter, elegant four-posters in some of the rooms, and three rooms opening straight onto the award-winning half acre of gardens. **£150**

The Queensberry Hotel 4-7 Russel St, BA1 2QF ⊕ 01225 447928, ⊛ thequeensberry.co.uk; map p.117. Spread across four Georgian townhouses at the top end of town, The Queensberry combines a clubhouse feel with a quirky boutique vibe. Rooms are tastefully minimalist

– and most have a fabulous bathroom – and there are stylish communal areas, a peaceful walled garden, and a superb basement restaurant (see below). Book direct for ten percent cashback. **£130**

The Roseate Villa Henrietta Rd, BA2 6LX, ☎01225 466329, ⓦroseatevillabath.com; map p.117. Luxurious boutique hotel with 21 stylish rooms. Some have views of the garden, where you can enjoy afternoon tea. **£98**

★**Royal Crescent Hotel & Spa** 16 Royal Crescent, BA1 2LS ☎01225 823333, ⓦroyalcrescent.co.uk; map p.117. Super-luxe five-star hotel in, you've guessed it, Bath's famous Royal Crescent. Step into some very fancy Georgian shoes and live like the aristocracy in beautiful bedrooms overlooking the gardens and lawn. The spa has a heated pool, hydrotherapy and sauna as well as a Taittinger Spa Garden, while the Dower House restaurant has been awarded three AA rosettes for its superb fine dining. Book direct and you'll get complimentary valet parking. **£236**

Three Abbey Green 3 Abbey Green, BA1 1NW ☎01225 428558, ⓦthreeabbeygreen.com; map p.117.

Top-notch B&B in a superbly renovated Georgian house just steps from the abbey. The airy, spotless rooms are beautifully done; the larger ones overlooking a peaceful square are more expensive. **£95**

★**Tucking Mill** Midford, BA2 7DB, ☎07762 191161, ⓦbathselfcatering.net; map p.117. Three beautiful self-catering cottages in the hamlet of Tucking Mill, less than 15min from Bath city centre. The surroundings are gorgeous, with views over Midford Brook, and the cottages are finished to the highest standards. Tucking Mill View and Brooks View sleep two, Fishermen's Retreat sleeps three. There are also two luxury self-catering apartments in Bath city centre (from £170), both sleeping four in two bedrooms. **£105**.

The White Hart Widcombe Hill, BA2 6AA ☎01225 338053, ⓦwhitehartbath.co.uk; map p.117. The comfiest of Bath's hostels has a kitchen, a first-class bar/restaurant and a spacious courtyard. There are four clean doubles and twins available, two en suite. Accommodation not available Sun. Dorms **£20**, doubles **£50**

EATING AND DRINKING

★**Acorn Vegetarian Kitchen** 2 North Parade Passage, BA1 1NX ☎01225 446059, ⓦacornvegetariankitchen .co.uk; map p.117. Classy veggie and vegan restaurant offering dishes such as butternut squash terrine with pine-nut risotto in an unruffled, arty environment. There's a set menu (£28.90 for two courses) and a 5-course taster menu (£45) which can be served with matching wines (£32). Daily noon–3pm & 5.30–9.30pm.

The Bath Brew House 14 James St West, BA1 2BX, ☎01225 805609, ⓦthebathbrewhouse.com; map p.117. With a microbrewery on site there are always home-brewed beers on tap here, plus a menu of pub classics such as burgers (£11.50) and beer-battered fish and chips (£12). Gluten free and vegan options too. Mon–Thurs noon–midnight, Fri–Sat noon–1am, Sun noon–11pm.

The Circus 34 Brock St, BA1 2LN ☎01225 466020, ⓦthecircusrestaurant.co.uk; map p.117. There's a refined but relaxed atmosphere at this family-run café/restaurant, just a stroll from the Royal Crescent. It specializes in Modern European dishes such as chicken roasted with peaches, honey and lavender (£13.50 at lunch, £19.70 at dinner) and Wiltshire lamb rump (£23.30). There's also fish of the day from Devon and Cornwall. Mon–Sat 10am–late.

Coeur de Lion 17 Northumberland Place, BA1 5AR ☎01225 463568, ⓦcoeur-de-lion.co.uk; map p.117. Centrally located tavern on a flag-stoned shopping alley, with a few tables outside (and more upstairs). It's Bath's smallest boozer, serves local Abbey Ales, and is a regular tourist stop, with good lunchtime snacks. Mon–Thurs 11am–11pm, Fri & Sat 11am–midnight, Sun noon–10.30pm.

King William 36 Thomas St, BA1 5NN ☎01225 428096, ⓦkingwilliampub.com; map p.117. North of the centre,

the upstairs dining room at the King William pub regularly receives accolades for its locally sourced dishes, such as pork tenderloin with swede fondue (£18) and pan-fried cod with spiced lentils (£19). The beer and wine list is top-drawer, too. Bar Mon–Fri noon–3pm & 5–11pm, Sat noon–midnight, Sun noon–11pm; restaurant Wed–Fri 6–9pm, Sat 6–10pm, Sun noon–3pm.

The Kingsmead Kitchen 1 Kingsmead Square, BA1 2AA ☎01225 329002, ⓦkingsmeadkitchenbath.co.uk; map p.117. Big all-day breakfasts (£7.95), omelettes, ciabattas and salads are served at this café tucked away in a corner of one of Bath's most attractive squares. There are beers and wines, and outside seating to boot. Mon–Sat 8.30am–6pm, Sun 9am–5pm.

Koffmann & Mr White's Abbey Hotel, North Parade, BA1 1LF, ☎01225 461603, ⓦmpwrestaurants.co.uk; map p.117. Well-known chefs Pierre Koffmann and Marco Pierre White are behind this English and French brasserie, which serves affordable classic dishes such as French onion soup (£6.50) and shepherd's pie (£13.50) in a typically classy setting. Mon–Fri noon–10pm, Sat noon–10.30pm, Sun noon–9.30pm.

★**Olé Tapas** 1 John St, BA1 2JL ☎01225 424274, ⓦoletapas.co.uk; map p.117. Authentic Spanish tapas joint much beloved of the ex-pat community. Come for *jamón de bellota* (£15.95), *huevos rotos* (broken eggs, £4.95) and calamari (£4.95), all served to share tapas-style. Sun–Thurs noon–11pm, Fri & Sat noon–11pm.

★**Olive Tree** Queensberry Hotel, 4-7 Russell St, BA1 2QF ☎01225 447928, ⓦolivetreebath.co.uk; map p.117. One of Bath's top restaurants, this offers exquisite and inventively prepared dishes, a relaxed, contemporary ambience and attentive, friendly service. Whether you order from the tasting menus (£58–82) or opt for individual dishes (mains £26.50–£32), you can sample such dishes as lobster lasagne, pan-fried turbot and pigeon with asparagus and hazelnut. There are also menus for vegetarians, vegans and the dairy-free. Mon–Thurs 7–9.30pm, Fri & Sat 12.30–2pm & 6.30–10pm, Sun 12.30–2pm & 7–9.30pm.

The Pump Room Abbey Churchyard, BA1 1LZ ☎01225 444477, ⓦ romanbaths.co.uk; map p.117. Splash out on a smoked salmon brunch, sample the excellent lunchtime menu (one-course £14, two courses £19) or succumb to a Bath bun or a range of cream teas, all accompanied by a classical trio or pianist. You may have to queue, but you get a good view of the Baths. Daily 9.30am–4.30pm; July, Aug & Dec and during major festivals 9.30am–9pm.

The Raven 6–7 Queen St, BA1 1HE ☎01225 425045, ⓦ theravenofbath.co.uk; map p.117. A civilised spot with first-rate local ales, served both downstairs and in the less crowded upstairs room (unless one of the storytelling nights is being held there). Food available, including renowned pies (£9.80). Mon–Thurs 11am–11pm, Fri & Sat 11am–midnight, Sun 11am–10.30pm.

The Regency Tea Room 40 Gay St, BA1 2NT ☎01225 443000, ⓦ janeausten.co.uk; map p.117. Staff in full Regency regalia serve up afternoon teas "with Mr Darcy" (from £18) and "Mrs Bennet's cake of the day" (£6.95). Champagne is also available. April–June, Sep & Oct 10am–4.30pm, July & Aug 10am–5pm, Nov–March Sun–Fri 10am–3.30pm, Sat 10am–4.30pm.

The Salamander 3 John St, BA1 2JL ☎01225 428889, ⓦ bathales.com; map p.117. Local brewer Bath Ales' pub, with a traditional, dark-wood interior, relaxed atmosphere and tasty dishes available at the bar or in the upstairs restaurant (mains £10–18). Sun–Thurs 11am–11pm, Fri & Sat 11am–1am. Food served Mon–Fri noon–3pm & 6–9pm, Sat noon–9pm, Sun noon–6pm.

Sally Lunn's 4 North Parade Passage, BA1 1NX ☎01225 461634, ⓦ sallylunns.co.uk; map p.117. One of the oldest houses in Bath and where the original Bath "bunn" (like the best brioche you've ever tasted) was created by the eponymous Huguenot baker. The daytime menu (served until 6pm) features Sally Lunn bunns with both savoury and sweet toppings while from 6pm traditional trencher dishes are served, complete with trencher bread, used as a plate and eaten as part of the meal. Mon–Sat 10am–10pm, Sun 10am–9.30pm.

Same Same But Different 7a Prince's Buildings, Bartlett St, BA1 2ED ☎01225 466856, ⓦ same-same .co.uk; map p.117. Excellent café/restaurant that mixes a laidback ambience with quality food – try some of the unusual tapas dishes (from £4.50), or go for something a bit more substantial, such as smoked haddock kedgeree with duck egg (£10). Mon 8am–6pm, Tues–Fri 8am–11pm, Sat 9am–11pm, Sun 10am–5pm.

Sotto Sotto 10 North Parade, BA2 4AL ☎01225 330236, ⓦ sottosotto.co.uk; map p.117. Authentic Italian restaurant in cave-like, brick-vaulted subterranean rooms. The simple but heavenly dishes include orecchiette pasta with spinach and sausage (£11.25), and *pesce spada al salmoriglio* (grilled swordfish; £17.55). Service is superb. It's usually packed, so booking is essential. Daily noon–2pm & 5–10pm.

Wild Café 10a Queen St, BA1 1HE ☎01225 448673, ⓦ wildcafe.co.uk; map p.117. Hidden away down a cobbled side street behind Queen Square, the open kitchen at this popular café does a steady trade in burgers (from £8.95), salads and sandwiches (including an excellent BLT; £5.95), which can also be bought to take away. Mon–Fri 8am–5pm, Sat 9am–6pm, Sun 10am–5pm.

NIGHTLIFE

The Bell 103 Walcot St, BA1 5BW ☎01225 460426, ⓦ thebellinnbath.co.uk; map p.117. Easy-going, slightly grungy tavern with a great jukebox, live music (every Mon from 9pm, alternate Tue or Wed from 9pm, plus Sun lunchtime from 1pm) and DJs (Fri & Sat). There's are plenty of games to keep all amused, from bar billiards to pool, as well as a beer garden with table footy. Mon–Thur 11.30am–11pm, Fri & Sat 11.30am–midnight, Sun noon–10.30pm.

Komedia 22–23 Westgate St, BA1 1EP ☎0845 293 8480, ⓦ komedia.co.uk/bath; map p.117. Cabaret and burlesque, comedy, punk and ska bands, tribute acts and more are all staged at this venue. The popular Krater Comedy Club is held on Sat (6.30pm), after which you can stay on for club nights.

BATH'S FESTIVALS

Bath hosts a great range of festivals throughout the year, notably the **Bath Festival** (ⓦ bathfestivals.org.uk/the-bath-festival), held over ten days in late May and featuring some 130 events taking in jazz, classical and world music, author talks, readings, workshops and debates; the **Bath Fringe Festival** (late May to early June; ⓦ bathfringe.co.uk), with the accent on comedy, cabaret and the performance arts; and the **Jane Austen Festival** (ⓦ janeaustenfestivalbath.co.uk), ten days in mid-September. For further information on these and other festivals, contact **Bath Box Office**, housed in the tourist office at 2 Terrace Walk (☎01225 463362, ⓦ bathboxoffice.org.uk).

Moles 14 George St, BA1 2EN ☎ 01225 437537, ⓦ moles
.co.uk; map p.117. This much-loved Bath institution
features a mix of good live music, DJs and club nights.
Mon–Sat 5pm–late.

Sub 13 4 Edgar Buildings, George St, BA1 2EE ☎ 01225
466667, ⓦ sub13.net; map p.117. Settle into a white

leather booth in the Champagne Lounge or chill out on the
backyard terrace at this trendy basement bar, boasting the
best cocktails in town. Mon–Wed 5pm–midnight, Thurs
5pm–1am, Fri 5pm–3am, Sat 1pm–3am, Sun
1pm–11pm.

ENTERTAINMENT

Chapel Arts Centre St James's Memorial Hall,
Lower Borough Walls BA1 1QR ☎ 01225 463362,
ⓦ chapelarts.org; map p.117. Nice little venue for all
kinds of performing arts, including jazz, folk and comedy.
Arrive early to get one of the cabaret-style tables.

Theatre Royal Sawclose, BA1 1ET ☎ 01225 448844,

ⓦ theatreroyal.org.uk; map p.117. Theatre fans should
check out what's showing at this historic venue, which
opened in 1805 and is one of the country's finest surviving
Georgian theatres, if only for the atmosphere. More
experimental productions are staged in its Ustinov Studio,
with family shows at the egg.

SHOPPING

Bath Old Books 6A Margaret's Buildings, BA1 2LP
☎ 01225 422244 ⓦ forreadingaddicts.co.uk; map
p.117. Long-running bookshop that specialises in second-
hand and antique books and has a great collection of local
titles. Mon–Sat 10am–5pm.

Jolly's 13 Milsom St, BA1 1DD ⓦ houseoffraser.co.uk;
map p.117. Current owners House of Fraser have kept the
historic signage on this long-established and locally loved
department store. You'll find numerous international
brands inside, from Abercrombie & Fitch to Yves Saint

Laurent. Mon–Fri 9.30am–5.30pm, Sat 9am–6pm, Sun
11am–5pm.

Mr B's Emporium 14-15 John St, BA1 2JL ☎ 01255
331155 ⓦ mrbsemporium.com; map p.117. Excellent
independent bookshop, with the latest titles in every genre
displayed in a bright, quirky space. Literary events and talks
too. Mon–Fri 9am–6pm, Sat 9.30am–6.30pm, Sun
11am-5pm.

Paxton & Whitfield 1 John St, BA1 2JL ☎ 01225
466403 ⓦ paxtonandwhitfield.co.uk; map p.117.

JANE AUSTEN FESTIVAL

5

Churchill once said "a gentleman only buys his cheese at Paxton & Whitfield" and they were also the appointed cheesemonger of Queen Victoria. Mon–Sat 9.30am–6pm, Sun 11am–5pm.

SouthGate Centre Southgate St, BA1 1AQ ☎01225 469061 ⓦsouthgatebath.com; map p.117. Bath's largest shopping centre is home to more than fifty stores. Brands include Urban Outfitters, All Saints and Superdry and there are lot of places to eat and drink. Mon–Wed, Fri & Sat 9am–7pm, Thur 9am–8pm, Sun 9am–5pm.

Topping & Company The Paragon, BA1 5LS ☎01225 428111 ⓦtoppingbooks.co.uk; map p.117. Friendly bookstore with all the latest titles and a fantastic range of literary events, many from big-name writers. Daily 8.30am–7.30pm.

Vintage to Vogue 28 Milsom St, BA1 1DG ☎01225 337323 ⓦvintagetovoguebath.co.uk; map p.117. Carefully selected premium vintage clothing for both men and women, including from top-drawer designers. Tue–Sat 11am–5pm.

ACTIVITIES

Bath Golf Club Sham Castle, BA2 6JG ☎01225 466953, ⓦbathgolfclub.org.uk; map p.115. One of England's most attractive inland golf courses, this 6505-yard par 71 course was established in 1880. From £35.

Bailey Balloons ☎01275 375300, ⓦbaileyballoons .co.uk. See Bath from above on a serene hot air balloon flight, launching from Royal Victoria Park. From £110.

Better Bowling Bath Sports and Leisure Centre, North Parade Rd, BA2 4ET ☎01225 486905, ⓦbetter.org.uk; map p.117. Boutique, eight-lane bowling alley. Prices start at £5.95.

Better Extreme Trampoline Park Bath Sports and Leisure Centre, North Parade Rd, BA2 4ET ☎01225 486905, ⓦextreme.better.org.uk; map p.117. Better Extreme has a huge main jump area, basketball hoops and a trapeze as well as a special toddler area. From £8.50.

Original Wild ☎01225 582181, ⓦoriginalwild.com. Outdoor activities company offering guided kayaking adventures (£45) and stand-up paddle boarding, both try sessions for beginners (£15) and safaris for those who have paddled before (£35). A unique way to see the city.

SIDE TRIP

CHEDDAR GORGE AND WOOKEY HOLE

Just 15 miles southwest of Bath is the **Mendip Hills AONB**, a spectacular limestone landscape that is home to two of the area's most impressive natural sights, **Cheddar Gorge** and **Wookey Hole**. Of the two, Cheddar Gorge is the more natural, with gorge **walks** and plenty of **wildlife**, while Wookey Hole has been turned into something of a Disneyland, with numerous **attractions** of varying degrees of authenticity gathered around the eponymous village.

CHEDDAR GORGE

Cheddar, BS27 3QE (24 miles from Bath) • Daily dawn–dusk • Free • ☎01934 744689, ⓦnationaltrust.org.uk

The National Trust own the northern side of England's largest gorge and offer access to **clifftop walks** with dizzying views down into the 400ft-deep fissure. The gorge itself is about 3 miles long and formed about a million years ago when the last Ice Age caused a river of melted glacier water to form here and begin gradually carving its way through the rock. The Cheddar Yeo river is now underground, where it continued its forging of the landscape by creating a series of caves.

CHEDDAR GORGE CAVES

Cheddar, BS27 3QF (24 miles from Bath) • Daily 10am–5pm • £19.95 or £16.95 online in advance, with Longleat £46.95 or £41.98 online • ☎01934 742343, ⓦcheddargorge.co.uk

Climb to the top of **Jacob's Ladder**, a 274-step concrete staircase that heads up through woodland to the top of the gorge, then take on 48 more to reach the top of the metal **Lookout Tower** for views out over the Mendip Hills and Somerset Levels. Underground is **Gough's Cave**, a 500,000-year-old series of chambers that drip with stalactites and open out into cathedral-like spaces with appropriate names like St Paul's Cathedral and Solomon's Temple. An **audio guide** narrates the story of the caves formation, Stone Age occupation and Victorian exploration and tastefully placed lighting highlights the caves' most arresting formations, including the **Black Cat of Cheddar.** The caves are a constant 11°C year-round and are used to age the eponymous **cheese**.

WOOKEY HOLE

Wookey Hole, Wells, BA5 1BB (22 miles from Bath) • April–Oct daily 10am–5pm, Nov, Feb & March daily 10am–4pm, Dec & Jan weekends and hols 10am–4pm • £19 or £16.15 online in advance • ☎01749 672243, ⓦwookey.co.uk

Wookey Hole is the UK's largest **cave system** but it has been almost overshadowed in recent years by the dizzying array of attractions now on offer around this Somerset village – more than twenty of them are included in your ticket price. The caves themselves are certainly impressive and a series of **walkways** takes you through from cavern to cavern, including the **Great Hall** at more than 70ft high and the **Witch's Kitchen**, home to the largest stalagmite in Wookey Hole. The **Witch's Parlour** is especially impressive, a natural underground dome that stretches for more than 200ft. Standing here, more than 110,000 tonnes of rock stand between you and daylight.

Other attractions here include **Pirate Adventure Golf**, a 4D **cinema**, a mirror **maze** and the largest collection of vintage Penny Arcade machines in the country. A highlight for most kids is **Dinosaur Valley**, home to numerous dinosaurs including some animatronic figures.

ACTIVITIES

Escape Rooms at Cheddar ☎01934 742343, ⊛cheddargorge.co.uk. Two different Cheddar-themed escape rooms pit you and your team (2–6 people) against the clock to solve a series of brainteasers and puzzles. From £14.95.

Rocksport ☎01934 742343, ⊛cheddargorge.co.uk. Various climbing experiences at Cheddar Gorge including a beginners' climbing session with seven routes of varying degrees of difficulty to tackle (£22/90min) and the Black Cat Free Fall, jumping from the top of a 30ft ladder into the darkness of Black Cat Chamber (£22 for three jumps).

Wild Wookey ☎01749 677243, ⊛wildwookey.co.uk. Three-hour caving experiences through Wookey Hole caves, including climbing, abseiling and generally squeezing through some very tight spaces. £49.99.

Bristol

Just twelve miles from Bath, on the borders of Gloucestershire and Somerset, Bristol is a city surrounded by gorgeous countryside. And yet it has an unashamedly urban character, with all the trappings of any large English city, as well as being regarded as the unofficial capital of the southwest.

HIGHLIGHTS

❶ Aerospace Bristol Fascinating museum focused on all things flight and giving visitors the chance to board the last Concorde ever built. **See p.151**

❷ Brunel's SS *Great Britain* Moored in the dock in which she was built, this iconic ship is now a museum offering an interactive insight into life aboard a nineteenth-century steamer. **See p.144**

❸ Banksy street art Love graffiti or loathe it, most people can't fail to recognise the talents of Bristol's very own street artist, Banksy, and

some of his best work can be seen around the city. **See p.143**

❹ Clifton Suspension Bridge Brunel's soaring bridge across the plunging Avon Gorge – and the views from it – are best appreciated by walking across it. **See p.147**

❺ Bristol International Balloon Fiesta Europe's largest annual meeting of hot air balloons fills the sky with colour one weekend every August. If you aren't here in August you needn't miss out – Bailey Balloons have flights year-round. **See p.150**

6

The city's mercantile roots are overlaid with an innovative, modern culture, fuelled by technology-based industries, a large student population and a lively arts and music scene. As well as its vibrant nightlife, the city's sights range from medieval churches to cutting-edge attractions highlighting its maritime and scientific achievements.

Weaving through its centre, the River Avon forms part of a system of waterways that made Bristol a great inland port, in later years booming on the transatlantic trafficking of rum, tobacco and slaves. In the nineteenth century, the illustrious Isambard Kingdom Brunel laid the foundations of a tradition of engineering, creating two of Bristol's greatest monuments: the SS *Great Britain* and the lofty Clifton Suspension Bridge.

In 2017 Bristol was named a UNESCO City of Film, bringing it into the Creative Cities Network along with Manchester and international cities such as Sydney and Rome, and today the city is having something of a renaissance. With an influx of young people, many of them priced out of London, the city has taken its place as one of the most forward-thinking in England and there is a vibrant spirit here that few other cities in the country can match. You'll find one of the UK's largest Pride celebrations here, as well as thousands of students and a liberal vibe. All are welcome.

Bristol Cathedral

College Green, BS1 5TJ • Mon–Fri 8am–5pm, Sat & Sun 8am–3.15pm; evensong Mon–Fri 5.15pm, Sat & Sun 3.30pm • Free • Tours usually Tues 2.15pm & Sat 11.30am & 1.30pm; up to 1hr • Free (suggested donation £5) • ⓦ bristol-cathedral.co.uk

Founded as an abbey around 1140 on the supposed spot of St Augustine's convocation with Celtic Christians in 603, venerable **Bristol Cathedral** became a cathedral church with the Dissolution of the Monasteries in the mid-sixteenth century. The two towers on the west front were erected in the nineteenth century in a faithful act of homage to Edmund Knowle, an architect and abbot who lived in the fourteenth century.

The interior offers a unique example among Britain's cathedrals of a German-style medieval "**hall church**", in which the aisles, nave and choir rise to the same height. Abbot Knowle's immense **choir** offers one of the country's most exquisite illustrations of the early Decorated Gothic style, while the adjoining thirteenth-century **Elder Lady Chapel** contains some fine tombs and eccentric carvings of animals, including (between the arches on the right) a monkey playing the bagpipes accompanied by a ram on the violin. The **Eastern Lady Chapel** has some of England's finest examples of heraldic glass and in the nave you can see windows commemorating World War II.

From the south transept, a door leads to the **Chapter House**, a richly carved piece of Romanesque architecture which dates from around 1160.

6

BRISTOL AIRPORT

Bristol Airport (ⓦbristolairport.co.uk) is an excellent gateway for international visitors to the Great West Way (ⓦGreatWestWay.co.uk). Far smaller than London's Heathrow, it has just one terminal and handles a fraction of the traffic, making arriving and departing from here a more pleasant experience.

Located just eight miles southwest of the city centre, travelling in to Bristol from its airport is a breeze. A regular bus (daily 24hrs; from 6.40am–7.30pm at least every 10min, less regular at other times; journey 30min; from £7 one-way when booked in advance, (ⓦflyer.bristolairport .co.uk) runs directly into the city centre, calling at Bristol Temple Meads train station and the city's main bus station. All the major car rental companies have large fleets here and you'll find their offices within walking distance of the terminal building. The airport is just off the A38 main road, a 45min drive from Bath and 30min from the M4 motorway which speeds traffic eastwards towards Swindon and London.

The New Room

36 The Horsefair, BS1 3JE • Mon–Sat 10.30am–4pm • Free; museum £6 • ⓦ newroombristol.org.uk

Built in 1739, John Wesley's **New Room** is the oldest **Methodist building** in the world. The chapel has served many purposes over the years, from a school to a free medical dispensary, and before the death of John Wesley, who founded Methodism, it was the most important centre of Methodism outside London. Today regular worship is still held, including a Communion service on Fridays at 1pm which is open to all. There is

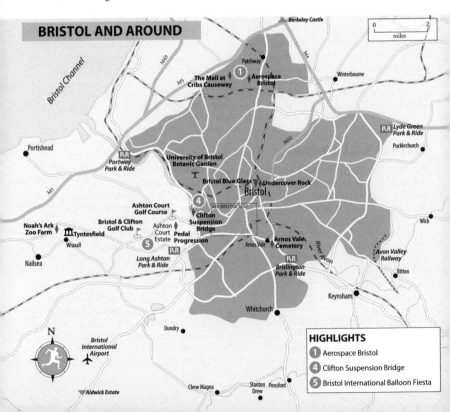

BANKSY AND THE BRISTOL STREET-ART SCENE

An integral part of Bristol's cultural profile, the street artist known as **Banksy** has (more or less) managed to maintain his anonymity, despite global fame which has seen exhibitions pulling in crowds from London to Los Angeles.

Banksy was born in Bristol in 1974 and it was here, in a city known since the 1980s for its **graffiti art**, that he first made his mark, leaving his stencilled daubs and freehand murals on walls throughout the inner city.

Websites such as Ⓦ bristol-street-art.co.uk will allow you to track down his surviving murals, though it's easy enough to locate his more iconic works such as *The Mild Mild West* (1999) on Stokes Croft and *The Naked Man* (2006) off the bottom of Park Street. One of his most recent is *The Girl with the Pierced Eardrum*, ono a building in Albion Docks in Hanover Place.

Banksy's global celebrity has led to his works becoming accepted and even protected by the city, and the council has given its blessing to **Upfest** (Ⓦ upfest.co.uk), touted as Europe's largest street-art and graffiti festival; it takes place in **Bedminster**, South Bristol, over a weekend in late July.

6

also a small **museum** with displays on how Methodism spread throughout Britain and the world; those on Wesley's stand against **slavery** are particularly interesting.

Bristol's Museums

Bristol's leading **museums** are home to artefacts spanning art, archaeology, geology and natural history. Although each museum has its own identity, all work together to promote this world-class collection and it is worth devoting a day or so to touring them. Even better, all are free.

The Georgian House Museum

7 Great George St, BS1 5RR · April–Dec Sat–Tues 11am–4pm · Free · ☎ 0117 921 1362, Ⓦ bristolmuseums.org.uk

Built in 1791, the deceptively large **Georgian House Museum** is the former home of a local sugar merchant, its spacious and faithfully restored rooms filled with sumptuous examples of **period furniture**. There are eleven rooms to visit, over four floors. The basement gives particular insight into domestic times past, while upstairs, illustrated panels tell the story of the family's dealings in the West Indies, including their involvement in slavery.

Bristol Museum and Art Gallery

Queen's Rd, BS8 1RL · Tues–Sun 10am–5pm, daily during school hols · Free · ☎ 0117 922 3571, Ⓦ bristolmuseums.org.uk

Housed in a grandiose Edwardian-Baroque building, the **Bristol Museum and Art Gallery** has sections on local archaeology, geology and natural history, as well as an important collection of Chinese porcelain and some magnificent Assyrian reliefs carved in the eighth century BC. Artworks by **Banksy**, the **Bristol School** and **French Impressionists** are mixed in with some choice older pieces, including a portrait of Martin Luther by Cranach the Elder and Giovanni Bellini's unusual *Descent into Limbo*.

This is a good place to get a handle on local affairs. On the ground floor there's a collection introducing the **wildlife** of southwest England, while the first floor houses a selection of fascinating **maps** and prints that show how Bristol has changed and developed over the centuries.

The Red Lodge Museum

Park Row, BS1 5LJ · April–Dec Sat–Tues 11am–4pm · Free · ☎ 0117 921 1360, ⓦ bristolmuseums.org.uk/red-lodge-museum

This Elizabethan house was originally a lodge to the Great House, which once stood on the site of the present **Colston Hall** and played host to Elizabeth I. Today it is a time capsule of a **museum**, with some of the oldest rooms in the city on display.

The **Original Lodge** is made up of three rooms that show the original 1580 design of the house, including the **Great Oak Room** – the last complete example of an Elizabethan room in Bristol. It took a team of craftsmen two years to carve the oak wall panelling, carve the intricate stonework of the fireplace and mould the dramatic ceiling and the room is a clear example of how showing off among local merchants reached fanatical levels.

The rest of the museum is a three-storey extension to the original building and shows how family life in the 1730s would have looked. Outside, the **Knot Garden** was restored in the 1980s, the design of the low hedges taken from the plasterwork in the master bedroom of the house.

Blaise Castle House Museum

Henbury Rd, BS10 7QS · April–Dec Thurs–Sun 11am–4pm · Free · ☎ 0117 903 9818, ⓦ bristolmuseums.org.uk

Bristol Museums' **social history collection** is housed in a vast nineteenth-century mansion set in 400 acres of parkland 5 miles north of the city centre.

The **Bristol at Home** galleries are particularly fascinating, with all manner of household equipment from the last three hundred years on display – including a collection of china toilets. There is also an extensive selection of **fashions** from the 1730s to the present day and an engaging display of **toys**, including train sets, dolls' houses, lead soldiers and a Sindy doll from the 1980s.

Bristol Harbourside

Bristol has tarted up its **waterfront** and what was once a noisy, dirty docks area is today a lively destination. You'll find yourself at the **HARBOURSIDE** at least once during your time in Bristol – not least because it's home to some of the city's best places to eat and drink, as well as nearby **Queen Square** - setting for several well-known TV shows.

Bristol Aquarium

Anchor Rd, BS1 5TT · Daily 10am–5pm · £15.30 (£13.77 online in advance) · ☎ 0117 929 8929, ⓦ bristolaquarium.co.uk

Bristol's **Aquarium** doesn't just jump straight in to showcasing exotic species from around the world (though it has plenty of them). Instead, it starts with a focus on native **marine life**, with species including a giant common lobster called Dale and a glowing family of moon jellyfish bred here at the aquarium on display. There's also a native shark collection that features a cast made up of some of the 33 different species found in UK waters.

The **Mighty Amazon** display holds numerous large freshwater fish, while the centrepiece **Coral Seas** exhibit, with its walk-through underwater tunnels, has more than 250 species swimming through it, including leopard sharks, pufferfish, eels and – of course – Nemo and Dory (aka clownfish and surgeonfish).

Brunel's SS *Great Britain*

Great Western Dockyard, Gas Ferry Rd BS1 6TY · Daily: April–Oct 10am–6pm; Nov–March 10am–4.30pm, last admission 1hr before closing; Go Aloft daily noon–5pm · £16.50, or £15.70 online in advance · ☎ 0117 926 0680, ⓦ ssgreatbritain.org

Harbourside's major draw, and one of Bristol's iconic sights, the SS *Great Britain* was the first propeller-driven, ocean-going iron ship in the world, built by Isambard Kingdom

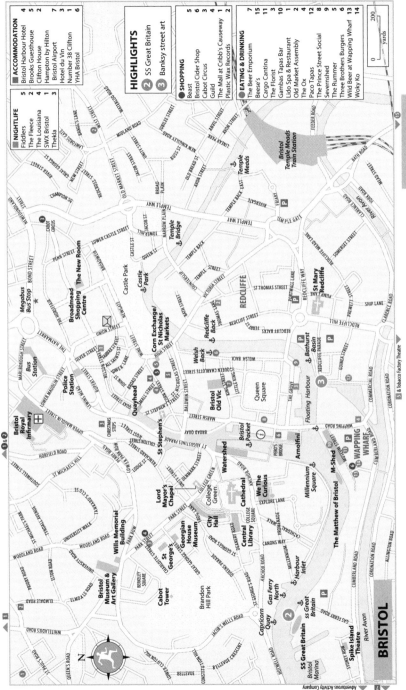

■ ACCOMMODATION
Bristol Harbour Hotel	4
Brooks Guesthouse	5
Clifton House	2
Hampton by Hilton	7
Bristol Airport	3
Hotel du Vin	1
Number 38 Clifton	3
YHA Bristol	6

■ NIGHTLIFE
Fiddlers	5
The Fleece	2
The Louisiana	4
SWX Bristol	1
Thekla	3

● HIGHLIGHTS
SS Great Britain	2
Banksy street art	3

● SHOPPING
Beast	5
Bristol Cider Shop	6
Cabot Circus	3
Guild	4
The Mall at Cribb's Causeway	1
Plastic Wax Records	2

● EATING & DRINKING
The Beer Emporium	7
Beese's	15
Cargo Cantina	11
The Florist	3
Gambas Tapas Bar	10
Lido Spa & Restaurant	1
Old Market Assembly	2
The Ox	4
Paco Tapas	12
The Prince Street Social	8
Sevenshed	9
The Rummer	5
Three Brothers Burgers	6
Wild Beer at Wapping Wharf	13
Woky Ko	14

6

Brunel in 1843. She initially ran between Liverpool and New York, then between Liverpool and Melbourne, circumnavigating the globe 32 times and chalking up over a million miles at sea. Her ocean-going days ended in 1886 when she was caught in a storm off Cape Horn, and she was eventually recovered and returned to Bristol in 1970. On board, you can see restored **cabins** and the immense **engine**, as well as the promenade deck and first-class **dining saloon**.

On the main deck **Go Aloft!** gives (brave) visitors the chance to step into a Victorian sailor's shoes and climb the rigging that rises 82ft in a lattice of ropes up from the deck before edging out onto the main yard, or mast, a further 30ft above the **Great Western Dockyard**. The views down over the Harbourside and city are quite literally breathtaking.

The ship stands in the dry dock in which she was built and a watery ceiling gives the impression of standing underwater as you walk around her hull, bathed in a constant stream of dry air to dehumidify the iron and keep it from corroding. The adjoining **Dockyard Museum** gives the background of the vessel and of Bristol's long shipbuilding history, while the new **Being Brunel museum** hosts an exhibition about the man himself and features a recreation of Brunel's London office as well as the restored clerks' office – from which the view out over the ship is exactly as it was in 1850 during the build.

We The Curious

One Millennium Sq, Anchor Rd, BS1 5DB • Mon–Fri 10am–5pm, Sat, Sun & hols 10am–6pm • From £15.95. Model-making workshops £3.50 • ☎ 0117 915 1000, ⓦ wethecurious.org

This massive hands-on **science centre** is the sort of place you can happily lose yourself for a few hours – especially if you have **kids** in tow. The exhibits are set up to induce curiosity and offer all sorts of fun and frolics, including the chance to walk through a tornado, create a TV show and cover yourself in a giant bubble.

The centre is also home to the UK's first **3D planetarium** and hosts model making workshops with **Aardman Animations**, based in Bristol and known for their *Wallace and Gromit* films.

M Shed

Princes Wharf, Wapping Rd, BS1 4RN • Tues–Sun & hols 10am–5pm • Free • ☎ 0117 352 6600, ⓦ bristolmuseums.org.uk/m-shed

Housed in an old harbourside transit shed, the superb **M Shed** museum is dedicated to Bristol itself, past and present. It's an enjoyable, unashamedly populist survey, full of memorabilia and anecdotes and casting light on everything from the city's mercantile history to its festivals and street life.

On the ground floor, **Bristol Places** charts the city's changing face, taking in its development as a port and the hardships of World War II. On the floor above, **Bristol People** and the adjoining **Bristol Life** galleries look at the people who have shaped the city, with the former including a small display on Bristol's links with the transatlantic slave trade. Afterwards, head out to the long terrace for fantastic harbour views.

The *Matthew* of Bristol

Prince's Wharf, BS1 4RN • Free • March–Nov Tues–Sun 10am–4pm, Dec–Feb Sat & Sun 10am–4pm • ☎ 0117 927 6868 • ⓦ matthew.co.uk

The *Matthew* that cruises around Bristol harbour today is a replica of the original ship that John Cabot sailed across the Atlantic to "discover" North America in 1497 and was built in 1997 to celebrate the 500th anniversary of his sailing to Newfoundland.

When she is moored in her usual spot at Prince's Wharf all are welcome to step aboard and explore her wooden decks. There is also a calendar of public sailing

THE SLAVE TRADE IN BRISTOL

Over two hundred years after the abolition of the British slave trade, Bristol is still haunted by the instrumental part it played in the trafficking of African men, women and children to the New World – indeed, according to some interpretations, it was Bristol-born Sir John Yeamans, a Barbados planter, who effectively introduced slavery to North America.

The slave trade in Britain was monopolized by the London-based **Royal African Company** until 1698, when the market was opened to all. For the next hundred years, Bristol's merchants were able to participate in the "triangular trade" whereby brass pots, glass beads and other manufactured goods were traded for slaves on the coast of West Africa, who were then shipped to plantations in the Americas, the vessels returning to Europe with cargoes of sugar, cotton, tobacco and other slave-labour-produced commodities. By the 1730s, Bristol had become – along with London and Liverpool – one of the main beneficiaries of the trade; in 1750 alone, Bristol ships transported some eight thousand of the twenty thousand slaves sent that year to **colonies** in the Caribbean and America. The direct profits, together with the numerous spin-offs, helped to finance some of the city's finest Georgian architecture.

Bristol's primacy in the trade had been long supplanted by Liverpool by the time opposition to slavery began to gather force: first the Quakers and Methodists, then more powerful forces voiced their discontent. By the 1780s, the Anglican Dean Josiah Tucker and the Evangelical writer Hannah More had become active **abolitionists**, and Samuel Taylor Coleridge made a famous anti-slavery speech in Bristol in 1795.

The British slave trade was finally **abolished** in 1807, but its legacy is still felt strongly in the city, particularly in the divisive figure of Edward Colston. The eighteenth-century sugar magnate is revered by many as a great philanthropist – his name given to numerous buildings, streets and schools in Bristol – but also reviled as a leading light in the Royal African Company. His statue on Colston Avenue has more than once been the subject of graffiti attacks and calls for its removal, and famous Bristol band **Massive Attack** refused to play the Colston Hall because of the connotations of its name, which is scheduled to be changed for the venue's reopening in 2020.

trips, including fish and chips and cream tea cruises around the harbour and longer jaunts along Avon Gorge.

Clifton

On the western side of the city, **CLIFTON**, once an aloof spa resort, is now Bristol's stateliest neighbourhood. At the top of Blackboy Hill, the wide green expanses of **Durdham Down** and **Clifton Downs** stretch right up to the edge of the **Avon Gorge**, a popular spot for picnickers, joggers and kite-flyers. On the southern edge of the Downs is the select enclave of **Clifton Village**, centred on the Mall, where **Royal York Crescent**, the longest Georgian crescent in the country, offers splendid views over the steep drop to the River Avon below.

Clifton Suspension Bridge

Bridge Rd, BS8 3PA • Free, £1 for motor vehicles • Visitor Centre Daily 10am–5pm • Free • Guided tours Easter–Oct Sat & Sun 3pm; 45min • ☎ 0117 974 4664 • ⊕ cliftonbridge.org.uk

A few minutes' walk from Clifton Village is Bristol's most famous symbol, **Clifton Suspension Bridge**, 702ft long and poised 245ft above the high water line. Money was first put forward for a bridge to span the Avon Gorge by a Bristol wine merchant in 1754, though it wasn't until 1829 that a competition was held for a design – won by **Isambard Kingdom Brunel** in a second round – and not until 1864 that the bridge was completed, five years after Brunel's death. Hampered by financial difficulties, the bridge never quite matched the engineer's original ambitious design, which included Egyptian-style towers topped by sphinxes at each end.

You can see copies of his plans in the **visitor centre** at the far side of the bridge, alongside designs proposed by Brunel's rivals, some of them frankly bizarre. There's also a coffee cart here in summer.

Clifton Observatory

Bridge Rd, BS8 3PA · **Camera obscura & museum** £2.50, **Giant's cave** £2.50, both £4 · Summer daily 10am–5pm, winter daily 10am–4pm, last admission 15min before closing· Free · ☎ 0117 974 1242 · ⓦ cliftonobservatory.com

The **Clifton Observatory** started life as a mill and was once Bristol's main "snuff", or tobacco, mill. After a fire in 1777 it was left derelict until artist William West took it as his studio and added a telescope in 1828; he added the **camera obscura** in 1829.

The camera obscura projects an image of the surrounding area, including Clifton Suspension Bridge, Avon Gorge and Clifton Downs, and is one of only a handful to still be operating in the UK.

West also built a 200ft-long tunnel from his observatory to **St Vincent's Cave**, in Bristolian folklore the home of two giants Goram and Ghyston. The cave opens out onto the cliff face at the side of Avon Gorge, 250ft above the River Avon for spectacular views.

Bristol Zoo Gardens

Clifton, BS8 3HA · Daily 9am–5.30pm, last admission 1hr before closing· From £12 (£10 online), **ZooRopia** £7.65 · ☎ 0117 428 5300, ⓦ bristolzoo.org.uk

Bristol Zoo was opened in 1836 by Henry Riley, a local physician, and is the world's fifth oldest zoo. The zoo's goal is conservation and they can be credited with helping to save more than 175 species from extinction. The 12 acres of gardens harbour some four hundred species of animals from around the world; highlights include gorillas, red pandas, African penguins and ring-tailed lemurs.

There are a variety of animal **experiences** you can book (from £69), including "meet and greets" with the zoo's most popular animals (including those penguins and red pandas), the chance to hand-feed an Asiatic lion and a day spent helping one of the zoo's keepers.

The zoo is also home to **ZooRopia**, a high ropes course, and a particularly adventurous **adventure playground**.

RIVER AVON TRAIL

The 23-mile **River Avon Trail** (ⓦ riveravontrail.org.uk) runs along the eponymous waterway from the village of Pill, just west of Bristol, to Bath. For most of the route the path is well-made, with loose stone tracks and paved sections making it an easy stroll for most walkers. Through Bristol the path is surprisingly pleasant, keeping away from the roads most of the time and running through **Harbourside**.

The short section between Conham and Hanham, just to the east of Bristol, is also a **public bridleway** and open to horses. From Pill to Hanham it is possible to **cycle** most of the trail. At Hanham cyclists can take the A431 to Bitton and pick up the Bristol & Bath Railway Path for the last 8 miles to Bath.

A route guide with clear, useful **maps** can be downloaded from the website.

Leigh Woods National Nature Reserve

Valley Rd · Daily dawn–dusk · Free · ☎ 0117 973 1645, ⓦ nationaltrust.org.uk/leigh-woods

Get a different view on the famous Clifton Suspension Bridge by taking a walk in this area of diverse **woodland**, made up of oak, small leaf lime and ash, which fills the plateau on the far side of Avon Gorge. In spring this is a great place to see carpets of bluebells – a quintessential English scene – and in summer there are plenty of shady **strolls**. At any time of year there are fine views back to the city.

The woods are looked after by the **National Trust** and are well-maintained, with established footpaths marked by colour-coded **waymarks**. A **map** can be downloaded from the website, which shows the trails, including a section of the **River Avon Trail**. The rangers hut has **information** and maps as well as a compost toilet. Picnic tables are provided; no barbecues.

Ashton Court Estate

Long Ashton, BS41 9JN · **Grounds** Daily Nov–Jan 8am–5.15pm, Feb 8am–6.15pm, March & Oct 8am–7.15pm, April & Sept 8am–8.15pm, May–Aug 8am–9.15pm · Free; parking £1.20/day · ☎ 0117 963 9176 · ⓦ bristol.gov.uk · **House** Wed–Sun 11am–4pm · Free · ☎ 0117 963 3438, ⓦ artspacelifespace.com · **Miniature railway** March–Oct & Dec Sun noon–5pm · 90p · ☎ 0117 946 7110, ⓦ bristolmodelengineers.co.uk

Once a family home but now owned by the local council and open to all, **Ashton Court Estate** has 850 acres of grounds presided over by stately ancient oak trees and a herd of deer. This is where Bristol decamps to on weekends and holidays and you're sure to see local families playing games and having picnics.

There are also plenty of more organised **activities**. A **miniature railway**, operated by Bristol Model Engineers, runs on two looped tracks through the grounds and on Saturdays at 9am there's a free 5km timed **run** operated by Parkrun (ⓦparkrun.org.uk).

The house itself currently has an uncertain future, though local arts company Artspace Lifespace hope to turn it into an arts venue for performances and community activities.

Arnos Vale Cemetery

Bath Rd, BS4 3EW · Daily 9am–5pm · Free (donations welcome) · ☎ 0117 971 9117, ⓦ arnosvale.org.uk

A cemetery might not sound like the most enjoyable place to visit, but this is no ordinary cemetery. Arnos Vale is one of Britain's best examples of a Victorian garden cemetery, with numerous self-guided walks (dogs on leads welcome) running through its 45 acres of

---

BRISTOL INTERNATIONAL BALLOON FIESTA

Every August the **Bristol International Balloon Fiesta** (ⓦbristolballoonfiesta.co.uk), Europe's largest annual meeting of **hot air balloons**, takes place at **Ashton Court Estate**. Well over a hundred balloons congregate here from around the globe and over four days fill the sky above the city with colour.

There are balloon **rides**, **food stalls** and a **fairground** with a carousel and helter skelter, plus daily balloon lifts (Fri–Sun 6am & Thurs–Sun 6pm) when the balloons take off en masse across Bristol. The highlight is the **Nightglows and Fireworks Finale** (Thurs & Sat 9pm) when a handful of balloons tethered to the ground are lit up to a backdrop of fireworks.

Admission is **free** but parking isn't and should be booked in advance (from £11.79). Several operators offer balloon flights as part of the fiesta, as well as at other times. Bailey Balloons (☎01275 375300, ⓦbaileyballoons.co.uk) offers flights year-round, including taking off from Ashton Court for views of Clifton and the Suspension Bridge. From £110.

woodland dotted with classical buildings, historical monuments and sculptures. The woodland is a mix of numerous species including horse chestnut, Chilean pines and English yews and there's plenty of wildlife, including a roe deer which makes a regular appearance. On summer Saturdays there's a themed guided tour (May–Oct, 1.30pm, £5).

Aerospace Bristol

Filton Airfield, Hayes Way, Patchway, BS34 5BZ · Daily 10am–5pm, last admission 1hr before · £15 · ☎ 0117 931 5315, ⓦ aerospacebristol.org

Bristol has played a starring role in British **aviation history** and hundreds of planes were built at **Filton**, a few miles north of the city. By far the most famous is **Concorde**, the supersonic jet plane that whisked travellers from England to New York in an average of just 3.5 hours. Every British Concorde ever built made her maiden flight from **Filton Airfield** and a glittering new **museum** here has finally given the last Concorde ever built, which long languished on a strip of disused runway, the home she deserves.

A former World War I hangar houses a museum of flight, with exhibits covering more than a century of aviation achievements and tells the story of the **British and Colonial Aeroplane Company** that was founded here in 1910. Concorde herself, *Alpha Foxtrot*, is now resting in a specially constructed hangar next door and visitors can follow in the footsteps of rock stars by boarding her for a look around.

Avon Valley Railway

Bitton Station, Bath Rd, BS30 6HD · Weekends and selected weekdays 11am–5pm · diesel £7, steam £8 · ☎ 0117 932 5538,
ⓦ avonvalleyrailway.org

A **heritage railway** that has been kept alive by passionate volunteers. Once part of British Rail, the Avon Valley line was axed by the infamous Dr Beeching in the 1960s. Today three miles of track has been preserved and both diesel and steam locomotives run through bucolic scenery from the Victorian train station at Bitton. There's a small **museum** as well as **train rides** and a station **buffet** serving breakfast, lunch and afternoon tea.

University of Bristol Botanic Garden

The Holmes, Stoke Park Rd, Stoke Bishop BS9 1JG · Feb & March Mon–Fri 10am–4.30pm, Sat & Sun 10.30am–3pm, April–end Nov daily
10am–4.30pm, Dec & Jan Mon–Fri 10am–4.30pm · £5.50 · ☎ 0117 932 5538, ⓦ bristol.ac.uk/botanic-garden

The five-acre **University of Bristol Botanic Garden** is home to a whopping 4,500 plant species. These include many native plants but there are also Chinese and Western medicinal herb gardens and a Mediterranean plant collection.

The three glasshouses feature diverse environments such as the Amazon rainforest, the highveld in South Africa and even cloud forests. They are packed with exotic plants including the Giant Amazon Waterlily and the largest collection of Sacred Lotus in the country.

Tyntesfield

Wraxall, BS48 1NX · Daily house 11am–pm, gardens until 6pm · £17.20, £10.60 gardens and estate only; free for National Trust members ·
☎ 01275 461900, ⓦ nationaltrust.org.uk

What is most staggering about **Tyntesfield** is that it was built as a family home – its Victorian Gothic architecture is imposing enough to have served as something far grander. The Gibb family lived here for four generations, each one adding their own touches to the place, and today the house is a confection of stylish bits and bobs that make it quite the treasure trove. In the grounds there is a splendid Gothic chapel with a mosaic floor and brass chandelier.

Noah's Ark Zoo Farm

6

Clevedon Rd, Wraxall, BS48 1PG • Feb–Nov Mon–Sat 10.30am–5pm, Dec & Jan 10.30am–4pm • £18 • ☏ 01275 852606, Ⓦ noahsarkzoofarm.co.uk

Noah's Ark is a hands-on zoo and working farm that is firmly focused on conservation and sustainability. The animals that live here range from farmyard favourites such as donkeys and pigs to more exotic species such as Bengal tigers and African lions and there are a variety of experiences available, from spending the morning as an elephant keeper to feeding the big cats their breakfast (from £20). There's also a gigantic hedge maze and a large indoor play area for rainy days.

Berkeley Castle

GL13 9BQ • Castle: late March–end Oct Sun–Wed 10.30am–5pm, last admission 4pm; Butterfly house: May–Sept Sun–Wed 10.30am–5pm • £12.50 • ☏ 01453 810303, Ⓦ berkeley-castle.com

Originally built to "keep out the Welsh", Berkeley Castle has been inextricably linked with England's history for nine centuries and the family still live in their ancestral home – this is the oldest castle in the country to still be lived in by the family who built it.

Since it was built for defence, there are trip steps, arrow slits and murder holes as well as battlements that drop some 60ft to the Great Lawn below, but the castle has always been a family home first and there are tapestries, paintings and ceramics collected over centuries on display too: look out for Queen Elizabeth I's bedspread.

Outside there are extensive grounds, including an old walled kitchen garden that is now home to the Butterfly House,, a tropical environment where you can see around forty species of butterfly flying freely. There is also a range of family activities, including games, trails and crafts.

ARRIVAL AND INFORMATION   BRISTOL

BY TRAIN

Bristol Temple Meads train station is a 20min walk east of the city centre. There are regular direct trains to London Paddington on the Great Western Railway (every 30min, 1hr 40min; from £20 single; Ⓦ gwr.com), which stop at Great West Way gateways: Bath Spa (15min), Chippenham (30min), Swindon (45min) and Reading (1hr 15min). There are also trains to Wiltshire which call at Bradford on Avon (25min), Trowbridge (30min) and Westbury (40min) en route to Salisbury (1hr 10min) and Southampton (1hr 40min), England's main cruise ship port. Great Western Railway also run trains from Bristol Temple Meads to Filton Abbey Wood (10min, from £4 return), which is a one-mile walk from Aerospace Bristol.

BY BUS

Bristol's bus and coach station is centrally located off Marlborough St. First Group (Ⓦ firstgroup.com) run local services and have an app which can plan your route for you.

The most useful routes are the A1 airport flyer to Bristol Airport (24hrs; 30min; from £7 one-way in advance, Ⓦ flyer.bristolairport.co.uk) and the T2 which runs north to Filton Gipsy Patch Lane (30min), half a mile from Aerospace Bristol, and Cribbs Causeway shopping centre (40min). Both stops are in the Inner Bristol zone (single journey £3). To reach Arnos Vale, take bus 1, X39, 57, 178 or 349 from the city centre (single £3).

National Express (☏ 0871 781 8181, Ⓦ national express.com) run non-stop coach services from Bristol to London, calling at Earl's Court and Victoria coach station (daily every 1hr 15min, 2hr 35min, from £5 one way). There is also a daily non-stop service to Bath bus station (4.15pm, 50min, from £3.30 one way). This service continues on to Swindon (2hr 10min, from £5.10), calling at Corsham (1hr 20min) and Chippenham (1hr 35min).

Megabus (☏ 0141 352 4444, Ⓦ megabus.com) have direct non-stop services to London from their stop outside

RIGHT, FROM TOP AEROSPACE BRISTOL; BERKELEY CASTLE

6

Black's camping shop on Bond St, calling at Victoria coach station only (roughly every hour throughout the day, 2hr 35min, from £1).

BY CAR

Park & Ride Like most major UK cities, traffic and parking can be a problem in Bristol and leaving the car outside the city centre is advisable. If you're visiting for the day the best place to park is in one of the Park & Ride car parks (ⓦtravelwest.info). There are four: at Portway to the north west (BS11 9QE), Long Ashton to the southwest (BS3 2HB), Brislington to the south east (BS4 5LR) and Lyde Green (BS4 5LR) to the north east (BS4 5LR). Parking is free with no ticket needed; you just pay for the bus into the city (from £3 return). The last bus back is around 9pm and overnight parking is not permitted.

Parking If you must take your car into the city centre and plan to leave it overnight you can expect to pay around £15–20 a day. Cabot Circus car park is open 24 hours a day and is perhaps the easiest to find, just off the M32 (BS2 9AB, 7am–5pm £2.30 for the first hour then £1/hr, over 7hr £18/day, 5pm–7am £2). It has 2,500 spaces, 74 dedicated family spaces and 18 free electric car charging points.

BY BIKE

The 13-mile Bristol & Bath Railway Path (ⓣ0117 922 4325, ⓦbristolbathrailwaypath.org.uk) connects the two cities along the route of a disused railway line and the course of the River Avon.

Bike rental Bristol Cycle Shack (ⓣ0117 955 1017, ⓦbristolcycleshack.co.uk) rents out bikes from £15/day including helmet and lock; Cycle the City (ⓣ07873 387167, ⓦcyclethecity.org) have bikes made in Bristol from £16/day (closed Mon & Tues). **Bristol Tandem Hire** (ⓣ07470 311592, ⓦbristoltandemhire.co.uk) hires tandems and there are various pick up points around Bristol, seats for babies and recommended routes you can follow. Half day £40.

INFORMATION AND TOURS

Brewerism ⓣ07564 017670, ⓦbrewerism.co.uk. Group tours (minimum 10) around Bristol's best microbreweries and pubs. From £35pp.

Bristol Brewery Tours ⓣ0203 189 1742, ⓦbristolbrewerytours.com. Craft beer tasting aboard HMS *Hops* including a tour of Moor Brewery and tastings at the Beer Emporium. Sat 11.45am–4pm, £50.

Bristol Community Ferry Boats ⓣ0117 927 3416, ⓦbristolferry.com. Hop-on-hop-off ferry service using heated, covered boats. The 17 stops include Temple Meads train station, the city centre and SS *Great Britain*. In summer there are also trips along Avon Gorge, departing from the SS *Great Britain* (3hr 30min, £18). Trips to Beese's too.

Bristol Insight: The Open Top Bus Company ⓣ0117 971 9279, ⓦbristolinsight.co.uk. Open-top hop on hop off bus tours which run around the city in two loops: the Clifton Loop and West End takes in the Harbourside, Clifton village, the suspension bridge and the zoo; the Old City loop calls at Temple Meads and Cabot Circus. £13.

★**Bristol Packet Boat Trips** ⓣ0117 926 8157, ⓦbristolpacket.co.uk. Various cruises of the harbour, including cream tea cruises (Wed 2.30pm, 1hr 45min, £16) and the short City Docks Tour (weekends 11am–3.45pm, every 45min, 45min, £6.75).

Number Seven Boat Trips ⓣ0117 929 3659, ⓦnumbersevenboattrips.com. Scheduled ferry service through the harbour from Hotwells to Temple Meads via SS *Great Britain* (weekends & hols 10.30am–5.50pm, 40min, from £1.50). Also trips to Beese's tea garden. Mar–Sept Sat noon & 2pm, 1hr each way, £14 return.

Street Art Walking Tours ⓣ07748 632663, ⓦwherethewall.com. Enlightening tour of the city's graffiti and street art, with a particular focus on Banksy. Weekends & selected weekdays 11am, 2hr, £9.80.

The Ultimate Bristol Walking Tour ⓣ07909 221684, ⓦblackbeard2banksy.com. Walking tour starting from the cathedral and taking in Bristol's street art and key sites in the city's history. Thurs–Sun 11.30am, £8.

ACCOMMODATION

Bristol Harbour Hotel & Spa 55 Corn St, BS1 1HT ⓣ0117 203 4445, ⓦharbourhotels.co.uk; map p.132. Bristol's best hotel is located in a gorgeously ornate stone pile that was once the Lloyds and Midland Bank HQ. Service is just short of five-star but rooms are spacious, with vast beds. The spa is in the old vault and features a hydrotherapy pool. £139

★**Brooks Guesthouse** St Nicholas St BS1 1UB ⓣ01179 300 066, ⓦbrooksguesthousebristol.com; map p.132. Unbeatable central location just opposite St Nicholas Markets in the heart of Old Bristol. Rooms are spread over three floors, with four funky aluminium Rocket caravans on the rooftop for those willing to trade space for cool points. Can be noisy. Breakfast is served in the open kitchen downstairs, where there's a pleasant lounge area with honesty bar. £69

Clifton House 4 Tyndall's Park Rd, Clifton, BS8 1PG ⓣ0117 973 5407, ⓦcliftonhousebristol.com; map p.132. This handily located B&B close to both Clifton and the city centre offers plush rooms with modern bathrooms and plenty of space – superior rooms, costing £20 extra, are huge – and there's off-street parking too. £85

Hampton by Hilton Bristol Airport North Side Rd, Bristol International Airport, BS48 3AQ ☎ 01275 405966 ⓦ hamptoninn3.hilton.com; map p.132. Modern hotel within walking distance of Bristol airport – ideal for first and last nights. Rooms are spacious (the sofa pulls out to form an extra bed) and there's a 24hr gym. **£89**

Hotel du Vin The Sugar House, Narrow Lewins Mead, BS1 2NU ☎ 0330 016 0390, ⓦ hotelduvin.co.uk; map p.132. Chic conversion of an old dockside warehouse, centrally located, with dark, contemporary decor. Rooms have big beds and grand bathrooms, and there's an excellent restaurant to boot. **£99**

Number 38 Clifton 38 Upper Belgrave Rd, BS8 2XN ☎ 0117 946 6905, ⓦ number38clifton.com; map p.132.

Funky new bed and breakfast with luxurious rooms decorated in soothing tones; many feature roll-top baths. There's also a lovely rooftop terrace ideal for sundowners and cream teas are served in the comfy reception rooms. **£115**

YHA Bristol 14 Narrow Quay, BS1 4QA ☎ 0345 371 9726, ⓦ yha.org.uk/hostel/bristol; map p.132. In a refurbished grain house on the quayside, this warm and friendly hostel is everything a modern hostel should be. The dorms are single sex and mostly four-beds and there are some small private doubles, while the kitchen is a decent size and well-equipped. Prices include an abundant breakfast and the Grainhouse Café & Bar has burgers, pizzas and drinks. Dorms **£12**, doubles **£25**

EATING AND DRINKING

★ **The Beer Emporium** 15 King St, BS1 4EF ☎ 0117 379 0333, ⓦ thebeeremporium.net; map p.132. Bristol's craft beer scene is booming and this friendly bar and bottle shop is the best place to up your knowledge. The shop has a full wall of local brews plus other beers from around the world while downstairs in the bar come beer hall you'll find plenty of options on tap. Mon–Sat noon–2am, Sun 1pm–midnight.

Beese's Wyndham Crescent, BS4 4SX ☎ 0117 977 7412, ⓦ beeses.co.uk; map p.132. Bucolic riverside spot that feels a million miles from the city centre but is easily reached by ferry. There are scones and cakes, as well as hot dishes such as burgers (from £9.95) and lunchtime boards including a cracking Ploughmans (£11.50). Lots of choice for veggies and vegans, as well as gluten free cakes. Roasts on Sundays, live music on Fridays. End Mar–end Sept Fri & Sat noon–11pm, Sun & hols noon–7pm.

Cargo Cantina Unit 15, Cargo 2, Wapping Wharf, BS1 6ZA ⓦ cargocantina.co.uk; map p.132. Inspired by Mexico's cantinas, this laidback spot serves up botanas (bar snacks) such as guacamole and roasted peanuts as well as a range of tacos including shredded pork shoulder and roasted cauliflowers (£2.95 each). Large selection of mezcals and tequilas too. Mon–Sat 11.30am–11pm, Sun 11.30am–5pm.

The Florist 69 Park St, BS1 5PB ☎ 0117 203 4284, ⓦ theflorist.uk.com; map p.132. Highly Instagrammable joint serving photo-ready nibbles plus grilled dishes such as hanging kebabs (from £10.95) and hearty mains including vegan tagine (£9.50) and lamb rump (£16.95). There's a separate gluten-free menu and plenty that's dairy free, even for dessert. Sun–Wed noon–midnight, Thurs noon–1am, Fri & Sat noon–2am.

Gambas Tapas Bar Unit 12, Cargo 2, Wapping Wharf, BS1 6ZA ☎ 0117 934 9256, ⓦ gambasbristol.co.uk; map p.132. Located upstairs at Cargo's development of shipping container restaurants, Gambas has lovely harbour views to accompany its seafood-focused tapas menu. Classics such as

patatas bravas and *gambas pil pil* are here as well as Cornish mussels and fried aubergine with molasses. Dishes start from just £2.90. They also have their own local gin and the wine list is all Spanish. Mon–Sat 11.30am–11pm, Sun 12–5pm.

Lido Spa & Restaurant Oakfield Place, Clifton, BS8 2BJ ☎ 0117 933 9530, ⓦ lidobristol.com; map p.132. This members-only Victorian outdoor swimming pool allows non-members to swim Mon–Fri 1–4pm or if booking a package with lunch or dinner (from £40). Alternatively simply come to eat – wood-roasted scallops followed by slow roast lamb shoulder from the wood oven perhaps. You'll have a view through floor to ceiling glass of the pool. Starters from £7.50, mains from £17.50. Daily noon–3pm & 6–10pm.

★ **Old Market Assembly** 25 West St, Old Market, BS2 0DF ☎ 0117 373 8199, ⓦ oldmarketassembly.co.uk; map p.132. This lively venue hosts live music, a storytelling slam and family events both in the bar itself and in the Wardrobe Theatre beyond. The food menu focuses on sustainability and caters for everyone from vegans to gluten intolerants. Dishes change with the seasons but expect Cornish seafood and a great line-up of pizzas, from £9. Mon–Thurs 11am–11pm, Fri 11am–1am, Sat 10am–1am, Sun 10am–10pm.

★ **The Ox** The Basement, 43 Corn St, BS1 1HT ☎ 0117 922 1001, ⓦ theoxbristol.com; map p.132. Moody basement steakhouse serving some of the best cuts of beef in Bristol. Steaks are local and cooked on a Josper grill for extra succulence; fillet is £26, T-bone to share £72. Starters include hickory-smoked ribs (£7.50) and the wine list is expertly-chosen with some real bargains. Mon–Fri 12–2.30pm & 5–10.30pm, Sat 5–10.30pm, Sun 12–4pm.

★ **Paco Tapas** 3a Lower Guinea St, BS1 6FU ☎ 0117 925 7021, ⓦ pacotapas.co.uk; map p.132. Probably the best dining experience in Bristol. Authentic tapas dishes served in a casual atmosphere by knowledgeable staff and attracting a Michelin star within a year of opening. The menu changes regularly but you can expect delicious just-carved *jamon*, *padron* peppers roasted over a wood fire and

6

Galician octopus. Tapas dishes start at £2, larger dishes from £11 and there's a tasting menu for £50. The wines and sherries have been selected meticulously; ask for a recommendation and you won't be disappointed. Tues–Thurs 5–11pm, Fri & Sat 12–3pm & 5–10pm.

The Prince Street Social 37-41 Prince St, BS1 4PS, ☎ 0117 405 8949, ⓦ princestreetsocial.com; map p.132. Welcoming all-day joint serving modern classics such as burgers in a brioche bun (£10.50) and posh kebabs (£10.50). There are great cocktails too and local beers from sister company King Street Brewhouse. Mon–Thurs 10am–11.30pm, Fri & Sat 10am–11.30pm, Sun 10am–6pm.

Severnshed The Grove, BS1 4RB ☎ 0117 925 1212, ⓦ severnshedrestaurant.co.uk; map p.132. Right on the water in the heart of Bristol, this long-running restaurant serves generous breakfasts daily as well as modern European dishes for lunch and dinner. Seafood linguine is £13.95, haddock fishcakes £11.95. The terrace overlooking the river is one of Bristol's most sought-after dining spots and there's a cosy lounge inside for cooler days. Mon–Thurs 10am–11pm, Fri 10am–1am, Sat 9am–1am, Sun 9am–11pm.

The Rummer All Saints Lane ☎ 0117 929 0111, ⓦ therummer.net; map p.132. Cocktail-focused bar in the heart of Old Bristol. Also the home of Bristol Dry Gin,

produced in the micro distillery here and served with tonic for just £5.50. Mon–Thurs 10am–11pm, Fri 10am–midnight, Sat 11am–midnight, Sun noon–6pm.

Three Brothers Burgers Welsh Back, BS1 4SB ☎ 0117 927 7050, ⓦ threebrothersburgers.co.uk; map p.132. Outdoor seating overlooking the harbour in summer and roaring fires in winter make this hip burger joint popular year-round. More than a dozen burgers to choose from; the classic is just £5 at lunchtime (noon-5pm), the pulled mushroom burger is vegan and the mega burger will keep you going all day – it has double patty, double bacon and double cheese. Mon–Thurs noon–11pm, Fri 11.45am–11pm, Sat 11.30am–11pm, Sun 11.30am–8pm.

Wild Beer at Wapping Wharf 6-8 Gaol Ferry Steps, BS1 6WE ☎ 0117 329 4997, ⓦ wbwappingwharf.com; map p.132. A beer-lover's dream, with twenty brews on tap, some from their own brewery in Shepton Mallet. The bottled beer list has rare and unusual beers selected by the expert staff. Mon–Sat noon–11pm, Sun noon–10pm.

Woky Ko Unit 7, Cargo, Wapping Wharf, BS1 6WP ⓦ wokyko.com; map p.132. Sit at simple wooden tables beneath a ceiling of parasols and feast on Asian street food such as Korean fried chicken bao (£4.25) and Singapore noodles (£7.95). Mon–Thurs 11.30am–10pm, Fri & Sat 11.30am–10.30pm, Sun 11.30am–late but closed 3–4.30pm Mon–Fri.

ENTERTAINMENT

Arnolfini 16 Narrow Quay BS1 4QA ☎ 0117 917 2300, ⓦ arnolfini.org.uk; map p.132. Bristol's centre for contemporary arts was founded in 1961 and stands on Narrow Quay in the city centre. It is dedicated to the visual arts, dance, film and music and is home to one of the country's best independent art bookshops.

Bristol Old Vic King St, BS1 4ED ☎ 0117 987 7877, ⓦ bristololdvic.org.uk; map p.132. Britain's oldest working theatre, dating from the 1760s, retains its Georgian interior but has modern facilities. It lays on a full programme of mainstream and more experimental productions in its main auditorium and the Studio.

St George's Great George St, BS1 5RR ☎ 0845 402 4001, ⓦ stgeorgesbristol.co.uk; map p.132. Elegant Georgian church with superb acoustics, staging a packed programme of lunchtime and evening concerts covering

classical, world, folk and jazz music.

Tobacco Factory Raleigh Rd, Southville, BS3 1ET ☎ 0117 902 0344, ⓦ tobaccofactorytheatres.com; map p.132. South of the river, this theatre offers a broad spectrum of drama, dance, comedy and other performing arts on two stages.

Spike Island 133 Cumberland Rd, BS1 6UX ☎ 0117 929 2266, ⓦ spikeisland.org.uk; map p.132. This contemporary arts space houses more than seventy artists and designers in low-cost studios and has a year-round programme of exhibitions and talks in its gallery.

Watershed 1 Canon's Rd, BS1 5TX ☎ 0117 927 5100, ⓦ watershed.co.uk; map p.132. This is the southwest's leading film and digital media centre, with three cinemas screening a line-up of contemporary films, from blockbusters to documentaries.

SHOPPING

Beast St Nicholas Markets, BS1 1HQ ☎ 0117 927 9535, ⓦ beast-clothing.com; map p.132. Amusing T-shirts, hoodies and hats emblazoned with snippets of the local lingo. Mon–Sat 9.30am–5pm.

Bristol Cider Shop Unit 4, Cargo, Wapping Wharf, BS1 6WE ☎ 0117 929 3203 ⓦ bristolcidershop.co.uk; map p.132. Bristol's best – and surely most passionate – cider shop stocks more than 100 varieties of local cider and

perry, with around eight on tap. Tues–Sat 11am–7pm, Sun 11am–4pm.

Cabot Circus BS1 3BX ☎ 0117 952 9361 ⓦ cabotcircus. com; map p.132. Ultra-contemporary shopping precinct filled with the usual big-name brands such as Hollister, Apple, All Saints, plus the only Harvey Nichols in the South West. Mon–Sat 10am–8pm, Sun 11am–5pm.

Guild 68 Park St, BS1 5JY ☎ 0117 926 5548 ⓦ bristol

guildgallery.co.uk; map p.132. Quality independent retailer operating in Bristol for over a century, containing various departments from designer kitchen goods to a gourmet food hall, plus an outside terrace for a quick coffee break. Mon–Sat 10am–6pm.

The Mall at Cribbs Causeway BS34 5DG ☎0117 903 0303 Ⓦmallcribs.com; map p.132. More than 150 stores in a modern mall just outside the city centre. There are large outposts of department stores John Lewis and Marks & Spencer as well as fashion brands such as Topshop, Superdry and River Island. Mon–Fri 9.30am–8pm, Sat 9am–8pm, Sun 11am–5pm.

Plastic Wax Records 222 Cheltenham Rd, BS6 5QU ☎0117 942 7368 Ⓦplasticwaxrecords.com; map p.132. Bristol's largest record dealer, with wall-to-wall used vinyl and CDs across all genres. Mon 9.30am–5.30pm, Tues–Fri 9.30am–7pm, Sat 9am–6pm, Sun noon–5pm.

6

NIGHTLIFE

Fiddlers Willway St, Bedminster, BS3 4BG ☎0117 987 3403, Ⓦfiddlers.co.uk; map p.132. Mainly roots bands, good-time retro acts and niche artists perform at this relaxed, family-run venue (formerly a prison) south of the river.

The Fleece 12 St Thomas St, BS1 6JJ ☎0117 945 0996, Ⓦthefleece.co.uk; map p.132. Stone-flagged ex-wool warehouse, now a loud, sweaty pub staging everything from acoustic blues and alt-country to punk and deathcore.

The Louisiana Wapping Rd, BS1 6UA ☎0117 926 5978, Ⓦthelouisiana.net; map p.132. Established music pub with a well-earned reputation for helping break bands (The White Stripes, Florence + the Machine) and promoting local artists. It's a mite cramped, but the acoustics and atmosphere are excellent.

SWX Bristol 15 Nelson St, BS1 2JY ☎0117 945 0325, Ⓦswxbristol.com; map p.132. A real super-club, one of the largest in Bristol, and home to various club nights, as well as live music and comedy.

Thekla The Grove, East Mud Dock, BS1 4RB ☎0117 929 3301, Ⓦtheklabristol.co.uk; map p.132. Ex-cargo boat, now a much-loved venue staging a varied line-up of live bands plus indie, house and club nights.

ACTIVITIES

Adventurous Activity Company Underfall Yard, Baltic Wharf, Cumberland Rd, BS1 6XG ☎01275 394 558. Ⓦadventurousactivitycompany.co.uk. Introductory climbing sessions and abseiling at Avon Gorge, plus canoeing, archery, mountain biking and orienteering. One activity from £39.50, two from £57.50.

Aldwick Estate Redhill, BS405RF, ☎01934 864404, Ⓦaldwickcourtfarm.co.uk. Tours and tastings at an award-winning English vineyard. Group tours (£15) last around 90 minutes and include a tasting of the estate's highly regarded wines. Private tours can also be arranged.

Ashton Court Golf Course Ashton Court, BS8 3PX ☎0117 973 8508, Ⓦbristol.gov.uk. Pay and play public golf course with two 9-hole courses. The flat course is suitable for families and beginners, the hilly course more challenging. A further 9-hole course offer FootGolf, where players kick the ball instead of hitting it. £7; equipment £5.

Bristol Blue Glass 357-359 Bath Rd, BS4 3EW, ☎0117 972 0818, Ⓦbristol-glass.co.uk. Have a go at glass blowing at this local company's studio. There's also a shop selling their range of products, both here and at 47 High St.

Bristol & Clifton Golf Club Beggar Bush Lane, BS8 3TH ☎01275 393 474, Ⓦbristolandcliftongolfclub.co.uk. Mature parkland course over 6,413 yards that celebrated its 125th anniversary in 2016. Green fees from £30.

Bristol Disc Golf Club Ashton Court, BS8 3PX ☎07422 521214, Ⓦbristoldiscgolf.org.uk. With similar rules to golf and otherwise not similar at all – disc golf involves chucking a frisbee into a basket over either 9 or 18 "holes". Bristol's course is at Ashton Court and is free to play. Frisbees can be hired or bought from Mr Frisbee.

Bristol Nordic Walking ☎07886 885213, Ⓦbristol nordicwalking.co.uk. The UK's biggest Nordic walking club offers beginners workshops (£15/75min including poles), regular classes and longer walks around the local area (from £15), including in Bath.

Bristol Orienteering Klub Ashton Court, BS8 3PX Ⓦbristolorienteering.org.uk. Pick up a map (£1.50) from the golf kiosk at Ashton Court Golf Club and navigate three different permanent orienteering courses which run through the Ashton Court park.

Pedal Progression Ashton Court, BS8 3PX ☎0117 973 1298, Ⓦpedalprogression.com. Bike hire for tackling the trails at Ashton Court. The four-mile Nova Cycle Trail is graded blue (intermediate), Super Nova's half mile is Red (difficult). £12/1hr.

SUP Bristol ☎0117 422 5858, Ⓦsupbristol.com. See Bristol's waterfront in a unique way by taking a lesson in stand-up paddle boarding. There are taster sessions on weekday evenings (£25) and longer adventures on weekends (£37.50).

Undercover Rock St Werburgh's Church, Mina Rd, BS2 9YT ☎0117 941 3489, Ⓦundercover-rock.com. Indoor rock climbing with walls up to 13 metres high and a dedicated bouldering area. Entry from £7, taster sessions £15/90min.

HOLLY BLUE BUTTERFLY

Contexts

159 History

176 Film and TV

178 Music

179 Wildlife

182 Books

History

England's history is long and densely woven. From obscure beginnings, it came to play a leading role in European affairs and, with the expansion of the British Empire, the world. Naturally, the history of the Great West Way and especially its larger cities, is inextricably wound up in this story and so this is necessarily a pared down version of events. We have provided some more resources on wider English history on page 182.

Early history

It is thought that England has been inhabited for the best part of half a million years and some of the earliest evidence of man living in the country can be found just off the Great West Way at **Cheddar Caves**. **Neolithic** culture arrived with nomadic hunters in around 3500BC and, for the first time, land was cleared for farming and livestock were kept. This Neolithic Age gave way to the **Bronze Age** around 2500BC with the importation from northern Europe of artefacts attributed to **Beaker Culture** – named for the distinctive cups found at many burial sites. Beaker Culture spread along European trade routes and stimulated the development of a more organised social structure with an established aristocracy. Around this time many of England's stone circles were completed, including **Stonehenge** and **Avebury**. By 500BC Britons, including by now a significant **Celtic** population, had established a sophisticated farming economy and a social hierarchy. The subsequent **Iron Age** saw the development of better methods of metalworking and the forging of weapons, coins and ornamental works – the first recognizable English art.

The Romans

The **Roman** invasion of Britain was hesitant at first, beginning with small cross-Channel incursions led by **Julius Caesar** in 55 and 54BC. Britain's rumoured mineral wealth was a primary motive, but the spur to the eventual conquest that came nearly a century later was anti-Roman collaboration between the British Celts and their cousins in France. **Emperor Claudius** led the invasion in August AD 43 when a substantial Roman force landed in Kent, soon establishing a base along the estuary of the Thames. Resistance to the Romans was patchy. The East Anglian Iceni, under their queen Boudica (or Boadicea) in AD 60, sacked Camulodunum (Colchester in Essex) and Verulamium (St Albans just north of London), and even reached the undefended new port of Londinium (London), but the Romans rallied and the rebellion was the last major act of resistance with most of the southern tribes – along the present Great West Way – acquiescing to their absorption into the empire.

The written history of England begins with the Romans, whose rule lasted nigh on four centuries. For the first time, the country began to emerge as a clearly identifiable entity with a defined political structure. Peace also brought prosperity. Commerce

c.5000BC	**c.3000BC**	**55BC**
End of the last Ice Age; British Isles split from European mainland	The first Stonehenge is built	First Roman invasions of Britain, under Julius Caesar

flourished and cities prospered, including Londinium, which soon assumed a pivotal role in the commercial and administrative life of the colony, and **Bath**, which became an important settlement due to its natural hot spring and the Romans penchant for bathing. Arguably the most important legacy of the Roman occupation was the introduction of **Christianity** from the third century on, becoming firmly entrenched after its official recognition by the **Emperor Constantine** in 313.

The Anglo-Saxons

By the middle of the fourth century, Roman England was subject to regular **raids** by a confusing medley of Germanic Saxons, Picts from Scotland and itinerant Scots from northern Ireland. Economic life declined, rural areas became depopulated and, as central authority collapsed, a string of military commanders usurped local authority. By the start of the fifth century England had become irrevocably detached from what remained of the Roman Empire and within fifty years the **Saxons** had begun settling England themselves. This marked the start of a gradual conquest that culminated in the defeat of the native Britons in 577 at the **Battle of Dyrham** (near Bath) and, despite the despairing efforts of such semi-mythical figures as **King Arthur**, the last independent Britons were driven deep into Cumbria, Wales and the southwest. So complete was the Anglo-Saxon domination, through conquest and intermarriage, that some ninety percent of English place names today have an Anglo-Saxon derivation.

The Anglo-Saxons went on to divide England into the kingdoms of Northumbria, Mercia, East Anglia, Kent and **Wessex**. In the eighth century, the central English region of Mercia was the dominant force, its most effective ruler being King Offa, who was responsible for the greatest public work of the period, Offa's Dyke, an earthwork marking the border with Wales from the River Dee to the River Severn, near **Bristol**. Yet, after Offa's death, Wessex – which covered much of present-day Dorset, Hampshire and **Wiltshire** – gained the upper hand, and by 825 the Wessex kings had taken fealty from all the other English kingdoms.

At first, the pagan Anglo-Saxons had little time for **Christianity**, but this was soon to change. In 597, at the behest of Pope Gregory I, **St Augustine** landed on the Kent coast accompanied by forty monks. **Ethelbert**, the overlord of all the English south of the River Humber, received the missionaries and gave Augustine permission to found a monastery at Canterbury in Kent, where the king himself was soon baptized, followed by ten thousand of his subjects at a grand Christmas ceremony. Despite some short-term reversals thereafter, the Christianization of England proceeded quickly, so that by the middle of the seventh century all of the Anglo-Saxon kings had at least nominally adopted the faith.

The Viking onslaught

The supremacy of Wessex in the early ninth century was short-lived. Carried here by their remarkable longboats, the **Vikings** – by this time mostly Danes – had started to raid the east coast towards the end of the eighth century. Emboldened by their success, these raids grew in size and then turned into a migration. In 865, a substantial Danish army landed in East Anglia, and within six years they had conquered Northumbria, Mercia and East

43AD	60–70AD	313
Emperor Claudius invades from Kent, beginning the Roman conquest of Britain	Temple in Bath constructed, the beginnings of the bathing complex	Emperor Constantine makes Christianity the official religion of the Roman Empire

Anglia. The Danes then set their sights on Wessex, whose new king was the formidable and exceptionally talented **Alfred the Great**. Despite the odds, Alfred successfully resisted the Danes and eventually the two warring parties signed a truce, which fixed an uneasy border between Wessex and Danish territory – the Danelaw – to the north. Ensconced in northern England and the East Midlands, the Danes soon succumbed to Christianity and internal warfare, while Alfred modernized his kingdom and strengthened its defences.

Alfred died in 899, but his successor, **Edward the Elder**, capitalized on his efforts, establishing Saxon supremacy over the Danelaw to become the de facto overlord of all England. The relative calm continued under Edward's son, **Athelstan** and his son, **Edgar**, who became the first ruler to be crowned king of England in 973. However, this was but a lull in the Viking storm. Returning in force, the Vikings milked Edgar's son **Ethelred the Unready** ("lacking counsel") for all the money they could, but payment of the ransom (the Danegeld) brought only temporary relief and in 1016 Ethelred hot-footed it to Normandy, leaving the Danes in command. The first Danish king of England was **Cnut**, a shrewd and gifted ruler, but his two disreputable sons quickly dismantled his carefully constructed Anglo-Scandinavian empire and the Saxons promptly regained the initiative.

1066 and the Normans

In 1042, the resurgent **Saxons** anointed Ethelred's son, **Edward the Confessor**, as king of England. It was a poor choice. Edward was more suited to be a priest than a king and he allowed power to drift into the hands of his most powerful subject, Godwin, Earl of Wessex, and his son **Harold**. On Edward's death, the Witan – effectively a council of elders – confirmed Harold as king, ignoring several rival claims including that of William, Duke of Normandy. William's claim was a curious affair, but he always insisted – however improbable it may seem – that the childless Edward the Confessor had promised him his crown. Unluckily for Harold, his two main rivals struck at the same time. First up was his alienated brother Tostig along with his ally King Harald of Norway, a giant of a man reckoned to be seven feet tall. They landed with a Viking army in Yorkshire and Harold marched north to meet them. Harold won a crushing victory at the battle of Stamford Bridge, but then he heard that William of Normandy had invaded the south. Rashly, he dashed south without gathering reinforcements, a blunder that cost him his life: Harold was famously defeated at the **Battle of Hastings** in 1066 and, on Christmas Day, **William the Conqueror** was installed as king in Westminster Abbey in London.

William I imposed a **Norman** aristocracy on his new subjects, reinforcing his rule with a series of strongholds, the grandest of which was the Tower of London. Initially, there was some resistance, but William crushed these sporadic rebellions with great brutality. Perhaps the single most effective controlling measure was the compilation of the **Domesday Book** in 1085–86. Recording land ownership, type of cultivation, number of inhabitants and their social status, it afforded William an unprecedented body of information about his subjects, providing a framework for the administration of taxation, judicial structure and ultimately feudal obligations.

William died in 1087, and was succeeded by his son William Rufus, an ineffectual ruler but a notable benefactor of religious foundations. Rufus died in mysterious circumstances – killed by an unknown assailant's arrow while hunting in the New Forest just south of the Great West Way in Hampshire – and the throne passed to **Henry I**, William I's

577	597	865
Battle of Dyrham; Saxons take control	St Augustine lands in Britain with instructions to convert it to Christianity	Vikings land in Britain

youngest son. Henry spent much of his time struggling with his unruly barons, but at least he proved to be more conciliatory in his dealings with the Saxons, even marrying into one of their leading families. On his death in 1135, the accession was contested, initiating a long-winded civil war that was only ended when **Henry II** secured the throne.

The Plantagenets (1154–1399)

Energetic and far-sighted, Henry II, the first of the **Plantagenets**, kept his barons in check and instigated profound administrative reforms, most notably the introduction of trial by jury. Nor was England Henry's only concern, his inheritance bequeathing him great chunks of France. This territorial entanglement was to create all sorts of problems for his successors, but Henry himself was brought low by his attempt to subordinate Church to Crown. This went terribly awry in 1170, when he (perhaps unintentionally) sanctioned the murder in Canterbury Cathedral of his erstwhile drinking companion Thomas Becket, whose canonization just three years later created an enduring Europe-wide cult.

The last years of Henry's reign were riven by quarrels with his sons, the eldest of whom, **Richard I** (or Lionheart), spent most of his ten-year reign crusading in the Holy Land. Neglected, England fell prey to the scheming of Richard's brother John, the villain of the Robin Hood tales, who became king in his own right after Richard died of a battle wound in France in 1199. Yet John's inability to hold on to his French possessions and his rumbling dispute with the Vatican over control of the English Church alienated the English barons, who eventually forced him to consent to a charter guaranteeing their rights and privileges, the **Magna Carta**, which was signed in 1215 at Runnymede, on the Thames.

The power struggle with the barons continued into the reign of **Henry III**, but Henry's successor, **Edward I**, who inherited the throne in 1272, was much more in control of his kingdom than his predecessors. Edward was a great law-maker, but he also became preoccupied with military matters, spending years subduing Wales and imposing English jurisdiction over Scotland. Fortunately for the Scots – it was too late for Wales – the next king of England, **Edward II**, proved to be completely hopeless, and in 1314 Robert the Bruce inflicted a huge defeat on his guileless army at the battle of **Bannockburn**. This spelled the beginning of the end for Edward, who ultimately died under suspicious circumstances – likely murdered by his wife Isabella and her lover Roger Mortimer – in 1327.

Edward III began by sorting out the Scottish imbroglio before getting stuck into his main enthusiasm – his (essentially specious) claim to the throne of France. Starting in 1337, the resultant **Hundred Years War** kicked off with several famous English victories, principally Crécy in 1346 and Poitiers in 1356, but was interrupted by the outbreak of the **Black Death** in 1349. The plague claimed about one and a half million English souls – some one third of the population – and the scarcity of labour that followed gave the peasantry more economic clout than they had ever had before. Predictably, the landowners attempted to restrict the concomitant rise in wages, thereby provoking the widespread rioting that culminated in the **Peasants' Revolt** of 1381. The rebels marched on London under the delusion that they could appeal to the king – now **Richard II** – for fair treatment, but they soon learned otherwise. The king did indeed meet a rebel deputation in person, but his aristocratic bodyguards took the opportunity to kill the peasants' leader, **Wat Tyler**, a prelude to the enforced dispersal of the crowds and mass slaughter.

973	1042	1066
Edgar crowned first King of England	Saxon Edward the Confessor becomes king	Battle of Hastings; William the Conqueror crowned king

The houses of Lancaster and York (1399–1485)

In 1399, **Henry IV**, the first of the **Lancastrian** kings, supplanted the weak and indecisive Richard II. Henry died in 1413 and was succeeded by his son, the bellicose **Henry V**, who promptly renewed the Hundred Years War with vigour. Henry famously defeated the French at the battle of **Agincourt**, a comprehensive victory that forced the French king to acknowledge Henry as his heir in the Treaty of Troyes of 1420. However, Henry died just two years later and his son, **Henry VI** – or rather his regents – all too easily succumbed to a French counter-attack inspired by **Joan of Arc** (1412–31); by 1454, only Calais was left in English hands.

It was soon obvious that the new monarch, **Henry VI,** was mentally unstable. Consequently, as he drifted in and out of sanity, two aristocratic factions attempted to take control: the Yorkists, whose emblem was the white rose, and the Lancastrians, represented by the red rose – hence the protracted **Wars of the Roses**. The Yorkist **Edward IV** seized the crown in 1471 and held onto it until his death in 1483, when he was succeeded by his twelve-year-old son **Edward V**, whose reign was cut short after two months: he and his younger brother were murdered in the Tower of London, probably at the behest of their uncle, the Duke of Gloucester, who was crowned **Richard III.** Richard did not last long either: in 1485, he was defeated (and killed) at the battle of Bosworth Field by **Henry Tudor**, Earl of Richmond, who took the throne as Henry VII.

The Tudors (1485–1603)

The opening of the **Tudor** period brought radical transformations. A Lancastrian through his mother's line, **Henry VII promptly** reconciled the Yorkists by marrying Edward IV's daughter Elizabeth, thereby ending the Wars of the Roses at a stroke. It was a shrewd gambit and others followed. Henry married his daughter off to James IV of Scotland and his eldest son Arthur to Catherine, the daughter of Ferdinand and Isabella of Spain – and by these means England began to assume the status of a major European power.

Henry's son, **Henry VIII**, is best remembered for his multiple marriages, but much more significant was his separation of the English Church from Rome and his establishment of an independent Protestant Church – the **Church of England.** This is not without its ironies. Henry was not a Protestant himself and the schism between Henry and the pope was triggered not by doctrinal issues but by the failure of his wife **Catherine of Aragon** – widow of his elder brother – to provide Henry with male offspring. Failing to obtain a decree of nullity from Pope Clement VII, he dismissed his long-time chancellor Thomas Wolsey and turned instead to **Thomas Cromwell**, who helped make the English Church recognize Henry as its head. One of the consequences was the **Dissolution of the Monasteries**, which conveniently gave both king and nobles the chance to get their hands on valuable monastic property in the late 1530s.

In his later years, Henry became a corpulent, syphilitic wreck, six times married but at last furnished with an heir, **Edward VI,** who was only nine years old when he ascended the throne in 1547. His short reign saw **Protestantism** established on a firm footing, with churches stripped of their images and Catholic services banned, yet on Edward's death most of the country readily accepted his fervently Catholic half-sister **Mary**, daughter of Catherine of Aragon, as queen – England's first female monarch to reign in her own right. She returned England to the papacy and married the future Philip II of Spain, forging an alliance whose immediate consequence was war with

1085-6	1215	1220
The Normans compile the Domesday book	Magna Carta signed at Runnymede	Works begins on Salisbury cathedral

France. The marriage was deeply unpopular and so was Mary's decision to begin persecuting Protestants, executing the leading lights of the English Reformation – Hugh Latimer, Nicholas Ridley and Thomas Cranmer, the archbishop of Canterbury.

Queen Mary, or "Bloody Mary" as many of her subjects called her, died in 1558 and the crown passed to her half-sister, **Elizabeth I**. The new queen looked very vulnerable. The country was divided by religion – Catholic against Protestant – and threatened from abroad by Philip II of Spain, the most powerful ruler in Europe. Famously, Elizabeth eschewed marriage and, although a Protestant herself, steered a delicate course between the two religious groupings. Her prudence sat well with the English merchant class, who were becoming the greatest power in the land, its members mostly opposed to foreign military entanglements. An exception, however, was made for the piratical activities of the great English seafarers of the day, captains like Walter Raleigh, Martin Frobisher, John Hawkins and Francis Drake, who made a fortune raiding Spain's American colonies. Inevitably, Philip II's irritation with the raiding took a warlike turn, but the **Spanish Armada** he sent against England in 1588 was defeated, thereby establishing England as a major European sea power. Elizabeth's reign also saw the efflorescence of a specifically English Renaissance – **William Shakespeare** (1564–1616) is the obvious name – the only major fly in the royal ointment being the queen's reluctant execution of her cousin and rival **Mary, Queen of Scots**, in 1587.

The early Stuarts (1603–49)

James VI of Scotland – son of Mary, Queen of Scots – succeeded Elizabeth as **James I** of England in 1603, thereby uniting the English and Scottish crowns. James quickly moved to end hostilities with Spain and adopted a policy of toleration towards the country's Catholics. Inevitably, both initiatives offended many Protestants, whose worst fears were confirmed in 1605 when **Guy Fawkes** and a group of Catholic conspirators were discovered preparing to blow up king and Parliament in the so-called **Gunpowder Plot**. During the ensuing hue and cry, many Catholics met an untimely end and Fawkes himself was hanged, drawn and quartered. At the same time, many Protestants felt that the English state was irredeemably corrupt and some of the more dedicated **Puritans** fixed their eyes on establishing a "New Jerusalem" in North America following the foundation of the first permanent **colony** in Virginia in 1608. Twelve years later, the **Pilgrim Fathers** landed in New England, establishing a colony that would absorb about a hundred thousand Puritan immigrants by the middle of the century.

Meanwhile, James was busy alienating his landed gentry. He clung to an absolutist vision of the monarchy – the **divine right of kings** – that was totally out of step with the Protestant leanings of the majority of his subjects and he also relied heavily on court favourites. It could only lead to disaster, but in the end it was to be his successor who reaped the whirlwind.

Charles I inherited James's penchant for absolutism, ruling without Parliament from 1629 to 1640, but he over-stepped himself when he tried to impose a new Anglican prayer book on the Scots, who rose in revolt, forcing Charles to recall Parliament in an attempt to raise the money he needed for an army. This was Parliament's chance and they were not going to let it slip. The **Long Parliament**, as it became known, impeached several of Charles's allies – most notably Archbishop Laud, who was hung out to dry by the king and

1337–1453	1349	1415
Hundred Years War with France	The Black Death reaches England	Henry V defeats France at Battle of Agincourt

ultimately executed – and compiled its grievances in the Grand Remonstrance of 1641.

Facing the concerted hostility of Parliament, the king withdrew to Nottingham where he raised his standard, the opening act of the **Civil War**. The Royalist forces ("Cavaliers") were initially successful, leading to the complete overhaul of key regiments of the Parliamentary army ("Roundheads") by **Oliver Cromwell** and his officer allies. The **New Model Army** Cromwell created was something quite unique: singing psalms as they went into battle and urged on by preachers and "agitators", this was an army of believers whose ideological commitment to the parliamentary cause made it truly formidable. Cromwell's revamped army cut its teeth at the battle of Naseby and thereafter simply brushed the Royalists aside. Meanwhile, an increasingly desperate Charles attempted to sow discord among his enemies by surrendering himself to the Scots, but as so often with Charles's plans, they came unstuck: the Scots handed him over to the English Parliament, by whom – after prolonged negotiations, endless royal shenanigans and more fighting – he was ultimately **executed** in January 1649.

The Commonwealth and Restoration

For the next eleven years, England was a **Commonwealth** – at first a true republic, then, after 1653, a **Protectorate** with Cromwell as the Lord Protector and commander in

---

THE GREAT BATH ROAD

The **Great Bath Road** (the modern day A4) is the backbone of the Great West Way and was for a long time the main route west out of London. Before the route was formalised there would have been a lattice of routes crossing the countryside from London to Bristol, but in 1632 Charles I tasked Thomas Witherings, the Postmaster of Foreign Mails, with building six "Great Roads" to speed up postal deliveries.

At first the **Royal Mail** opposed the use of coaches to deliver the post, favouring the traditional method of sending a **postboy** on a horse. However this was unreliable (and often subject to robberies). John Palmer, the manager of Bath's original Theatre Royal, saw a better way and petitioned William Pitt, then Chancellor of the Exchequer, to allow him to trial sending the Bristol to London mail by coach in 1784. Since the coach could carry more mail than a postboy, as well as an armed guard, the trial was a resounding success and in time all mail was travelling by coach.

The Great Bath Road rose in prominence in the eighteenth century when Queen Anne began visiting **Bath** and the city became a fashionable resort. Road conditions improved over the years and as stagecoaches got faster (reaching 10mph by the 1830s) journey times halved in a period of about fifty years, a similar improvement seen in more modern times with the opening of the motorways.

During the heyday of coach travel, the maroon and black **mail coaches** left London by night and arrived in Bath in time for breakfast, while the very wealthy travelled by private coach and **yellow post chaises** could be rented to travel from inn to inn. Coach travel was very expensive as it needed numerous horses – who could only work one stage of the route (generally 10–20 miles) each day and required a day off each week. It was said at the time that to travel 100 miles required a hundred horses. It is no surprise then that once the railways came – with their cheaper, faster, safer and more comfortable carriages – that coach travel became a thing of the past.

Today the A4 has been usurped by the M4 motorway but remains a major road connecting towns and villages along the Great West Way.

1455–85	1534	c.1592
Wars of the Roses	Church of England established	First performance of Shakespeare's *Henry VI, Pt 1*, at the Rose Theatre, London

chief. Cromwell reformed the government, secured advantageous commercial treaties with foreign nations and used his New Model Army to put the fear of God into his various enemies. The turmoil of the Civil War and the pre-eminence of the army unleashed a furious legal, theological and political debate throughout the country. This milieu spawned a host of leftist sects, the most notable of whom were the **Levellers**, who demanded wholesale constitutional reform, and the more radical **Diggers**, who proposed common ownership of all land. Nonconformist religious groups also flourished, prominent among them the pacifist **Quakers**, led by the much-persecuted George Fox (1624–91), and the **Dissenters**, to whom the most famous writers of the day, John Milton (1608–74) and John Bunyan (1628–88), both belonged.

Cromwell died in 1658 to be succeeded by his son **Richard**, who ruled briefly and ineffectually, leaving the army unpaid while one of its more ambitious commanders, **General Monk**, conspired to restore the monarchy. Charles II, the exiled son of the previous king, entered London in triumph in May 1660.

A **Stuart** was back on the English throne, but **Charles II** had few absolutist illusions – the terms of the **Restoration** were closely negotiated and included a general amnesty for all those who had fought against the Stuarts, with the exception of the regicides – that is, those who had signed Charles I's death warrant. Nonetheless, there was a sea change in public life with the re-establishment of a royal court and the foundation of the **Royal Society**, whose scientific endeavours were furthered by Isaac Newton (1642–1727). The low points of Charles's reign were the **Great Plague** of 1665 and the 1666 **Great Fire of London**, though the London that rose from the ashes was an architectural showcase for Christopher Wren (1632–1723) and his fellow classicists. Politically, there were still underlying tensions between the monarchy and Parliament, but the latter was more concerned with the struggle between the **Whigs** and **Tories**, political factions representing, respectively, the low-church gentry and the high-church aristocracy. There was a degree of religious toleration too, but its brittleness was all too apparent in the anti-Catholic riots of 1678.

James II and the Glorious Revolution

James II, the brother of Charles II, came to the throne in 1685. He was a Catholic, which made the bulk of his subjects uneasy, but there was still an indifferent response when the Protestant **Duke of Monmouth**, the favourite among Charles II's illegitimate sons, raised a rebellion in the West Country. Monmouth was defeated at Sedgemoor, in Somerset, in July 1685 and nine days later he was beheaded at Tower Hill. Neither was any mercy shown to his supporters: in the **Bloody Assizes** of Judge Jeffreys, hundreds of rebels and suspected sympathizers were executed or deported. Yet if James felt secure he was mistaken; he showed all the traditional weaknesses of his family, from his enthusiasm for the divine right of kings to an over-reliance on sycophantic favourites. Even worse, as far as the Protestants were concerned, he built up a massive standing army, officered it with Roman Catholics and proposed a **Declaration of Indulgence**, removing anti-Catholic restrictions. The final straw was the birth of James's son, which threatened to secure a Catholic succession, and, thoroughly alarmed, powerful Protestants now urged **William of Orange**, the Dutch husband of James II's Protestant daughter Mary, to save them from "popery" – and that was precisely what he did. William landed in Devon in 1688 and, as James's

1603	1608	1642
King James unites the crowns of England and Scotland	England founds its first American colony, in Virginia	The Civil War begins when Charles I raises his standard at Nottingham

forces melted away, he speedily took control of London in the **Glorious Revolution** of 1688.

The last Stuarts

William and Mary became joint sovereigns after they agreed a **Bill of Rights** defining the limitations of the monarchy's power and the rights of its subjects. This, together with the **Act of Settlement of 1701**, made Britain a **constitutional monarchy**, in which the roles of legislature and executive were separate and interdependent. The model was broadly consistent with that outlined by the philosopher and political thinker **John Locke** (1632–1704), whose essentially Whig doctrines of toleration and social contract were gradually embraced as the new orthodoxy. Meanwhile, William, ruling alone after Mary's death in 1694, mainly regarded England as a prop in his defence of Holland against France, a stance that defined England's political alignment in Europe for the next sixty years.

After William's death, the crown passed to **Anne**, the second daughter of James II. Anne was a Protestant – an Anglican to be exact – but her popularity had more to do with her self-proclaimed love of England, which came as something of a relief after William's marked preference for the Dutch. During Anne's reign, English armies won a string of remarkable victories on the Continent, beginning with the Duke of Marlborough's triumph at Blenheim in 1704, followed the next year by the capture of Gibraltar, establishing a British presence in the Mediterranean. These military escapades were part of the Europe-wide **War of the Spanish Succession**, a long-winded dynastic squabble that rumbled on until the 1713 Treaty of Utrecht pretty much settled the European balance of power for the rest of the century. Otherwise, Anne's reign was distinguished mainly for the 1707 **Act of Union**, uniting the English and Scottish parliaments.

Despite her seventeen pregnancies, none of Anne's children survived into adulthood. Consequently, when she died in 1714, the succession passed from the Stuarts to the Hanoverians in the person of the Elector of Hanover, a non-English-speaking Protestant who became George I of England – all in accordance with the terms of the Act of Settlement.

The Hanoverians

During **George I**'s lacklustre reign, power leached into the hands of a Whig oligarchy led by a chief minister – or prime minister – the longest serving of whom was **Robert Walpole** (1676–1745). Elsewhere, plans were being hatched for a **Jacobite Rebellion** in support of **James Edward Stuart**, the "Old Pretender", son of the usurped James II. Its timing appeared perfect: Scottish opinion was moving against the Union, which had failed to bring Scotland tangible economic benefits, and many English Catholics supported the Jacobite cause too, toasting the "king across the water". In 1715, the Earl of Mar raised the Stuart standard in Scotland and gathered an army of more than ten thousand men. Mar's rebellion took the government by surprise. They had only four thousand soldiers in the north, but Mar dithered until he lost the military advantage and by the time the Old Pretender landed in Scotland in December 1715, six thousand veteran Dutch troops had reinforced government forces. The rebellion disintegrated rapidly and James slunk back to exile in France with his tail between his legs.

1649	1660	1665–6
Charles I executed; England becomes a Commonwealth under Cromwell	The Restoration: Charles II takes the throne	The Great Plague kills 100,000 people in London in 18 months

Under **George II**, England became embroiled in yet another dynastic squabble, the War of the Austrian Succession (1740–48), but this played second fiddle to another **Jacobite Rebellion**, this one in 1745, when the "Young Pretender", **Charles Stuart** (Bonnie Prince Charlie), assembled a Highland army and marched south, reaching Derby, just 100 miles from London. There was panic in the capital, but the Prince's army failed to press home his advantage, and the Jacobites turned tail. A Hanoverian army under the Duke of Cumberland caught up with them at **Culloden Moor** near Inverness in April 1746 and hacked them to pieces. The prince lived out the rest of his life in drunken exile, while in Scotland wearing tartan, bearing arms and playing bagpipes were all banned. Most significantly, the government prohibited the private armies of the highland chiefs, thereby destroying the military capacity of the clans.

Empire and colonies

Towards the end of George II's reign, the **Seven Years War** (1756–63) harvested England a bounty of overseas territory in India and Canada at the expense of France; and then, in 1768, with **George III** now on the throne, **Captain James Cook** stumbled upon New Zealand and Australia, thereby extending Britain's empire still further. Amid the imperial bonanza, the problem was the deteriorating relationship with the thirteen colonies of North America, which came to a head with the **American Declaration of Independence** and Britain's subsequent defeat in the **Revolutionary War** (1775–83). The debacle helped fuel a renewed struggle between king and Parliament, enlivened by the intervention of John Wilkes, first of a long and increasingly vociferous line of parliamentary radicals. It also made the British reluctant to interfere in the momentous events taking place across the Channel, where France, long its most consistent foe, was convulsed by revolution. Out of the turmoil emerged the most daunting of enemies, **Napoleon Bonaparte** (1769–1821), whose stunning military progress was interrupted by Nelson at **Trafalgar** in 1805 and finally stopped ten years later by the Duke of Wellington (and the Prussians) at **Waterloo**.

The Industrial Revolution

England's triumph over Napoleon was underpinned by its financial strength, which was itself born of the **Industrial Revolution**, the switch from an agricultural to a manufacturing economy that transformed the face of the country within a century. The earliest mechanized production was in the northern **cotton mills**, where cotton-spinning progressed from a cottage industry to a highly productive factory-based system. Initially, river water powered the mills, but the technology changed after James Watt patented his **steam engine** in 1781. Watt's engines needed **coal**, which made it convenient to locate mills and factories near coal mines, a tendency that was accelerated as **ironworks** took up coal as a smelting fuel, vastly increasing the output from their furnaces. Accordingly, there was a shift of population towards the Midlands and the north of England, where the great coal reserves were located. Commerce and industry were also served by improving transport facilities, principally the digging of a network of **canals** (including the **Kennet & Avon Canal**), but the great leap forward came with the arrival of the **railway**. This greatly facilitated trade but also tourism, and the **Great Western Railway** brought parts of the Great West Way into far easier reach for many people.

1684	1688	1701
Isaac Newton discovers gravity – but is probably not hit on the head by an apple	The Glorious Revolution installs William & Mary on the throne	The Act of Settlement makes Britain a constitutional monarchy

Boosted by a vast influx of immigrant workers, the country's population rose from about eight and a half million at the beginning of George III's reign to more than fifteen million by its end. As the factories and their attendant towns expanded, so the rural settlements of England declined, inspiring the elegiac pastoral yearnings of Samuel Taylor Coleridge and William Wordsworth, the first great names of the Romantic movement. Later Romantic poets such as Percy Bysshe Shelley and Lord Byron took a more socially engaged position, but much more dangerous to the ruling class were the nation's factory workers, who grew restless when mechanization put thousands of them out of work.

Industrial discontent coalesced in the **Chartists**, a broad-based popular movement that demanded parliamentary reform – the most important of the industrial boom towns were still unrepresented in Parliament – and the repeal of the hated **Corn Laws**, which kept the price of bread artificially high to the advantage of the large landowners. Tensions continued to run high throughout the 1820s, and in retrospect it seems that the country may have been saved from a French-style revolution by a series of judicious parliamentary acts: the **Reform Act** of 1832 established the principle (if not actually the practice) of popular representation; the **New Poor Law** of 1834 did something to alleviate the condition of the most destitute; and the repeal of the Corn Laws in 1846 cut the cost of bread.

Significant sections of the middle classes supported progressive reform too, as evidenced by the immense popularity of **Charles Dickens** (1812–70), whose novels railed against poverty and injustice. Indeed, they had already played a key reforming role in the previous century when John Wesley (1703–91) and his **Methodists** led the anti-slavery campaign. As a result of their efforts, **slavery** was banned in Britain in 1772 and throughout the British Empire in 1833 – albeit long after the seaport of **Bristol** had grown rich from the trade.

THE KENNET & AVON CANAL

The idea of an east–west waterway across the south of England was first raised in the late sixteenth century but there was opposition from turnpike operators on the **Great Bath Road** who feared losing their income if freight was transported by water and so the plans were shelved. In the early eighteenth century the River Kennet was made navigable from Reading to Newbury; around the same time the River Avon between Bath and Bristol was restored to its previous state as a navigable river (which had been altered by the construction of watermills).

Surveys for what would become the **Kennet & Avon Canal** began in the last decades of the eighteenth century and the route was agreed by 1794, when construction began. The first section to be completed ran from Newbury to Hungerford and the canal was finished in 1810 when the famously steep locks at **Devizes** were constructed.

At first trade on the canal flourished, with costs lower than sending freight by road and by 1818 some seventy 60-ton barges were ploughing up and down the canal, completing journeys from Newbury to Bath in about three and a half days.

But it was not to last. With the opening of the **Great Western Railway** in 1841 a better method of transporting freight had been found and the canal fell into decline. By the 1950s large sections of the canal had closed but almost immediately there were plans afoot to save it and in 1962 the Kennet & Avon Canal Trust was formed. Gradually restoration works were completed and on August 8 1990 the Queen officially reopened the canal. Maintenance and upgrade works continue but today the canal is a popular cruising route and hundreds of narrowboats carry holidaymakers on its waters every year.

1707	1783	1815	1819
The Act of Union unites English and Scottish parliaments	End of the American War of Independence – American colonies break from Britain	Final defeat of Napoleon at the battle of Waterloo	Isambard Kingdom Brunel builds the SS *Great Eastern*, the largest ship in the world

The Victorians

Blind and insane, **George III** died in 1820. His two sons, **George IV** and **William IV,** were succeeded in their turn by his niece, **Victoria,** whose long reign witnessed the zenith of British power. The economy boomed – typically the nation's cloth manufacturers boasted that they supplied the domestic market before breakfast, the rest of the world thereafter – and the British trading fleet was easily the mightiest in the world. The fleet policed an empire upon which, in that famous phrase of the time, "the sun never set" and Victoria became the symbol of both the nation's success and the imperial ideal. There were extraordinary intellectual achievements too – as typified by the publication of **Charles Darwin's** *On the Origin of Species* in 1859 – and the country came to see itself as both a civilizing agent and the hand of (a very Protestant) God on earth. Britain's industrial and commercial prowess was best embodied by the engineering feats of **Isambard Kingdom Brunel** (1806–59) – including his Great West Way works, the **Clifton Suspension Bridge** and the Great Western Railway itself.

In 1854 troops were sent to protect the Ottoman empire against the Russians in the **Crimea,** an inglorious fiasco whose horrors were relayed to the public by the first-ever press coverage of a military campaign and by the revelations of Florence Nightingale, who was appalled by the lack of medical care for the soldiers. The **Indian Mutiny** – or more accurately Indian Rebellion – of 1857 was a further shock to the imperial system, exposing the fragility of Britain's hold over the Indian subcontinent, though the status quo was brutally restored and Victoria took the title Empress of India after 1876. Thereafter, the British army was flattered by a series of minor wars against poorly armed Asian and African opponents, but promptly came unstuck when it faced the Dutch settlers of South Africa in the **Boer War** (1899–1902). The British ultimately fought their way to a sort of victory, but the discreditable conduct of the war prompted a military shake-up at home that was to be of significance in the coming European conflict.

World War I and its aftermath (1914–39)

Victoria died in 1901, to be succeeded by her son, **Edward VII,** whose leisurely lifestyle has often been seen as the epitome of the complacent era to which he gave his name. It wasn't to last. By 1910, all the major European powers were enmeshed in a network of rival military alliances and these were switched on – almost accidentally – by the assassination of the Habsburg Archduke Franz Ferdinand in late June 1914; a few weeks later, with **George V** now on the throne, the British declared war on Germany in alliance with France and Russia. Hundreds of thousands volunteered for the British army, but their enthusiastic nationalism was not enough to ensure a quick victory and **World War I** dragged on for four miserable years, its key engagements fought in the trenches that zigzagged across northern France and Belgium. Britain and its allies eventually prevailed, but the number of dead – tragically increased by 1918's devastating **Spanish flu** pandemic – beggared belief, undermining the authority of the British ruling class, whose generals had shown a lethal combination of incompetence and indifference to the plight of their men.

After the war ended in 1918, the sheer weight of public opinion pushed Parliament into extending the vote to all men 21 and over and to women over thirty. This tardy liberalization of women's rights owed much to the efforts of the Suffragists and the

1892	1926	1946	1962
The *Titanic* sinks, and Captain Scott and his men die in the Antarctic	Britain's first-ever General Strike: a nine-day walkout in support of the coal miners	Britain's first supermarket opens in south London	The Beatles hit the big time with their first single, *Love Me Do*

THE GREAT WESTERN RAILWAY

The **Great Western Railway** was founded in 1833, largely to help Bristol maintain its status as England's second port as Liverpool rose in ascendency. **Isambard Kingdom Brunel** was appointed chief engineer in 1835 and set about determining a route. This proved controversial, with his chosen route running north of the Marlborough Downs and prioritising potential link-ups with Oxford and Gloucester over passing through any existing significant towns. This led to the railway being built along a route that is not the most direct – and earning the later moniker the "Great Way Round".

The railway opened in sections, the first being the London-Maidenhead section which opened in 1838. The railway finally linked London with Bristol on completion of the Box Tunnel (between Bath and Chippenham) in 1841. Most of the original locomotives were built at the company's **Swindon workshop** which was operational from 1843 until 1986; they were painted a dark green colour known as Brunswick green, while the livery for passenger coaches was chocolate and cream.

During the nineteenth century the GWR became known as the "**holiday line**", transporting people out of London to the holiday resorts of the Bristol Channel and far southwest of England. At the outbreak of **World War I** the line was taken under government control (along with most other railways in Britain) and many of its staff joined the armed forces. Post-war it was decided that the railways would be amalgamated into four large groups; the Great Western Railway was the only one to keep its name, though this did not survive the post Second World War **nationalisation** of the railways, when it became known as the Western Region of British Railways.

After some 40 years the railway was privatised and its name reverted back. After a period as First Great Western under FirstGroup, since 2015 it has once again be officially called the Great Western Railway.

---

more radical **Suffragettes**, led by Emmeline Pankhurst and her daughters Sylvia and Christabel, but the process was only completed in 1929 when women were at last granted the vote at 21. The royal family itself was shaken in 1936 by the **abdication of Edward VIII**, following his decision to marry a twice-divorced American, Wallis Simpson. In the event, the succession passed smoothly to his brother **George VI**, but the royals had to play catch-up to regain their popularity among the population as a whole.

During this period, the **Labour Party** supplanted the Liberals as the second-largest party, its strength built on an alliance between the working-class trade unions and middle-class radicals and Labour formed its first government in 1923 under **Ramsay MacDonald** (1866–1937). Two years later, a bitter dispute between the nation's pit men and the mine-owners spread to the railways, the newspapers and the iron and steel industries, thereby escalating into a **General Strike**. The strike lasted nine days and involved half a million workers, provoking the government into draconian action – the army was called in, and the strike was broken. The economic situation deteriorated even further after the crash of the New York Stock Exchange in 1929, which precipitated a worldwide depression.

Abroad, the structure of the **British Empire** was undergoing profound changes. After the cack-handed way in which the British had dealt with Dublin's 1916 Easter Rising, the status of **Ireland** was bound to change. There was a partial resolution in 1922 with the establishment of the Irish Free State, but the six counties of the mainly Protestant North (two-thirds of the ancient province of **Ulster**) chose to "contract out" and stay part of the United Kingdom – and this was to cause endless problems later. In 1926, the **Imperial**

1967	1970	1975	1985
First withdrawal from an ATM in Britain – at a branch of Barclays in Enfield, north London	First Glastonbury Festival held – music lovers get used to mud	First North Sea oil comes ashore	The bitter, year-long miners' strike is crushed by Margaret Thatcher

Conference recognized the autonomy of the British dominions, comprising all the major countries that had previously been part of the empire. This agreement was formalized in the 1931 Statute of Westminster, whereby each dominion was given an equal footing in a **Commonwealth of Nations**, though each still recognized the British monarch.

World War II

When Hitler set about militarizing Germany in the mid-1930s, the British government adopted a policy of appeasement. Consequently, when Britain declared war on Germany after Hitler's invasion of Poland in September 1939, the country was poorly prepared. After embarrassing military failures during the first months of **World War II**, the discredited government was replaced in May 1940 by a national coalition headed by the charismatic **Winston Churchill** (1874–1965)– days before the British army made a forced evacuation from Dunkirk. These were bleak and uncertain days for Britain, but the tide turned when the Germans invaded the **USSR** in 1941, and Churchill found he had a new and powerful ally. Further reinforcements arrived in December 1941, when the **US** declared war on both Germany and Japan after the Japanese had made a surprise attack on Pearl Harbor. The involvement of both the United States and the Soviet Union swung the military balance, and by early 1943 the Germans were doomed to defeat – though it took two more years to finish Hitler off.

In terms of casualties, World War II was not as calamitous as World War I, but its impact upon British civilians was much greater. In its first wave of **bombing** of the UK, the Luftwaffe caused massive damage to industrial centres such as London and **Bristol**. Later raids, intended to shatter morale rather than factories and docks, battered the cathedral cities of England, including **Bath**. By 1945, nearly a third of the nation's houses had been destroyed or damaged, over 58,000 civilians had lost their lives, and nearly a quarter of a million soldiers, sailors and airmen had been killed.

Postwar England (1945–79)

Hungry for change, voters in 1945's postwar election replaced Churchill with the Labour Party under **Clement Attlee** (1883–1967), who set about a radical programme to **nationalize** the coal, gas, electricity, iron and steel industries. In addition, the early passage of the National Insurance Act and the National Health Service (NHS) Act gave birth to what became known as the **welfare state**. However, despite substantial American aid, rebuilding the economy was a huge task that made **austerity** the keynote, with the rationing of food and fuel remaining in force long after 1945. This cost the Labour Party dearly in the general election of 1951, which returned the Conservatives to power under the leadership of an ageing Churchill. The following year, King George VI died and was succeeded by his elder daughter, who, as **Queen Elizabeth II**, remains on the throne today.

Meanwhile, Britain, the United States, Canada, France and the Benelux countries defined their postwar international commitments in 1949's **North Atlantic Treaty**, a counterbalance to Soviet power in Eastern Europe. Nevertheless, there was continuing confusion over Britain's imperial – or rather post-imperial – role and this bubbled to the surface in both the incompetent **partition of India** in 1947 and the **Suez Crisis** of 1956, when Anglo-French and Israeli forces invaded Egypt to secure control of the

1994	1999	2005
The Channel Tunnel opens to traffic	The Scottish Parliament and the National Assemblies for Wales and Northern Ireland take on devolved powers	The Civil Partnership Act gives same-sex couples legal recognition of their relationships

Suez Canal, only to be hastily recalled following international (American) condemnation; the resignation of the Conservative prime minister, **Anthony Eden** (1897–1977), followed. His replacement, pragmatic, silky-tongued **Harold Macmillan** (1894–1986), accepted the end of empire, but was still eager for Britain to play a leading international role – and the country kept its nuclear arms.

The dominant political figure in the 1960s was Labour's **Harold Wilson** (1916–95), a witty speaker and skilled tactician who was prime minister twice (1964–70 and 1974–76). The Sixties saw a boom in consumer spending, pioneering social legislation (primarily on homosexuality and abortion),and a corresponding cultural upswing, with London becoming the hippest city on the planet. But the good times lasted barely a decade: the Conservatives returned to office in 1970 and although the new prime minister, the ungainly **Edward Heath** (1916–2005), led Britain into the brave new world of the **European Economic Community (EEC)**, the 1970s was an era of recession and industrial strife. Labour returned to power in 1974, but ultimately a succession of public-sector strikes and mistimed decisions handed the 1979 general election to the Conservatives under new leader **Margaret Thatcher** (1925–2013). The pundits were amazed by her success, but as events proved, she was primed and ready to break the unions and anyone else who crossed her path.

Thatcher and Major (1979–97)

Thatcher went on to win three general elections but pushed the UK into a period of sharp social polarization. While taxation policies and easy credit fuelled a consumer boom for the professional classes, the erosion of manufacturing and weakening of the welfare state impoverished a swathe of the population. Thatcher won an increased majority in the 1983 election, thanks largely to the successful recapture of the **Falkland Islands**, a remote British dependency in the south Atlantic, retrieved from the occupying Argentine army in 1982. Her electoral domination was also assisted by the fragmentation of the Labour opposition, particularly following the establishment of the Social Democratic Party, which had formed in response to what it perceived as the radicalization of the Labour Party but ended up amalgamating with what remained of the Liberal Party to form the **Liberal Democrats** in 1988.

Social and political tensions surfaced in sporadic urban rioting and the year-long **miners' strike** (1984–85) against colliery closures, a bitter industrial dispute in which the police were given unprecedented powers to restrict the movement of citizens. The violence in Northern Ireland also intensified, and in 1984 IRA bombers came close to killing the entire Cabinet, who were staying in a Brighton hotel during the Conservatives' annual conference. The divisive politics of Thatcherism reached their apogee when the desperately unpopular **Poll Tax** led to her overthrow by Conservative colleagues who feared annihilation if she led them into another general election. The beneficiary was **John Major** (b.1943), a notably uninspiring figure who nonetheless managed to win the Conservatives a fourth term of office in 1992, albeit with a much-reduced Parliamentary majority. While his government presided over a steady growth in economic performance, they gained little credit amid allegations of mismanagement, incompetence and feckless leadership, all overlaid by endless tales of Tory "sleaze", with revelations of

2007	**2009**	**2011**
Smoking banned in enclosed public places in England and Wales	Economic crisis prompts the Bank of England to reduce interest rates to a record low of 0.5 percent	Murdoch media empire in crisis over illegal phone-hacking: *News of the World* newspaper closes

extramarital affairs and financial crookery gleefully recounted by the British press. There was also the small matter of ties with Europe: a good chunk of the Conservative Party wanted a European free-trade zone, but nothing more, whereas the **Maastricht Treaty** of 1992, which the UK government signed, seemed to imply an element of political union with the EEC (now rebranded as the **European Union** or **EU**); right-wing Tories were apoplectic and their frequent and very public demonstrations of disloyalty further hobbled the Major government.

The Blair years

Wracked by factionalism in the 1980s, the **Labour Party** regrouped under Neil Kinnock and then John Smith, though neither of them reaped the political rewards. These dropped into the lap of a new and dynamic young leader, **Tony Blair** (b.1953), who soon pushed the party further away from traditional left-wing socialism. Blair's cloak of idealistic, media-friendly populism worked to devastating effect, sweeping the Labour Party to power in the **general election of May 1997** on a wave of genuine popular optimism. There were immediate rewards in enhanced relations with the EU and progress in the Irish peace talks, and Blair's electoral touch was soon repeated in Labour-sponsored **devolution referenda**, whose results semi-detached Scotland and Wales from their more populous neighbour in the form of a Scottish Parliament and Welsh Assembly.

Labour won the **general election of June 2001** with another thumping parliamentary landslide. This second victory was, however, accompanied by little of the optimism of the one before. Few voters fully trusted Blair, and his administration had by then established an unenviable reputation for the laundering of events to present the government in the best possible light. Nonetheless, the ailing Conservative Party failed to capitalize on these shortcomings, leaving Blair streets ahead of his political rivals in the opinion polls when the hijacked planes hit New York's World Trade Center on **September 11, 2001**. Blair rushed to support President Bush, joining in the attack on Afghanistan and then, to widespread horror, sending British forces into **Iraq** alongside the Americans in 2003. Saddam Hussein was deposed with relative ease, but neither Bush nor Blair had a coherent exit strategy, and back home Blair was widely seen as having spun Britain into the war by exaggerating the danger Saddam presented with his supposed – indeed nonexistent – **WMDs** (Weapons of Mass Destruction).

The financial crash and its aftermath

Blair won a third general election in May 2005, but only after promising to step down before the following one. Perhaps regretting his promise, Blair proceeded to huff and puff but eventually, in 2007, he stepped down and was succeeded by his colleague and arch-rival, **Gordon Brown** (b.1951). It was not a happy succession: Brown, previously Chancellor of the Exchequer, managed to secure little credit for his one major achievement, the staving-off of a banking collapse during the worldwide **financial crisis** that hit the UK hard in the autumn of 2007–08. Brown's bold decision to keep public investment high by borrowing vast sums of money almost certainly prevented a comprehensive economic collapse in 2008–09, though equally his failure to properly regulate the banks beforehand helped create the crisis in the first place.

2012	2013	2015
London hosts the Olympic Games	Same-sex marriage legalized in England	Conservatives win the general election under David Cameron

In the build-up to the **general election of 2010**, both main political parties, as well as the Liberal Democrats, spoke of the need to **cut public spending** more or less drastically, manoeuvring the electorate away from blaming the bankers for the crash. In the event, none of the three was able to secure a Parliamentary majority in the general election, but an impasse was avoided when the Liberal Democrats swapped principles for power to join a **Conservative–Liberal Democrat coalition**, which took office in May 2010 with Conservative David Cameron as prime minister.

An old Etonian with a PR background, **David Cameron** (b.1966) made a confident and sure-footed start as prime minister, while his government set about a concerted attack on the public sector on the pretext of the need for **austerity** following the financial crash. All seemed set fair, with the Liberals suitably supine, but key policy initiatives soon began to run aground and the coalition zigzagged between decision and revision, for example in its plans to transform (that is, part privatize) the NHS.

There was also the matter of Scotland, where the **Scottish National Party** (SNP) had galvanized support for Scottish independence. In the event, the **Scottish independence referendum** of September 2014 gave a slight victory to the unionists, and the United Kingdom survived. The most remarkable feature of the referendum, though, was the high turnout – an astounding 84 percent.

Despite the less than impressive record of his government, Cameron managed to win an overall majority in the **general election of 2015** by promising strong fiscal management – and yet more austerity. The Conservative election manifesto also committed to a referendum on the UK's membership of the EU – partly as a sop to Eurosceptics within the party and partly to head off an emergent **UKIP**, an EU-hating, right-wing party. Cameron, who wanted to stay in the EU, seems to have been quietly confident that the "remainers" would win by a country mile, but in the **EU membership referendum** of June 23, 2016, almost 52 percent of the population voted to leave the EU; Cameron promptly resigned.

Into the future

After Cameron's departure, **Theresa May** (b.1956) was elected Prime Minister from within the ranks of the Conservative Party. An experienced politician and long-serving Home Secretary, May was reckoned to be reliable and efficient but it soon became obvious that **Brexit** negotiations with the EU would both strain the resources of the British government and sharpen divisions within the Tory Party about the speed of leaving the EU – and what, exactly, leaving actually meant. Still, the Tories thought, they were in no electoral danger as the unexpected new leader of the Labour Party, **Jeremy Corbyn** (b.1949), was far too left-wing to gain any traction – and many more right-wing Labour MPs agreed, whispering away in order to plot Corbyn's downfall. May then called the **general election of June 2017**, which she presumed would be a romp.

It wasn't. May's campaign was extraordinarily inept, but rather more surprisingly a fair chunk of the population warmed to the much-maligned Labour leader. Then there was the Labour manifesto: no 'ifs', no more austerity, plus a renationalization of key industries and the abolition of student university fees. Suddenly there seemed to be a sea change in the popular mood and, although the Conservatives won the election by a nose – albeit with the help of a controversial confidence-and-supply deal with Northern Ireland's populist, right-wing **DUP** – austerity, their key policy plank, was left looking dead in the water.

2016	2017–19
UK narrowly votes to leave the EU (51.9 percent). Many leave voters express "Regrexit"; "Remainers" unimpressed	PM Theresa May calls a snap election in 2017. In 2019, her Brexit deal is defeated in the Commons and uncertainty reigns

Film and TV

The Great West Way is home to some of England's most scenic locations, so it's no surprise that the route has been seen on screen so many times. From blockbuster films to long-running TV dramas much beloved around the world, the Great West Way has featured in some of the best on screen moments of recent years. Those listed below are some of our favourites.

The GWW on screen

The ★ symbol indicates titles that are especially recommended.

Cranford (Simon Curtis, 2007). This five-part BBC drama might have been set in Cheshire, but Lacock in Wiltshire was the main filming location, standing in for the fictional village of Cranford. The story begins when a handsome young doctor moves into the village, causing quite a stir with the spinster and widowed ladies of the parish – whose determination to keep things "proper" is tested as modern life intervenes and the railway arrives.

★Downton Abbey (Julian Fellowes, 2010–2015). Unmissable ITV drama series that focuses on life both above and below stairs in the fictional Downton Abbey. Writer Julian Fellowes is said to have based the show on real-life estate Highclere Castle and the building was used for both exterior and interior filming. The story begins in 1912 with the sinking of the Titanic and ranges through the 20th century, following the fortunes of the aristocratic Crawley family and their three daughters Mary, Edith and Sybil as the First World War strikes and the upper-class way of life begins its ultimate demise. This is an entertaining show but also one that introduces early 20th century English history in an engaging and accessible way.

The Duchess (Saul Dibb, 2008). Drama based on Amanda Foreman's biography of the eighteenth-century Duchess of Devonshire, played on screen by Keira Knightley. Much of the filming took place in Bath, including at the Assembly Rooms, Royal Crescent and Holburne Museum.

Emma (BBC, 1996). Jane Austen's classic novel about great meddler Emma Wodehouse was brought to life by a stellar cast, including Kate Beckinsale playing the title role. Lacock in Wiltshire was the principle filming location.

The Guernsey Literary and Potato Peel Society (Mike Newell, 2018). This historical romance is set in 1946 and follows a London writer who begins communicating with the residents of Guernsey, an island under German occupation during the Second World War. Princes Wharf in Bristol appears on screen as Weymouth Docks.

★Harry Potter film series (Chris Columbus, Alfonso Cuarón, Mike Newell, David Yates, 2001–2011). JK Rowling's blockbuster series of novels about boy wizard Harry Potter was made into a series of eight big-budget films. Virginia Water, just west of London, was Hogwarts School's lake in the Prisoner of Azkaban, Swinley Forest appeared in the Deathly Hallows part one and Ashridge Wood just north of Newbury stood in as the setting for the Quidditch World Cup in the Goblet of Fire. It was Lacock though that saw the most action on screen, appearing in numerous scenes as Hogwarts locations including Professor McGonagall's classroom, the Room of Requirement and Professor Quirrell's Defence Against the Dark Arts classroom.

Lark Rise to Candleford (Bill Gallagher, 2008–2011). The idiosyncrasies of the English countryside are fodder for this costume drama, adapted from Flora Thompson's trilogy of semi-autobiographical novels. The story is set in Oxfordshire, in the hamlet of Lark Rise and wealthier neighbouring village of Candleford. The series was mostly filmed in Wiltshire, with the two villages recreated on two farms near Corsham. Great Chalfield Manor also appears.

Les Misérables (Tom Hooper, 2012). Oscar-winning big-budget adaptation of the 1862 Victor Hugo novel. The heavyweight cast includes Anne Hathaway (who won the Oscar for Best Supporting Actress), Hugh Jackman, Russell Crowe and Amanda Seyfried and some scenes were shot around Pulteney Bridge and weir in Bath.

Midsomer Murders Greys Court (ITV, 1997–present). Detective drama based on the Chief Inspector Barnaby book series by Caroline Graham. The fictional county of Midsomer sees a higher than average number of murders, one of which sees the grisly end of a nun in the chicken coop outside Grey's Court in the village of Rotherfield Greys near Henley on Thames.

The Other Boleyn Girl (Justin Chadwick, 2008). Not entirely accurate but enjoyable historical romance drama based around sisters Mary Boleyn, one-time mistress of King Henry VIII, and her more famous sister, Anne. The all-star cast included Natalie Portman, Scarlett Johansson and Eric Bana. Lacock Abbey and Great Chalfield Manor are both seen on screen.

Agatha Christie's Poirot, Elephants Can Remember
(Nick Dear, 2013). Based on the crime novels of Agatha
Christie, Poirot was one of the longest-running shows on
British TV, screening from 1989 to 2013 and starring David
Suchet. Episode one of series 13, Elephants Can Remember,
featured Zoe Wanamaker, as well as Greys Court near
Henley.

Poldark (BBC, 2015–2018) is a hugely popular historical
period drama - largely due to its often-shirtless hero,
played by Aidan Turner - who has returned to Cornwall after
the American War of Independence. Its fifth and final series
began filming in September 2018.

★ **Pride and Prejudice** (BBC, 1995). Probably the most
popular adaptation of Jane Austen's most famous novel
ever made, this BBC drama screened in six parts and
featured Lacock as the fictional village of Meryton. It also
featured Colin Firth as Mr Darcy, a role the actor has since
never quite escaped.

The Secret Garden (Mark Munden). The latest
adaptation of Frances Hodgson Burnett's 1911 novel,
starring Colin Firth and Julie Walters, was filmed in Iford
Manor, among other locations in the UK. At the time of
writing, the film was in post production.

★ **Sherlock** (Mark Gatiss and Steven Mofatt, 2010–
2017). Wonderfully engaging interpretation of Sir Arthur
Conan Doyle's detective stories, starring Benedict
Cumberbatch and Martin Freeman. Set in the present day,
the 13 episodes are irreverent and modern, bringing the
world-famous detective bang up to date. Bristol was used
for much of the filming and the 2016 special the
Abominable Bride used the city as its production base.
You'll see Queen Square, the Old Vic theatre and Tyntesfield
on screen among many other locations around the city.

Vanity Fair (Mira Nair, 2004). Historical drama based on
William Makepeace Thackeray's novel of the same name
and starring Reese Witherspoon as main character Becky
Sharp.Great Pulteney Street in Bath was turned into a film
set and Beauford Square and the Holburne Museum were
also used as filming locations.

★ **Wallace and Gromit** (Nick Park, 1989–present). Two
of the most famous film stars to come out of the Great West
Way are made of clay. Wallace and his dog Gromit are the
creation of Nick Park's Aardman Animations, based in
Bristol, and have appeared on screen in a series of short
films including A Grand Day Out, The Wrong Trousers and A
Close Shave. This is the stuff of Christmas Day family
viewing and you'll be hard pressed to find any English
person who doesn't love these two characters.

War Horse (Steven Spielberg, 2011). This highly emotive
war drama was based on Michael Morpurgo's 1982 novel
and the 2007 play adaptation of it and tells the story of
Albert Narracott and his horse Joey, who both see action in
World War One. Despite Devon being the setting for the
film, Castle Combe appeared on screen as Albert's village,
and the location of his enlistment.

Wolf Hall (BBC, 2015). This six-part historical drama was
adapted by the BBC from two novels by Hilary Mantel, Wolf
Hall and Bring Up the Bodies. The story follows the rapid
rise to power of Oliver Cromwell and features scenes shot at
Lacock Abbey, Great Chalfield Manor and Bristol Cathedral.

The Wolfman (Joe Johnston, 2010). Benicio del Toro,
Anthony Hopkins and Emily Blunt star in this horror movie
about werewolves. Lacock's tithe barn and Castle Combe
both feature.

Music

The Great West Way has given the world some top music acts and its biggest city, Bristol, has been associated since the 1990s with trip hop, a catch-all term encompassing artists such as Portishead and Massive Attack, who rejected the guitar-led Britpop scene in favour of a darker, spacier and more down-tempo sound. Fewer musicians have come out of the quieter areas further east, though reality TV successes Will Young and Sarah Harding both hail from Berkshire.

Discography

Girls Aloud *Sound of the Underground, What Will the Neighbours Say?, Chemistry, Tangled Up, Out of Control*. You might well sniff at reality TV bands but Girls Aloud, formed in 2002 on *Popstars: The Rivals*, had 20 consecutive top 10 singles in the UK charts. Group member Sarah Harding hails from the Berkshire town of Ascot.

Massive Attack *Blue Lines, Protection, Mezzanine, 100th Window, Heligoland*. Trip hop band formed in Bristol in 1988 and releasing five studio albums with huge commercial success. Rumours abound that band member Robert "3D" Del Naja is also the street artist, Banksy, though this has, naturally, been denied.

Portishead *Dummy, Portishead, Third*. One of the pioneers of trip hop, formed in Bristol in 1991 and name after the town of the same name. Their first album, *Dummy*, was released in 1994 to critical acclaim and is considered not only their best work, but also a milestone in the development of the genre.

Propellerheads *Decksandrumsandrockandroll*. Electronic duo Will White and Alex Gifford from Bath released their one and only studio album in 1998, reaching number 6 on the UK charts. They are better known for their single *History Repeating* which featured Shirley Bassey and reached number one on the UK dance chart. It has been used on TV and in film numerous times.

Tears for Fears *The Hurting, Songs from the Big Chair, The Seeds of Love, Elemental, Raoul and the Kings of Spain, Everybody Loves a Happy Ending*. Synth pop turned mainstream pop and rock band, formed in Bath in 1981.

Their debut album *The Hurting* reached number one on the UK album charts in 1983 while second album *Songs from the Big Chair* featured their best-known single, *Everybody Wants to Run the World*.

The Verve *A Storm in Heaven, A Northern Soul, Urban Hymns, Forth*. Although this rock band were formed in Wigan, drummer Peter Salisbury hails from Chippenham in Wiltshire. The band released four studio albums but by far the most successful was the 1997 *Urban Hymns*, which featured hugely popular singles *Bitter Sweet Symphony* and *The Drugs Don't Work* and became one of the bestselling albums in UK chart history.

XTC *White Music, Go 2, Drums and Wires, Black Sea, English Settlement, Mummer, The Big Express, 25 O'Clock, Skylarking, Psonic Psunspot, Oranges & Lemons, Nonsuch, Apple Venus Volume 1, Wasp Star (Apple Venus Volume 2)*. Idiosyncratic punk and new wave band formed in Swindon in 1972 and producing multiple albums, of which *Skylarking* is arguably the best. A total of 18 of their singles made the UK top 40, including *Making Plans for Nigel* in 1979 and *Senses Working Overtime* in 1982.

Will Young *From Now On, Friday's Child, Keep On, Let it Go, Echoes, 85% Proof*. One of the UK's first reality TV success stories, Will Young won the first series of *Pop Idol* in 2002. The singer-songwriter and actor comes from Wokingham and has released six studio albums to date, four of which have reached number 1 in the UK charts. His debut single *Evergreen* went straight to number one in the singles chart and was the fastest selling debut single in UK chart history.

Wildlife

"It seems to me that the natural world is the greatest source of excitement; the greatest source of visual beauty; the greatest source of intellectual interest. It is the greatest source of so much in life that makes life worth living."

Sir David Attenborough.

England's most popular naturalist was himself born on the Great West Way, in Isleworth near Richmond. Even in this most urban section of the Way there is plenty of wildlife to spot, and as you explore the landscapes of the route, from dense ancient woodland to wildflower meadow, wending river to chalky hill, you are sure to come across all manner of plant life, birdlife and animal life, from the tiniest butterfly to a soaring red kite or even a rutting deer. These are some of the species you are most likely to encounter as you travel.

Butterflies

Butterflies are one of the most beguiling sights on a walk through the English countryside, flitting across your path in a sudden eruption of dancing colour. You will see butterflies pretty much everywhere along the Great West Way, and they fall into around fifty different species. Some of the most common are the Brimstone, a large lemon-yellow species often seen heading towards purple flowers; the Peacock, with its russet wings and dramatic eye-spot pattern; and the Holly Blue, which is the most common blue butterfly seen in English woodlands. One of the most loved species in England is the small tortoiseshell, which has a bright orange and black pattern, but sadly this species is in dramatic decline – although you are still very likely to see these beautiful butterflies, there are real fears for their future as global warming brings more and more parasitic flies, which seem to favour this species.

Although butterflies are common everywhere along the Great West Way, the best places to see them are gardens with plenty of flowers to attract them, and protected areas of countryside such as **Wiltshire Wildlife Trust Blakehill Farm** and the **Nature Discovery Centre, Thatcham**. For absolutely guaranteed butterfly sightings (and in large numbers) head to **Studley Grange Butterfly World**.

Deer

Perhaps the most impressive animal you are likely to see along the Great West Way is the deer. The species you are most likely to see are the **red deer** and **fallow deer**.

The red deer is the large land mammal in the UK and England's deer are often bigger than their more famous Scottish cousins. The males (stags) can reach heights of up to around four and a half feet with a weight of up to 400 pounds, while females (hinds) rise to four feet in height with weights up to around 260 pounds. These are a native species to Britain and are believed to have migrated from Europe around 11,000 years ago. Although these majestic animals have seen their numbers dwindle in the past (due to hunting and a loss of woodland cover) they are now thriving across Great Britain.

The fallow deer is much smaller than the red, with males (bucks) reaching only around three feet and weighing up to 200 pounds and females (does) a similar height with a weight of around 120 pounds. Most commonly fallow deer are a tan colour with white spotting and these are a more exotic species than their red counterparts, introduced deliberately in the eleventh century from the eastern Mediterranean. Although technically non-native, fallow deer are considered to be naturalized and their population is increasing. Many of those you see today are the descendants of escapees from ancient deer parks, which were once the height of fashion.

For both species the rutting season runs from the end of September until November and during this time males perform elaborate displays (roaring, clashing antlers) in order to attract a female. Although this time of year is the most dangerous time to approach deer, these are wild animals and should be respected at all times – try to keep at least 150ft away and don't even think about feeding them.

Deer can be seen wild along the Great West Way but for the best chance of a sighting head to **Richmond Park** in West London, home to a population of around 650 red and fallow deer; **Ashton Court Estate** in Bristol or **Dyrham Park** near Chippenham (fallow deer only).

Ducks, geese and swans

Ducks, geese and swans can all commonly be seen along the waterways of the Great West Way. One of the most picturesque sights you might encounter is a brilliant white swan seemingly floating along the surface of the water and most common is the **mute swan**, a large snow-white bird with a long S-shaped neck and bright orange bill – these can weigh up to around 25 pounds and have a wingspan of more than seven feet. The population across the UK is increasing, with some 74,000 birds wintering here, so you can be fairly certain of spotting at least one or two on any trip that includes the rivers or the **Kennet & Avon Canal**.

You are also very likely to see the non-native **Canada goose**, most often found on grassland and in parks. They are not universally popular, often making a lot of noise, and their numbers are strong (around 190,000 in the UK). They have a wingspan of more like 6ft and can be seen all year round.

Much more popular are ducks, and especially their tiny fluffy ducklings who are born each year in the spring and early summer. The Great West Way is home to several common species, including the **teal**, the **tufted duck** and the **mallard**. The mallard is most commonly seen, the males distinctive green head and yellow bill spotted regularly along all waterways, even in the most urban of areas. The male is by far the more exotic looking, with females mainly brown to aid camouflage.

Grey heron

One of the UK's most familiar birds is the **grey heron**, an often solitary creature that is unmistakable when seen standing tall and entirely still in the shallow waters of a lake or stream waiting to catch a fish. Herons have grey, black and white feathering, long legs and a long slender neck that is often seen stretched out in search of food – mostly fish, but also ducklings and small mammals such as voles. The grey heron does not migrate and so can be seen along the Great West Way all year round, generally near water, such as a lake, river, estuary or even just a garden pond. Two places that are particularly good for sighting grey herons are the protected wet woodlands at **Wiltshire Wildlife Trust Lower Moor** and **Wiltshire Wildlife Trust Jones's Mill**.

Owls

The RSPB (Royal Society for the Protection of Birds, ⓦ rspb.org.uk) lists five species of **owl** as resident to the UK: the barn owl, little owl, long-eared owl, short-eared owl and tawny owl. Although it is possible to see all of these along the Great West Way, the long-eared owl is nocturnal and highly secretive and the short-eared owl is generally found further north, so both of these are unlikely to be spotted.

You do though have a good chance of seeing barn owls, which can often be seen along the edges of fields and at riverbanks. It's a distinctive bird, with a white heart-shaped face, buff back and wings and white underparts and there are around four thousand breeding pairs in the UK. They are sizeable enough to be spotted fairly easily, standing a foot or so tall and with a wingspan of around three feet.

Tawny owls are similar in size to barn owls but have a more rounded head and a mottled brown plumage that can be trickier to pick out when sitting in the trees. Since they are most active at night, you are more likely to hear them than you are to see them, though **Wiltshire Wildlife Trust Blakehill Farm** is a good bet for sightings.

Little owls are, unsurprisingly, smaller than both barn and tawny owls, typically around nine inches in length and with a wingspan just under two feet. These small owls are the most likely of the three species to be seen in the daytime, using perching somewhere like a telegraph pole or tree. It particularly likes lowland farmland, which the Great West Way has in abundance. They also favour hedges, copses and orchards.

Red kites

The Great West Way is the best place in Britain to see **red kites**. This graceful bird of prey is most commonly seen in the Chilterns AONB where a population was reintroduced between 1989 and 1994. These birds were brought in from Spain to replace a population driven to extinction by the end of the nineteenth century. It is now thought that there could be around a thousand breeding pairs in the area – indeed, the reintroduction has been so successful that it has become impossible to monitor all the nests.

Red kites are only partially a reddish-brown, through the mid-section of their body, and have black and white wings and a distinctive deeply forked tail. Their wingspan typically tops 6ft but the birds only weigh around two pounds and the males are slightly smaller than the females. The red kite is an opportunistic bird – their nests are often the abandoned nests of other birds and are made of large sticks lined with wool and found items such as clothing, while they will happily feast on chicks and small mammals if the opportunity to catch one arises. Otherwise they mainly eat carrion. Their chicks are usually hatched in May and fledge within about six or seven weeks.

Red kites are seen across the mid and southern **Chilterns**, with the best sightings between October and April. Look out for their nests high up in areas of woodland.

Books

England not only has a substantial literary pedigree – from Shakespeare to Rowling – but also an enticing yet rather confusing culture and mindset that warrants some explanation. This bibliography therefore includes not only works focused on the Great West Way but also books that discuss England, and the English, more generally.

Bibliography

The bibliography we've given here is necessarily selective, and entirely subjective. The ★ symbol indicates titles that are especially recommended.

Peter Ackroyd *Albion*. In the massively erudite *Albion*, Ackroyd traces the very origins of English culture and imagination.

Peter Aughton *Bristol: A People's History*. This accessible history of Bristol presents the story of the city that played a major part in the discovery and colonisation of America, as well as the industrial revolution of the Victorian era and the slave trade, which is examined here in full detail.

Jane Austen *Persuasion* and *Northanger Abbey* were both published posthumously, in 1817, and both set in Bath, where Austen herself lived from 1801 to 1806.

★**Bill Bryson** *Notes From A Small Island*. After twenty years living and working in England, Bryson set off on one last tour of Britain before returning to the States – though in the end he couldn't resist his new country and now lives in Hampshire. His hilarious observations set the tone for his future travel, history and popular science bestsellers.

Bill Bryson *Icons of England*. Bryson also edited this collection of rather wonderful essays on rural England. The book celebrates everything from the weather (by Floella Benjamin) to cattle grids (Leo Hickman) and the Great West Way's white horses (Peter Marren).

Martin Crocker *Avon Gorge*. Illustrated guide to climbing at Avon Gorge, including plenty of information about the history of the gorge and of climbing here.

Paul Kingsnorth *Real England*. Kingsnorth's personal journey through his own "private England" is partly a lament for what's being lost – village greens, apple varieties, independent shops, waterways, post offices – and partly a heartfelt howl against globalization.

Ian Marchant *The Longest Crawl*. The pub – so central to English life and landscape – is dissected in this highly entertaining account of a month-long pub crawl across the country, involving pork scratchings, funny beer names and lots of falling over.

Paul Theroux *The Kingdom by the Sea*. Travelling around the coast in its entirety in 1982 to find out what the British are really like leaves Theroux thoroughly bad-tempered. No change there then.

Julian Baggini *Welcome to Everytown: A Journey into the English Mind*. The prolific Baggini's "Everytown" is Rotherham – or rather postcode S66, supposedly containing the most typical mix of household types in the country. As a philosopher, his six-month stay there wasn't in search of the English character, but rather their "folk philosophy" (ie, what they think). The result? A surprising, illuminating view of mainstream English life as of 2007.

Andy Beckett *When the Lights Went Out*. Enough time has elapsed to make 1970s Britain seem like a different world (the title refers to the power cuts during the industrial unrest of 1974), but Beckett's lively history brings the period to life.

John Campbell *The Iron Lady: Margaret Thatcher*. Campbell has been mining the Thatcher seam for years now and this abridged paperback version, published in 2012, hits many political nails right on the head. By the same author, and equally engaging, is his 1987 *Aneurin Bevan and the Mirage of British Socialism*, plus his biography of Roy Jenkins.

★**Kate Fox** *Watching the English*. Exceptionally well observed account of the English, which takes on everything from the class system and endless discussion of the weather to home decor, fashion and all manner of other quirks you might notice on your travels.

Lynsey Hanley *Estates*. The story of social housing (the council "estates" of the title) hardly sounds like a winning topic, but Hanley's "intimate history" brilliantly reveals how class structure is built into the very English landscape (albeit a land that tourists rarely see).

Christopher Hill *The World Turned Upside-Down; God's Englishman: Oliver Cromwell and the English Revolution*. A pioneering Marxist historian, Hill (1912–2003) transformed the way the story of the English Civil War and the Commonwealth was related by means of a string of superbly researched, well-written texts – among which these are two of the best.

★**Eric Hobsbawm** *Industry and Empire*. Ostensibly an economic history of Britain from 1750 to the late 1960s charting Britain's decline and fall as a world power, Hobsbawm's (1917–2012) great skill was in detailed analysis of the effects on ordinary people. See also *Captain Swing*, focusing on the eponymous labourers' uprisings of nineteenth-century England; *Age of Extremes: The Short Twentieth Century 1914–1991*; and his magnificent trilogy, *The Age of Revolution 1789–1848*, *The Age of Capital 1848– 1875*, and *The Age of Empire: 1875–1914*.

David Horspool *Why Alfred Burned the Cakes*. Little is known of the life of Alfred the Great, king of Wessex, and arguably the first king of what would become "England", but Horspool adds a welcome new dimension to the myths and legends. And in case you were wondering about the cakes, Alfred probably didn't.

Roy Jenkins *Churchill: A Biography*. Churchill biographies abound (and the man himself, of course, wrote up – and magnified – his own life), but politician and statesman Jenkins adds an extra level of understanding. Jenkins (1920–2003) specialized in political biographies of men of power, so you can also read his take on the likes of Gladstone, Asquith and Roosevelt.

Owen Jones *Chavs: The Demonization of the Working Class*. A trumpet blast from the political left – and a yell of moral/political outrage at the way the media treat the working class. The youthful Jones is articulate, fiery and witty – and followed up *Chavs* with the equally trenchant, howl-inducing *The Establishment: And How They Get Away With It*.

★**David Kynaston** *Austerity Britain, 1945–51*. Comprehensive vox pop that gives the real flavour of postwar England. Everything is here, from the skill of a Dennis Compton cricket innings through to the difficulties and dangers of hewing coal down the pit, all in a land where there were "no supermarkets, no teabags, no Formica, no trainers … and just four Indian restaurants". Also recommended are Kynaston's follow-up volumes *Family Britain, 1951–57* and *Modernity Britain, 1957–1962*.

Diane Purkiss *The English Civil War: A People's History*. The story of English revolution, given a human face – the clue is in the subtitle. Purkiss dodges the battles and armies, focusing instead on the men who fought and the women who fed and tended to them. If you like it, try Purkiss's follow-up *Literature, Gender and Politics During the English Civil War*.

★**Andrew Rawnsley** *The End of the Party*. Arguably Britain's most acute political journalist, Rawnsley cross-examines and dissects New Labour under Blair and Brown to withering effect. Different target, same approach – in *In It Together: The Inside Story of the Coalition Government*.

Sheila Rowbotham *Hidden from History*. Last published in 1992, this key feminist text provides an uncompromising account of three hundred years of women's oppression in Britain alongside a cogent analysis of the ways in which key female figures have been written out of history.

Simon Schama *A History of Britain* (3 vols). British history, from 3000 BC to 2000 AD, delivered at pace by the TV-famous historian and popularizer, Simon Schama. The prolific Schama can't half bang it out – even in his seventies, he's showing no signs of slowing down.

James Sharpe *Remember, Remember the Fifth of November; Dick Turpin*. A crisp retelling of the 1605 Gunpowder Plot, *Remember, Remember* also puts the whole episode – and the resultant Bonfire Night – into historical context. In *Dick Turpin*, subtitled "The Myth of the English Highwayman", Sharpe stands and delivers a broadside to the commonly accepted notion of Turpin and his ilk – not romantic robbers but brutal villains after all. If you warm to Sharpe's themes, then move on to his *A Fiery & Furious People: A History of Violence in England*.

Lytton Strachey *Queen Victoria*. Strachey (1880–1932) is often credited with establishing a warmer, wittier, more all-encompassing form of biography with his *Queen Victoria* (1921), following on from his groundbreaking *Eminent Victorians* (1918). Many others have followed in trying to understand the long-serving monarch, but few match Strachey's economy and wit.

A.J.P. Taylor *English History 1914–45*. Thought-provoking, scintillatingly well-written survey by one of Britain's finest populist historians (1906–90). When it first appeared in 1965 it was the fifth and final volume of the Oxford History of England. See also *The Origins of the Second World War*, *The Struggle for Mastery of Europe 1848– 1918* and *The First World War: An Illustrated History*, a penetrating analysis of how the war started and why it went on for so long, including a savage portrayal of Britain's high command; first published in 1963, never surpassed.

Richard and Sheila Tames *A Traveller's History of Bath*. A history of Bath that will appeal to visitors, with a good balance of the Roman and Georgian periods with the rest of the city's story, including its fashions, theatrical heritage, music and architecture.

★**E.P. Thompson** *The Making of the English Working Class*. A seminal text – essential reading for anyone who wants to understand the fabric of English society. It traces the trials and tribulations of England's emergent working class between 1780 and 1832.

John Betjeman *Ghastly Good Taste, Or, A Depressing Story of the Rise and Fall of English Architecture*. Classic one-hundred-page account of England's architecture written by one of the country's shrewdest poet-commentators. First published in 1970.

William Gaunt *Concise History of English Painting*. Books covering the broad sweep of English painting are thin on the ground, but this succinct and excellently illustrated book provides a useful introduction to its subject, covering the Middle Ages to the twentieth century in just 288 pages; it is, however, a little dated – it was published in 1964.

Owen Hatherley *A Guide to the New Ruins of Great Britain*. There's no good news from this angry rant of a book, which rails against – and describes in detail – the devastating 1990s architectural desecration of a string of British cities in the name of speculation, masquerading as modernization.

Nikolaus Pevsner *Pevsner Architectural Guides: Buildings of England*. If you want to know who built what, when, and how (rather than why), look no further than this landmark architectural series, in 46 county-by-county volumes. This serious-minded, magisterial project was initially a one-man show, but after Pevsner died in 1983 later authors revised his text, inserting newer buildings but generally respecting the founder's tone.

Rod Priddle and David Hyde *GWR to Devizes*. Two Great Western Railway experts take on the history – and ultimate demise – of the Devizes branch line of this great railway.

Francis Pryor *Home: A Time Traveller's Tales from Britain's Prehistory*. The often arcane discoveries of working archeologists are given fascinating new exposure in Pryor's lively archeological histories of Britain. Everything from before the Romans to the sixteenth century is examined through the archeologist's eye, unearthing a more sophisticated native culture than was formerly recognized along the way. This latest book concentrates on family life, but other Pryor titles include *Britain in the Middle Ages*; *Britain BC* and *Britain AD*.

Brian Sewell *Naked Emperors: Criticisms of English Contemporary Art*. Trenchant, idiosyncratic, reviews on contemporary art from the late critic and arch debunker of pretension, who died in 2015. Few would want to plough through all 368 pages of the assembled reviews – but dip in and yelp with glee, or splutter with indignation.

Bruce Watkin *A History of Wiltshire*. A comprehensive (and partially illustrated) history of the fascinating county of Wiltshire, including a comprehensive account of the social and economic changes that have taken place in one of England's oldest counties over six thousand years.

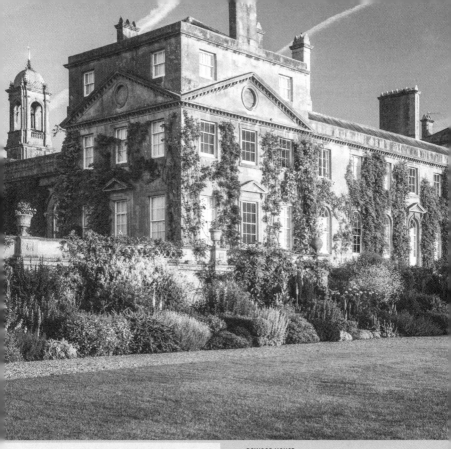

BOWOOD HOUSE

Did you know…?

The Great West Way is not just a touring route. This is a journey through England's heart and soul, taking in some of the country's finest architecture, cultural sites and countryside. Here are some nuggets of Great West Way knowledge to inspire your trip.

- The Great West Way is some 125 miles long and can be travelled by road, rail, boat, bike, on horseback or on foot.

- The Great West Way links three designated Areas of Outstanding Natural Beauty (AONB) – the North Wessex Downs, the Cotswolds and the Chilterns.

- The Queen's best-loved castle is on the Great West Way. Windsor Castle is said to be her favourite residence, and it's also the oldest and largest occupied castle in the world.

- The only place in the UK outside of London where you can get a three Michelin-starred meal is on the Great West Way – in the Berkshire village of Bray, at either *The Fat Duck* or *The Waterside Inn*.

- The earliest surviving photographic negative was taken on the Great West Way: at Lacock Abbey, by William Fox Talbot in 1835.

- There are 15 National Trust sites along the route, from the prehistoric stone circles of Stonehenge and Avebury to fine Victorian mansions, such as Cliveden and Tyntesfield.

- The UK's only natural hot springs are found on the Great West Way, in the ancient city of Bath. You can bathe in them at Thermae Bath Spa.

- There are three UNESCO World Heritage Sites on the Great West Way: the City of Bath, the Royal Botanic Gardens, Kew, and Stonehenge, Avebury and Associated Sites – all selected for their cultural importance.

- The world's oldest pot plant lives on the Great West Way: a prickly cycad, planted in 1775, and still thriving at the Royal Botanic Gardens, Kew.

- The Kennet & Avon Canal runs along the Great West Way and is home to the longest continuous lock flight in the UK. Caen Hill lock flight rises 237ft in just two miles and takes around half a day to tackle in either direction.

- The Great West Way was where the Magna Carta was first signed, at Runnymede on the banks of the River Thames.

- Europe's largest annual meeting of hot air balloons takes places on the Great West Way, at the Bristol International Balloon Fiesta, held every August.

- The UK's oldest surviving hedge maze is on the Great West Way, at Hampton Court Palace just outside London.

- The Great West Way is home to England's largest gorge, the spectacular Cheddar Gorge.

- The last flight of supersonic jet Concorde was along the Great West Way, from Heathrow Airport just west of London to Filton Airfield near Bristol, on 26 November 2003. That Concorde, Alpha Foxtrot, remains on display at Aerospace Bristol and you can step aboard it – though sadly not take to the skies.

- The real "Downton Abbey" is on the Great West Way. Highclere Castle in Berkshire was seen on screen in every episode of the popular show and visitors can check out the Dining

Room, the Library and even some of the bedrooms.

- Prince Charles' and the Duchess of Cornwall's private residence, Highgrove, is on the Great West Way – and the famous gardens he planted here are open to the public.

- Renowned landscape gardener Lancelot "Capability" Brown designed several of the gardens along the Great West Way, including Bowood, Corsham Court, Longleat and Cliveden.

- Lacock Abbey appeared on screen as Hogwarts School in three of the *Harry Potter* films. The room where Harry first saw his parents, in the *The Mirror of Erised*, is the Abbey's Chapter House and can be visited by the public.

- The greatest Royalist victory of the seventeenth-century English Civil War took place on the Great West Way, at Roundway Hill in Wiltshire.

- England's National Arboretum is on the Great West Way, at Westonbirt, and boasts some 2500 different tree species from around the world.

- If you travel the Great West Way by rail you'll be travelling along what was arguably Isambard Kingdom Brunel's greatest achievement – the Great Western Railway. Brunel forged this route in the early nineteenth century and a highlight is the Box Tunnel, a feat of engineering many people said could not be built. Until he built it.

- Travellers have been making journeys by coach along the Great West Way for more than 350 years – though in the eighteenth century coaches could only travel at 10mph and it was said to take 100 horses to complete a journey of 100 miles.

YOUR STORY STARTS HERE

Travel back 5,000 years to discover
the world of your ancestors.

Nr Amesbury, Wiltshire **SP4 7DE**

ENGLISH HERITAGE
STONEHENGE

CHERHILL DOWNS, WILTSHIRE

Great West Way®
Ambassador Network

The Great West Way Ambassador Network was launched to enable collaboration, storytelling and the future sustainability of the 125-mile long route. Our Ambassadors all share a pride of place and a common aim in creating outstanding experiences for curious visitors just like you. Together, we look forward to giving you a warm welcome filled with new discoveries...

Title Ambassadors

- Bristol Airport – Airport Ambassador
- Canal & River Trust – Waterways Ambassador
- Great Western Railway – Rail Ambassador
- National Trust – Houses & Gardens Ambassador

Destination Ambassadors

- Bath Business Improvement District
- Bradford on Avon Town
- Calne Town
- Chippenham Town
- Corsham Town
- Cotswolds Tourism
- Destination Bristol
- Devizes Town
- Henley on Thames
- Hungerford Town
- Malmesbury Town
- Marlborough Town
- Marlow
- McArthurGlen Designer Outlet
- North Wessex Downs AONB
- Reading UK
- Stonehenge & Avebury WHS
- Swindon Town
- Tourism South East
- Trowbridge Town
- Vale of Pewsey
- Visit Bath
- Visit Richmond
- Visit Thames
- Visit Newbury
- VisitWiltshire

Designated Attraction & Hotel Ambassadors

- Aerospace Bristol
- Alder Ridge Vineyard
- Bowood House & Gardens
- Cheddar Gorge & Caves
- Designer Outlet Swindon
- The Fashion Museum
- Longleat
- Roman Baths
- The Royal Crescent Hotel & Spa
- Stonehenge
- Thermae Bath Spa
- Wadworth Brewery & Tours
- West Berkshire Brewery
- Westonbirt, The National Arboretum
- Whatley Manor Hotel & Spa
- Windsor Castle

Gateway Ambassadors

- Abbey Hotel
- The Abbey Quarter
- a'Beckett's Vineyard
- Active England
- Aldermaston Tea Rooms, Visitor Centre, & Shop
- Aldwick Estate
- Alton Priors Church
- Apex Hotel Bath
- Arnos Vale Cemetery
- Around and About Bath
- Aspley House
- Atwell Wilson Motor Museum
- Avalon Lodge Bed and Breakfast
- Avebury Landscape Wiltshire
- Avon Valley Adventure & Wildlife Park
- Bailey Balloons
- Bailbrook House Hotel
- Bainton Bikes
- Barbara McLellan

- The Barn Theatre
- Barrington Court
- Bath Apartment Breaks
- The Bath Brew House
- Bath Bus Company
- Bath Self Catering
- Beanhill Farm B&B
- Berkeley Castle
- Best Western Plus Angel Hotel Chippenham
- Bombay Sapphire
- Bozedown Alpacas
- Bristol Blue Glass
- Bristol Cathedral
- Bristol Community Ferry Boats
- Bristol Packet Boats
- Bristol Tandem Hire
- Bristol Zoo
- Brooks Guest House B&B Bath
- Bruce Branch Boat
- Brunel's SS *Great Britain*
- Buttle Farm
- Canal Trust Café
- Castle Combe Circuit
- Cheddar Gorge
- The Chilterns View
- Chippenham Museum and Heritage Centre
- Church Farm Country Cottages
- Clifton Suspension Bridge and Visitor Centre
- Cobbs Farm Shop
- Compass Holidays
- The Courts Garden
- Cricklade Hotel
- Crofton Beam Engines
- Cumberwell Country Cottages
- Devizes Marina
- Devizes Marina Day Boat Hire
- Devizes Wharf Tea Room
- Didcot Railway Centre
- Donnington Grove
- DoubleTree by Hilton Swindon
- Dyrham Park
- The Engineman's Rest Café
- The Farm Camp
- Foottrails
- French Brothers
- Glenside Hospital Museum
- Great Northern Hotel
- Hampton by Hilton Bristol Airport
- Hampton Court Palace
- The Harrow at Little Bedwyn
- Henley Greenlands Hotel
- Helen Browning's Royal Oak
- Heritage Bed & Breakfast
- Hobbs of Henley
- The Holburne Museum
- Holiday Inn Salisbury - Stonehenge
- Honey Street Boats & Café
- Hungerford Wharf and Kintbury
- Iford Manor Gardens
- Inspirock
- Jane Austen Centre
- Kenavon Venture
- Koffmann & Mr. Whites
- Lacock Abbey, Fox Talbot Museum and village
- The Langley
- Liberty Car Tours
- Lido Bristol
- Lytes Cary Manor
- MacDonald Bath Spa Hotel
- Maidenhead Heritage Centre
- Manor Farm B&B
- Marlborough College Summer School
- The *Matthew* of Bristol
- Meadowbank House
- Merchants House
- Mompesson House
- Montacute House
- The Museum of English Rural Life
- MV *Jubilee*
- Newark Park
- The Newbury Pub
- Newbury Racecourse
- No. 1 Royal Crescent
- Noah's Ark Zoo Farm
- The Old Bell Malmesbury
- The Old Chapel
- Old Sarum
- Oldbury Tours
- Parkway Shopping Newbury

AMBASSADOR NETWORK

- Pound Arts
- Practical Car and Motorhome Hire
- Prince Street Social
- Prior Park Landscape Garden
- Queens Arms East Garston
- Reading Museum
- The Red Lion East Chisenbury
- REME Museum
- River & Rowing Museum
- Roseate House London
- The Roseate Villa Bath
- The Roseate Reading
- Rose of Hungerford
- Roves Farm
- Royal Borough Windsor & Maidenhead
- Royal Oak Yattendon
- The Royal Windsor Pub
- Salisbury Cathedral
- Salisbury, Stonehenge and Sarum Tours
- Salters Steamers Ltd
- Savouring Bath
- Shaw House
- Sheephouse Manor
- Skydive Netheravon
- Southwest Heritage Tours
- Southwestern Railway
- Stay in Bath
- Stonehenge Landscape Wiltshire
- Stonor Park
- Stourhead
- SUP Bristol
- Swinley Bike Hub
- The Swan, Bradford on Avon
- Thames Lido
- Thames Rivercruise
- Three Tuns Freehouse
- Tintinhull Garden
- Tour and Explore
- Tours 2 Order
- TransWilts Community Rail Partnership
- Troutbeck
- Tucking Mill Self Catering
- Tutti Pole
- Tyntesfield
- University of Bristol Botanic Garden
- Vaughan's Kitchen
- Vintage Classics
- The Watermill Theatre
- We The Curious
- Wellington Arch
- West Berkshire Museum
- Whitchurch Silk Mill
- Wiltshire Museum
- Wiltshire Music Centre
- Wiltshire Wildlife Trust, Blakehill Farm
- Wiltshire Wildlife Trust, Lower Moor
- Wiltshire Wildlife Trust, Jones's Mill
- Woolley Grange Hotel

Take your time on the K&A

The beautiful Kennet & Avon Canal (or K&A as its known) flows along 87 miles of the Great West Way®. From Bath to Reading, it winds through quintessential rolling Wiltshire hills, bustling towns and even a World Heritage Site.

Since 1810, narrowboats have drifted along at four miles an hour, plying their trade from Bristol to London. Today, you'll find a mixture of holiday and live-aboard boaters, all seeking the calm and tranquillity that comes from life on or by the water.

In fact, research by the Canal & River Trust, the charity that looks after the K&A, suggests spending time next to water is good for your wellbeing. So take a wander along the towpath, paddle away on a canoe, jump aboard a boat trip from one of the many wharves along the way, or discover one of the best canal-side cycling routes criss-crossing Bath Stone aqueducts and bridges. Or simply stop, stare and take it all in. And the best bit? The K&A is free and open for everyone to use and enjoy every day.

Canal & River Trust
Making life better by water

GREAT WEST WAY®

Great West Way® Waterways Ambassador

canalrivertrust.org.uk/GreatWestWay

Small print and index

195 Small print

197 Index

Rough Guide credits

Editor: Tatiana Wilde
Author: Helen Ochyra
Managing Editor: Carine Tracanelli
Head of DTP and pre-press: Dan May

Layout: Pradeep Thapliyal
Cartography: Katie Bennett
Picture editor: Aude Vauconsant
Proofreader and indexer: Penny Phenix

Publishing information

This 1st edition published 2019

Distribution
UK, Ireland and Europe
Apa Publications (UK) Ltd; sales@roughguides.com
United States and Canada
Ingram Publisher Services; ips@ingramcontent.com
Australia and New Zealand
Woodslane; info@woodslane.com.au
Southeast Asia
Apa Publications (SN) Pte; sales@roughguides.com
Worldwide
Apa Publications (UK) Ltd; sales@roughguides.com
Special sales, content licensing and co-publishing
Rough Guides can be purchased in bulk quantities
at discounted prices. We can create special editions,
personalized jackets and corporate imprints tailored to
your needs. sales@roughguides.com
roughguides.com
Printed in Poland

200pp includes index
A catalogue record for this book is available from the
British Library
ISBN: 978-1-78919-002-1

Help us update

We've gone to a lot of effort to ensure that the first
edition of **The Rough Guide to the Great West Way** is
accurate and up-to-date. However, things change – places
get "discovered", opening hours are notoriously fickle,
restaurants and rooms raise prices or lower standards. If
you feel we've got it wrong or left something out, we'd like
to know, and if you can remember the address, the price,
the hours, the phone number, so much the better.

Please send your comments with the subject line
"Rough Guide Great West Way Update" to mail@
roughguides.com. We'll credit all contributions and send a
copy of the next edition (or any other Rough Guide if you
prefer) for the very best emails.

Photo credits

(Key: T-top; C-centre; B-bottom; L-left; R-right)

Index

A

A4 165
a'Beckett's Vineyard 39, 99
accommodation......... 36, *See also* town and area listings
activities.... 39, *See also* town and area listings
afternoon tea 14, 38
Alder Ridge Vineyard 39, 78
All Saints Church, Alton Priors 99
Alton Priors 99
Ambassador Network 188
Anglo-Saxons.......................... 160
antiques 14
Apsley House 54
Arnos Vale Cemetery.............. 150
Ascot 11, 60
Ascot Racecourse 62
Ashton Court Estate 150
ATMs.. 42
Atwell-Wilson Motor Museum 105
author picks..................................5
Avebury.............................. 85, 159
Avon Gorge...................... 26, 147
Avon River 141, 148
Avon Valley Railway 16, 151

B

babies, travelling with 44
Banksy 143
Basildon Park............................. 73
Bath 4, 125, 165
  accommodation.................... 134
  activities 138
  American Museum & Gardens ...131
  arrival.................................. 132
  Bath Abbey.......................... 127
  Beckford's Tower.................. 131
  bike hire.............................. 132
  Bristol & Bath Railway Path 132
  buses 132
  Circus, The 128
  drinking 135
  eating.................................. 135
  entertainment...................... 137
  Fashion Museum 130
  festivals............................... 136
  Gainsborough Bath Spa 24, 134
  Herschel Museum of Astronomy 131
  Holburne Museum 28, 130
  Jane Austen Centre 128
  Museum of Bath Architecture....131
  nightlife............................... 136
  parking................................ 132
  Prior Park Landscape Garden 132
  Pulteney Bridge 130
  Queen Square 128
  Roman Baths 29, 126
  Royal Crescent 25, 130
  Royal Victoria Park 130
  self-catering..........................37
  shopping........................ 16, 137
  Thermae Bath Spa 13, 24, 127
  tours.............................. 132, 134
  Victoria Art Gallery 130
Bath Road............................... 165
Beale Park................................. 73
bed and breakfasts 37
beer 38
Berkeley Castle 152
bikes 36
bike rentals 36
birdlife 16, 180
Blair, Tony 174
boats 34
boat trips 64, 70, 102, 108
Bombay Sapphire Distillery 80
books 182
Bourton-on-the-Water............ 123
Bowood House and Gardens 26, 103, 105
Bradford on Avon 107
Bray 23, 29, 68
Brexit...................................... 175
Bristol 24, 140
  accommodation................... 154
  activities 157
  Aerospace Bristol 24, 151
  airport 142
  Arnos Vale Cemetery........... 150
  Ashton Court Estate............. 150
  Avon Gorge................... 26, 147
  Avon Valley Railway 151
  Banksy........................... 20,143
  Berkeley Castle.................... 152
  bike rental........................... 154
  Blaise Castle House Museum..144
  Bristol and Bath Railway Path...... 132
  Bristol Aquarium 144
  Bristol Cathedral.................. 141
  Bristol International Balloon Fiesta 45, 150
  Bristol Museum and Art Gallery 28, 143
  Bristol Zoo Gardens 14, 148
  Brunel's SS *Great Britain*.. 13, 25, 144
  Clifton.......................... 24, 147
  Clifton Observatory.............. 148
  Clifton Suspension Bridge 24, 147
  Concorde 19, 24, 151
  drinking 155
  Durdham Down.................... 147
  eating.................................. 155
  entertainment...................... 156
  Filton................................... 151
  Georgian House Museum...... 143
  Harbourside 144
  Leigh Woods National Nature Reserve.............................. 150
  M Shed................................ 146
  Matthew of Bristol, The 146
  New Room, The 142
  nightlife............................... 157
  Noah's Ark Zoo Farm............ 152
  Paco Tapas....................... 23, 155
  parking................................ 154
  Queen Square 25, 144
  Red Lodge Museum.............. 144
  Royal York Crescent 147
  St Vincent's Cave 148
  shopping.............................. 156
  slave trade........................... 147
  street art.............................. 143
  tours.................................... 154
  transport 152
  Tyntesfield 151
  University of Bristol Botanic Garden 151
  Upfest.................................. 143
  We The Curious.................... 146
Bristol Airport 142
British Empire.......................... 169
Brown, Lancelot "Capability".105
Brunel, Isambard Kingdom ...170, 171
Buckinghamshire....................... 68
Bucklebury Farm Park.............. 78
bureaux de change................... 43
butterflies............................... 179

C

Caen Hill Lock Flight.......... 25, 36, 99
cafés 38
Calne 104
canal *See* Kennet & Avon Canal
car rental................................... 33
Castle Combe..................... 25, 117
Castle Combe Circuit........ 20, 117
caving 139
Cheddar Caves................. 138, 159
Cheddar Gorge....................... 138
chemists.................................... 42
children, travelling with........... 44

Chilterns AONB 16, 69, 96, 181
Chilterns Cycleway.............. 27, 70
Chippenham 103
Chipping Campden 124
Churchill, Winston 172
cider...38
circus..123
Cirencester................................123
Clifton ....147 see also Bristol
climbing............................ 139, 157
Cliveden Estate........26, 66, 68, 71
coffee shops 38
Commonwealth of England
....165
Concorde....................19, 24, 151
Confetti Battle, Devizes............14,
45, 98
Cookham 68
Corsham 105
Corsham Court 105
costs 41
Cotswolds AONB............. 116, 120
Cotswold Water Park 27, 41
Cotswold Way 35, 124
Cotswolds....................4, 13, 115
Courts Garden 108
credit cards 42
cricket 40
crime 41
Crofton Beam Engines........30, 90
Cromwell, Oliver 165
crop circles....................................91
cycling 40
cycling tours.......................40, 100

D

deer 14, 179
Devizes..................................... 14, 98
disabilities, travellers with........43
doctors 42
Donnington Castle.....................77
Dorney Lake 60
Downton Abbey 25, 78, 176
drinks 22, 37
drinking...38
driving..33
Dyrham Park..............................117

E

electricity 41
Elizabeth II.........................58, 172
emergencies..................................41
entry requirements.....................41
equestrian routes 35

escape rooms.............................139
Eton College, Windsor 59
European Health Insurance Card
(EHIC) 42

F

Fat Duck, Bray 23, 71
Fay's Bistro, Calne 107
festivals 44
film and TV............................25, 176
Filton...151
food and drink......................22, 37
football..39

G

gardens 266
gastropubs....................................37
getting around 33
Girls Aloud 178
Great Bath Road.............. 165, 169
Great Bedwyn 90
Great Chalfield Manor 108
Great Western Railway....... 19, 34,
168, 169, 171
Greys Court, Henley...................69
guesthouses .....36, See also town
and area listings

H

Hampton Court Palace 20,
26, 54
Hanoverians, The 167
Harry Potter films 25, 82, 103,
104, 176
health...42
Heathrow Airport 53
Henley on Thames 60, 69
Henley Royal Regatta.......... 60, 69
Highclere Castle 25, 26,
30, 78, 105
Highgrove Royal Gardens
....26, 121
history...159
horse racing..................................62
horse riding 16, 35
hospitals 42
hot air balloon rides 28, 150
hotels ....36, See also town and
area listings
Hungerford 14, 78

I

Iford Manor Gardens 26, 108
industrial heritage...................... 24,
See also Kennet & Avon Canal,
steam trains
Industrial Revolution................168
itineraries.......................................22
Ivinghoe Beacon.........................96

K

Kennet & Avon Canal .. 13, 28, 35,
81, 90, 99, 168, 169
Kennet & Avon Cycle Route...100
Kew...16, 51

L

Lacock.....................................25, 104
Lacock Abbey and the Fox
Talbot Museum 11, 103, 104
Lancaster, House of 163
Legoland Windsor Resort..45, 60
Leigh Woods National Nature
Reserve....................................150
LGBTQ travellers...........................42
Longleat.....................19, 105, 111
Lower Slaughter........................124
Living Rainforest.........................77
luxury...24
Lydiard House and Park 94

M

M4 165
Magna Carta...................59, 62, 162
Maidenhead 25, 66
Major, John 173
Malmesbury 24, 29, 120
maps..42
Marlborough 89
Marlborough Downs.................16
Marlow 68
Massive Attack...........................178
Mendip Hills 138
money..42
motor racing 117
mountain biking..................13, 28
music...178